More
Days in the
Lives of
Social Workers

35 "Real-Life" Stories of Advocacy,
Outreach, and Other Intriguing
Roles in Social Work Practice

More
Days in the
Lives of
Social Workers

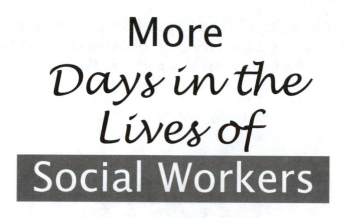

35 "Real-Life" Stories of Advocacy,
Outreach, and Other Intriguing
Roles in Social Work Practice

Linda May Grobman, Editor

Harrisburg, Pennsylvania

More Days in the Lives of Social Workers
35 "Real-Life" Stories of Advocacy, Outreach, and Other Intriguing Roles in Social Work Practice

Edited by Linda May Grobman

Published by:

Post Office Box 5390
Harrisburg, PA 17110-0390 U.S.A.
717-238-3787 (voice)
717-238-2090 (fax)
http://www.socialworker.com

The editor can be contacted by e-mail at: *linda.grobman@paonline.com*

Note: The names and identities of social work clients mentioned in this book have been carefully disguised in accordance with professional standards of confidentiality.

Library of Congress Cataloging-in-Publication Data

More days in the lives of social workers : 35 real-life stories of advocacy, outreach, and other intriguing roles in social work practice / Linda May Grobman, editor.
    p. cm.
Includes bibliographical references.
ISBN 1-929109-16-4 (pbk.)
1. Social workers—United States. 2. Social case work—United States. I. Grobman, Linda May.
HV40.8.U6M67 2005
361.3'2—dc22
                                2005000298

More Days in the Lives of Social Workers

Table of Contents

About the Editor

Linda May Grobman, ACSW, LSW, is the founder, publisher, and editor of *THE NEW SOCIAL WORKER*®, the magazine for social work students and recent graduates, editor of the book *DAYS IN THE LIVES OF SOCIAL WORKERS*, and co-author of *THE SOCIAL WORKER'S INTERNET HANDBOOK*. She has practiced social work in mental health and medical settings, and is a former interim executive director of the Pennsylvania and Georgia state chapters of the National Association of Social Workers. She received her MSW and BM (Music Therapy) degrees from the University of Georgia.

About the Contributors

Catherine Sperry Beckett, LCSW, is National Director of Curriculum, Training, and Evaluation at the national office of Friends of the Children. She also serves as an Instructor of Contemporary Family Issues at Portland State University, and has designed curricula and instructed courses for professionals who work with at-risk children and adolescents for institutions including St. Mary's College, U.C. Davis, and U.C. Berkeley. She received her MSW in clinical social work from Smith College.

Ann F. Biddlestone, MSW, LISW, is a play therapist at Family Resource Center of Hancock County and Family Service of Lucas County. She also serves as Interim Field Associate and Adjunct Instructor at the University of Toledo.

Mark O. Bigler, LCSW, Ph.D., is Associate Professor and Director of Social Work in the Department of Social Work and Gerontology, Weber State University, in Ogden, Utah.

Laura Boutwell, MSW, is United with Youth Coordinator at Family Service in Roanoke, Virginia. She also serves as Field Liaison for Radford University's social work program, where she received her MSW in May 2004. She spent the summer of 2003 in Ghana and has special interests in the areas of community development, leadership development with diverse populations, intercultural competencies, collaborative service learning, and refugee and immigrant resettlement processes.

Stephen C. Burke, Ph.D., MSW, is the BSW Program Director at Marywood University School of Social Work. He has written numerous articles on social work education and practice issues, and he received the 2002 Influencing State Policy award for MSW students and field instructors.

Suzanne Bushfield, Ph.D., MSW, LCSW, has over 30 years experience as a professional social worker. Her practice concentrations in health and mental health enrich her teaching, scholarship, and service. Professor Bushfield's research focuses on multiple factors of risk and resilience for vulnerable families across the life span, including divorce, imprisonment, pain, death, caregiving, and the role of spirituality, hope, and collaboration in fostering resilience. As Assistant Professor of Social Work at Arizona State University at the West Campus in Phoenix, she teaches human behavior, advanced practice, and research. She is actively involved in the Social Work Section of the National Hospice and Palliative Care Organization.

Regina D. Cassidy, MS, CSW, is a social worker at Bayley Seton Hospital, where she does mental health evaluation and referral. Her experience includes the areas of homelessness, parent education, and prenatal health. She received her MSW from New York University and lives in New York City with her husband Tom and three sons, Mike, John, and Jim.

Theresa Hancock, BSW, is a Policy Associate at Rhode Island KIDS COUNT, where she does research, writing, and policy analysis on children's health issues and provides program support on the National School Readiness Indicators Initiative. She received her BA in Social Work from Providence College. She has also worked in the fields of domestic violence, childhood lead poisoning prevention, and special education.

Dana K. Harmon, MSW, is a Licensed Graduate Social Worker and is currently a doctoral student at the University of Alabama. She has been employed at Family Counseling Service in Tuscaloosa, Alabama since 1997.

David V. Henton, LCSW, MSSW, is the Assistant Field Director in the School of Social Work at Texas State University in San Marcos. He holds BA and MSSW degrees from the University of Texas at Austin. His practice background is in the areas of developmental disabilities and mental health. He also teaches in the practice sequence and has research interests in social work education, as well as geriatric depression and loneliness.

Maureen Holland, BSW, MSW, is Director of Home Visiting Services at New North Citizens' Council in Springfield, Massachusetts, where she has held this position since 1990. She received her MSW from Springfield College in May 2004 and double bachelor's degrees in social work and Spanish from Elms College in 1985.

Carmela Isabella, BSW, interned in the Washington office of Senator Hillary Rodham Clinton from September to December 2003. She attended campaign training by the Institute for the Advancement of Political Social Work Practice, and her activities include Habitat for Humanity, America Counts, School Social Work Advisory Board, and serving as an advisor to the Social Work Organization. She received her BSW from Elms College in December 2003.

Mitchell Kahn, MSW, LSW, is Professor and Director of the BSW Program at Ramapo College of New Jersey. He also holds the positions of Organizing Vice President of the New Jersey Tenants Organization, Executive Director of the Bergen County Housing Coalition, and board member of New Jersey Citizen Action.

Heidi Ann Karns, BSW, is employed by the Hawaii State Department of Health, Developmental Disabilities/Mental Retardation Branch. She received her BSW from Hawaii Pacific University. Originally from upstate New York, she has also worked with the birth to three population of children with developmental disabilities. She would like to acknowledge and thank Mary Sheridan for her continuous support and dedication in assisting with her chapter for this book. Heidi enjoys waterskiing and going to the beach with her husband.

Karen Kimsey Lawson, MSW, is a Long-Term Care Policy Supervisor in the Virginia Department of Medical Assistance Services. She received her MSW from Virginia Commonwealth University and her BSW from James Madison University.

Susan Mankita, MSW, LCSW, was director of social work at Vencor Hospital in Coral Gables, Florida. She left that position to pursue completion of her Ph.D. at Barry University. She is an adjunct faculty member at Barry University, and serves as Social Work Forum Leader on America Online.

Valerie Scott (Scotty) Massimo, MSW, Ph.D., is Assistant Professor of Social Work at Ramapo College of New Jersey. She received her BA from Columbia School of General Studies and her MSW and Ph.D. from the State University of New York at Albany. She began her social work career in the fields of substance abuse and developmental disabilities. However, most of her time in the field was in child welfare, both in direct practice and in public adoption policy. She is a frequent presenter at conferences and has worked extensively in bringing together pedagogy and technology.

Donna McIntosh, MSW, is Chair of the Siena College Social Work Program. She has written widely on a variety of policy and practice issues.

Doris Nelson, LMSW, received her Master of Social Work degree from the University of South Carolina in 2003. She is a Disabled Veterans Outreach Program Specialist at the Georgia Department of Labor. She received an honorable discharge from the United States Army.

Kristi O'Dell, Ph.D., ACSW, LCSW, is Associate Professor at the University of Mississippi Department of Social Work. She previously served as Assistant Professor of Psychiatry and Assistant Dean of Medical Student Affairs at the University of Alabama School of Medicine-Huntsville Campus, and has held a number of other academic, research, and medical social work positions. She received her Ph.D. and MSW from the University of Kansas.

Jesus E. Reyes, AM, ACSW, is Director of Social Service of the Circuit Court of Cook County, Illinois, the largest unified court system in the nation. He is a graduate of the School of Social Service Administration (SSA) of the University of Chicago and former Assistant Dean for Enrollment and Placement at SSA. Reyes is the author of *The Social Work Graduate School Applicant's Handbook.*

Jill Rodriguez, BSW, is a Bridge Advocate at Rose Brooks Center in Kansas City, Missouri. She serves on the Professional Advisory Committee for Park University's social work degree program. Jill received dual degrees in social work and family studies/human services from Kansas State University in Manhattan, Kansas.

Mona C. Struhsaker Schatz, MSW, DSW, is a Full Professor in the School of Social Work, and the Founder and Director of the Education and Research Institute for Fostering Families (ERIFF), at Colorado State University. She also serves as the coordinator for an online graduate certificate program in Youth Development through the Great Plains-Interactive Distance Education Alliance. Dr. Schatz has worked with children and families and trained professionals who are involved with children and families and human services work. She has presented in over a dozen countries, particularly in Eastern Europe and Russia. She has published in a variety of social work journals, along with news articles, monographs, and several dozen original training manuals and accompanying video materials.

Scott P. Sells, Ph.D., LCSW, LMFT, teaches MSW students at Savannah State University and is clinical director of the Savannah Family Institute. He serves as a consultant to the Department of Juvenile Justice, and has written a book entitled *Treating the Tough Adolescent: A Family-Based, Step-by-Step Guide.*

Glenda F. Lester Short, Ph.D., MSW, LCSW, received her Ph.D. from the College of Social Work, University of South Carolina, and her MSW from Kansas University. She has received a wide variety of training, including marriage and family therapy, mediation, community leadership, clinical family social work, family advocacy, and substance abuse. She is on the social work faculty at Southwest Missouri State University.

Monica Sierra-Mayberry, BSW, is a Bridge Advocate at Rose Brooks Center, the University of Kansas Hospital. She is co-chair of the Immigrant/Refugee Committee of the Mayor's Task Force Against Domestic Violence. She received her BSW with a minor in Spanish language from Olivet Nazarene University.

Barbara E. Solt, Ph.D., LICSW, ACSW, is a Senior Program Associate at the Institute for the Advancement of Social Work Research (IASWR) in Washington, DC. Dr. Solt received her Ph.D. from the Catholic University of America National School of Social Service. Her dissertation research was a qualitative study of resilience in adult former hostages and their supportive others. She received her MSSW from Columbia University School of Social Work.

Mary Dunne Stewart, BA, MSW, has been Associate Director of the Virginia Interfaith Center for Public Policy since July 2002. Mary specializes in policy analysis and advocacy related to at-risk children and healthcare. She participates in direct advocacy at the Capitol, grassroots organizing, leading workshops and seminars, and coalition building; provides leadership for the organization's financial development; and manages the Center's Seminarian and Social Work internship programs. She received her MSW from Virginia Commonwealth University and an undergraduate degree from the College of William and Mary. She and her husband John, a special education teacher, have a son, Ethan.

Diane Strock-Lynskey, MSW, has more than 25 years of experience as a social worker in mezzo and macro direct practice, training, management, policy development/analysis, advocacy, and organizing. Since 1987, as President/ CEO of S-L Associates, she has assisted groups, organizations, and communities in developing just and human change efforts. Since 1990, she has combined this work with serving as Professor of Social Work in the Siena College BSW program. She has also served as Program Director and Coordinator of Field Education.

Roxana Torrico, MSW, is a Program Manager for the Youth Services Division of the Child Welfare League of America (CWLA). She provides direction and technical assistance specific to the development and knowledge regarding the intersection of foster care and homelessness. Prior to joining CWLA, she worked as a foster care social worker at Arlington County (VA) Department of Human Services. Ms. Torrico received her MSW from Virginia Commonwealth University.

Denise Travis, Ph.D., LCSW, is Director of the Graduate School of Social Work at Indiana University Northwest. She is also the Executive Director of Human Beginnings Outpatient Mental Health Center located in the Glen Park area of Gary, Indiana. Dr. Travis received her Bachelor of Arts degree in 1980 from Benedictine University in Lisle, Illinois. She then went on to pursue her MSW (1983) and Ph.D. (1998) from Jane Addams College of Social Work at the University of Illinois at Chicago. She has participated in several state-funded research projects on HIV/AIDS and includes this area as one of her major research interests.

Rob Udell, MSW, lives and works in Toronto, Canada, where he is Director of Community Services at Metropolitan United Church and a part-time social worker in the Emergency Department at Mt. Sinai Hospital. Rob has worked in all aspects of social work, from street and community work to program development and management, over the past twenty-five years. He holds BA and MSW degrees from the University of Toronto and is registered with the College of Social Workers and Social Service Workers of Ontario.

Lisa Villareal-Rios, JD, MSW, is Assistant Attorney General for the Crime Victim Services Division of the Texas Office of the Attorney General. Previously, Ms. Villareal-Rios served as an Equal Justice Works fellow for the South Texas Pro Bono Asylum Representation Project (ProBAR), where she represented immigrant children in detention. Ms. Villareal-Rios is a graduate of the Washington University joint degree program in law and social work (JD/ MSW). She also holds a BA in psychology and Spanish from Trinity University.

Wanda Whittlesey-Jerome, Ph.D., LMSW, received her MSW and Ph.D. in social work from the University of Texas at Arlington, and her BSW from the University of North Texas. She has been a full-time visiting professor at New Mexico Highlands University's School of Social Work since August 2001. She became the BSW Program Coordinator in January 2003 and Interim Director of the School of Social Work at Rio Rancho in July 2003. She has direct clinical and administrative experience in a variety of social service organizations, including those that assist male and female inmates, provide safe haven for victims of domestic violence, treat substance abusers and their families, and others.

Carole A. Winston, Ph.D., LCSW, ACSW, is Assistant Professor in the Department of Social Work of the College of Health and Human Services at the University of North Carolina at Charlotte. She is a native New Yorker who received her MSS from Columbia University School of Social Work and her doctorate in clinical social work from New York University. Dr. Winston's research interests include parenting grandparents, particularly in communities of color; and health and mental health issues in the African Diaspora, including disparities in the provision of health care services and barriers to end-of-life and palliative care services to communities of color.

Introduction

•••••••••••••••

Is *this social work?* You may ask yourself this question as you read some of the stories in this book. Many of the social workers whose stories are told here serve in roles that are quite different from the common perceptions in our society of what a social worker does.

There are many different kinds of social workers and many different roles that social workers play. This is one of the things that make it such an interesting career choice. As you read the stories, you will see that some social workers started out with a clinical or direct practice focus, or as foster care workers, or in other "traditional" social work roles, and later moved into more administrative roles, or advocacy roles, or research and teaching roles, where they use their clinical knowledge to inform their new roles. Others knew all along that they wanted to do macro work, and still others are in direct practice with people who are directly affected by the policies that advocates are working to change.

Much has been written about the different roles of "macro," "mezzo," and "micro" social workers. In reality, many social workers play a variety of these roles simultaneously in a single position, or in different positions throughout their careers. A social work manager in a hospital might also have a patient caseload. A social worker specializing in sex therapy may go into the community to do HIV/AIDS prevention and education. Still another social worker, specializing in mental health, might start her career as a psychotherapist, then move into a consultation and education role, and finally transition into a supervisory and administrative position, all within the same mental health system.

This book starts where my previous book, *DAYS IN THE LIVES OF SOCIAL WORKERS* (now in its third edition) leaves off. This volume has more of a macro focus than its predecessor, but it is not quite so easy to pinpoint a social worker as macro (working on "the big picture") or micro (working with "the individual"), and I am reluctant to do so. Many social workers do focus more on one than the other, but schools of social work teach us that those working with individuals and families, for example, need to know how policy affects their clients and how to advocate effectively for the individuals they are helping, and those doing advocacy, administration, and the like need to know how their work affects and relates to individuals and families.

As you read this book, you will see how the various roles interact. You will read about social workers in national organizations, in management, in advocacy, training, policy, and research. You will read about social workers in the boardroom, the courtroom, the classroom, and the bedroom. You will find social workers in roles from the Senate floor to the hospital floor to the playroom floor. You will read about social workers working to combat domestic violence, unemployment, and hunger. You will learn about social workers whose work incorporates faith and spirituality.

So, what do they all have in common? They are all professional SOCIAL WORKERS. They have MSW degrees, BSW degrees, Ph.D.s in social work. They work in different settings and in different roles, all coming from a social work perspective, all looking at the person in his or her environment. They look at both the "big picture" and the smallest details to find solutions to problems with individuals, families, groups, organizations, and society as a whole.

They are real-life social workers. Most likely, they became social workers for some of the same reasons that led you to the profession. If you are thinking about becoming a social worker, are a student in a social work program, or are a social worker thinking about changing direction, their stories will open your eyes and help you comprehend the broad scope of what social work is.

Maybe you will discover a new area of social work that appeals to you. Maybe you will find out why policy and research are important, even if all you want to do is be a psychotherapist. Maybe you will experience that "AHA!" moment in which you "get" what distinguishes social work from other helping professions.

As in the first *DAYS IN THE LIVES OF SOCIAL WORKERS* book, there are no "typical" days, but stories that show what social workers do from day to day, week to week, year to year. I hope their stories (and those in the first book, as well) will help you gain a new appreciation for the work that social workers at the bachelor's, master's, and doctoral levels are doing each and every day.

Regardless of your previous ideas about what social workers do, the answer to that question you were asking yourself is a definitive "YES! This IS social work!"

Linda May Grobman, ACSW, LSW, Editor

Acknowledgments

• •

This book grew out of my first book, *DAYS IN THE LIVES OF SOCIAL WORKERS*. As I read the manuscripts that poured in for the third edition of that book, I realized that there were so many interesting and important social work stories to be told that I had no choice but to expand the project to a second volume.

As with the first book, I was struck with how many people wrote to me to tell me how much they loved being social workers. They were excited to tell their stories, and I was excited to read them, and ultimately, to share them with you.

This book was possible only with the participation of the social workers who took time to write about what happens during their busy days. I would like to thank each of these professionals for the work they do, and especially for their contributions to this book.

Thanks also go to the BPD, AGE-SW, IASWR, and other e-mail mailing lists that provided a forum for getting the word out about this project, and to the readers of *THE NEW SOCIAL WORKER's Social Work E-News* for responding so heartily to my call for manuscripts.

I want to thank the many, many social work educators and students who have read and used *DAYS IN THE LIVES OF SOCIAL WORKERS,* and who have taken the time to give me their input by mail, telephone, e-mail, and at conferences throughout the country. Their comments helped shape the new content in the third edition of that book, as well as in this new volume.

I am especially grateful to my husband Gary for his editorial input, proofreading, spell-checking, and support. I thank my son, Adam, for always giving a big "thumb's up" for my work.

LMG

PART 1: Working on a National Level

Chapter 1
I Am Still a Social Worker

•••••••••••••••••••••••

by Linda May Grobman, ACSW, LSW

October 2004. It was almost 22 years ago that I began my first post-MSW position as a social worker. I earned $11,998 per year as a full-time employee in the inpatient adult mental health unit of a state hospital. I felt like Mary Richards from *The Mary Tyler Moore Show*. I could hear the familiar line from the theme song, "You're gonna make it after all," playing in my head as I happily practiced my new profession.

I am a social worker. My diploma says so. My state license says so. But mostly, I say so. I am a social worker.

The following is a composite "day" in my life. Some of these activities typically happen over a period of time, rather than in one day.

I wake up and, after the morning's activities at home, go to my office. I begin my morning by turning on my computer, checking and answering e-mail, and responding to telephone calls. I am going to the annual conference of the Association of Baccalaureate Social Work Program Directors (BPD) next week, so I pack several boxes of books and materials to ship to the conference for my booth in the exhibit hall.

I will spend about 3½ days at the conference talking to social work educators and students about the books I publish, *THE NEW SOCIAL WORKER* magazine, and other projects I am currently working on and may want to collaborate on with them, as well as discussing their current activities and projects. I cherish the two times a year (sometimes more) when I meet with colleagues at this and similar conferences. It is a time to renew friendships and professional connections, to make important contacts, to learn what is happening in the field nationally, and to get a refreshed perspective on things. I hope I'll be able to take some time away from my exhibit to attend some of the conference workshops. Conferences have so much to offer, both educationally and through informal networking.

I log on to the Internet again. This time, I check for new messages on the Socialworker.com online discussion forum. This site is one of my "publications." Social work skills come in handy in managing an electronic message board, which is really a form of online community. As in many aspects of social work, it is important to know when to sit back and let the process occur naturally, and when to actively participate or intervene. The discussions can take a controversial turn at times, which provides for some lively and healthy exchange among colleagues. Some non-social workers join the discussion, too, and at times, they express their frustrations with our profession. I recently added a "Posting Policy" to the Forum, to help keep the discussion on topic and in keeping with the purpose of the site. Today, there's not too much new—a social worker asking how to prepare for the social work licensing exam, and a student looking for resources on school social work. I respond with some suggestions. There are quite a few "regulars"— social workers from Canada, Chicago, Texas, and all over the world who visit the forum often—and I'm sure they will be around later today to respond to these information requests and to weigh in on the ongoing discussions on social justice issues, licensing, and other topics.

Next, I check the SocialWorkJobBank.com site. SWJB is an online job board I launched in 2001, where social work job seekers and employers go to, hopefully, find a "perfect match." I have always had an interest in social work career development, and I enjoy seeing people find the right job. Two new job postings so far today! And good ones, too—an administrative position in state government and an entry level BSW position.

I am a social worker. My current "job" is publisher and editor at White Hat Communications, a social work publishing company that I started. I am a social worker. It's what I am, but is it what I *do?*

It's time for lunch. I like to get away from the office at lunch time. It breaks the day into manageable chunks. I guess this is a throwback from my days as a hospital social worker. I always felt that a change in scenery in the middle of the day was a good, healthy idea.

My husband Gary and I go to the Chinese buffet down the road. A local social worker, someone Gary knows, stops by our table to say "hi." Gary introduces us to each other, saying, "You're both social workers," and pointing to each of us. The woman says, "Well, I used to be." *Hmmm,* I think. Then she says to me, "Are you *still* a social worker?" I think to myself, *I didn't know I could UN-become one once it was part of who I am!* (And I don't want to.)

I am a social worker. Does she mean do I *do* social work? Does she mean is social work my *job title*? What is the meaning of her question, "Are you *still* a social worker?"

When I got my MSW, I chose the mental health concentration. That was my main area of interest, and I figured that regardless of what setting I worked in, I would be working with people on emotional issues, so a mental health background would be good preparation. I also remember writing in my MSW application, as part of my personal statement, that I wanted to accomplish social work goals through my writing.

In my first professional job after graduate school, I worked in a mental health inpatient setting. A "state hospital." Every day started with reading patient charts. Then leading the morning "community" group. Then the morning team meeting, individual sessions, charting, and other paperwork, before lunch. After lunch (away from the hospital, with colleagues), there was therapy group, then more individual sessions, family sessions, charting, and more paperwork. Sometimes a hearing for involuntary commitment, and a couple of times a month, a family education and support group that I developed and co-led with another social worker at the hospital. My days were fairly structured, although never quite the same from one day to the next. And it was clear. I was a social worker. My job title said so. And I was doing social work.

My next job was at a children's hospital. Patients ranged in age from infancy to late adolescence. Their presenting problems could be anything from a life threatening illness to injuries suffered in an accident or other medical conditions. Social workers were assigned to patients and their families who needed some help with community resources, emotional coping, and other social issues. My job title was Social Worker, and I was employed in the Social Work Department. Every day, I would find out about any new patients in the hospital who were assigned to my caseload, and I would check to see who on my caseload from the previous day was still there. Then I would head out to "the floor." I would go to their hospital rooms, hoping to find their parents or other support people to talk to. Referrals came from doctors, nurses, and other staff. Social workers were involved if there was a specific reason to be involved. It might be suspected child abuse, emotional adjustment to a new diagnosis of cancer, a need for financial assistance, discharge planning issues, or something else. Most of my day would be spent going to rooms and talking to children and their parents, writing in charts, consulting with doctors and nurses, making phone calls, and sometimes meeting with an interdisciplinary team.

But back to today. I am a social worker. It is part of who I am, not just what I do. I have several manuscripts on my desk that people have sent to me for possible publication in *THE NEW SOCIAL WORKER*, the national magazine I started and edit and publish. I get excited each time I receive an article. I especially enjoy finding new and interesting social work writers!

The first article looks good. It's about networking when looking for a social work job. This is just the kind of article I want to publish in *THE NEW SOCIAL WORKER*. I insert the writer's name, title of the article, and other details on a publication agreement and send it to the writer, letting her know that the article has been accepted.

I read each manuscript carefully, paying attention to the content presented, the writing style, the writer's credentials, sources of information, and especially, the article's relevance to our unique niche of readers—social work students and recent graduates. I also need to be aware of warning signs for such things as plagiarism and inaccurate information.

I am a social worker. So, how did I get to be a publisher? I am often asked this question when I attend social work conferences, and someone will probably ask me again next week. It's sometimes difficult to explain. Even though I sometimes describe myself as a publisher, I know I'm really primarily a social worker. Even though I am an entrepreneur, social work is where my core professional values lie. I make decisions based on those core social work values.

To me, social work is not just a job that one learns and does. It is a way of thinking and being, as well. Social work education is a transformative process. It teaches you theories and skills, and gives you a professional title, and helps you understand the "why" and "how" of some things you may have already known instinctively.

But it doesn't just teach you *about* social work. If successful, it turns you *into* a social worker.

I became a social work publisher so I could use my skills in editing and writing, along with my social work values and skills, to help other social workers in their career development. This was one of my interests from the beginning of my own career. As I developed my own career path, I became interested in social work career development as a whole. I found it interesting and exciting to be able to help other social workers find their niche.

About 17 years ago, I had a part-time job working with a college student organization, and I enjoyed this population. It was a mix of association management, leadership development, and individual and group counseling. I became involved in the National Association of Social Workers, first as a volunteer leader, and then as a staff person. I worked at two state chapter offices of NASW, editing state newsletters, staffing committees, and performing other functions. I liked being able to serve other social workers.

Eventually, I had some ideas that I wanted to put into action. I wanted to publish a magazine for social workers. I wanted to write or edit a book or two, help social workers find jobs, and foster career development in social work colleagues. I created this niche in the form of a social work publishing company.

As the end of my work day nears, I think about the book I am editing, the third edition of *DAYS IN THE LIVES OF SOCIAL WORKERS*. It is a collection of social workers' stories—social workers in different roles, and in different settings. They all have different jobs, but they all have a professional social work education and do their work from a social work perspective. They are all social workers.

Before I leave for the day, I reach into my box of "I Am a Social Worker" buttons and pull out a few to take to the conference next week. I will proudly wear the big round, red buttons with these words in large letters, to let everyone at the conference know that I identify with and am a part of the social work profession.

I think that many social workers have careers that evolve and transform over time, as mine has. Their social work backgrounds sometimes take them places they never would have imagined. Who knows where mine will lead next? There is one thing that I know for certain.

I am a social worker. STILL.

Think About It

1. What does it mean to be a social worker?

2. How might a manager or business person who is a professional social worker act differently from a manager or business person who is trained in business?

Chapter 2
A Licensed Clinical Social Worker in Nonclinical Practice

● ● ● ● ● ● ● ● ● ● ● ● ● ● ● ● ● ● ●

by Catherine Sperry Beckett, LCSW

I t is mid-March, 2004, Thursday, 8:00 a.m. My first actions of every work day at the national office of Friends of the Children are always the same; I enter my cubicle and turn on my computer. The notion of how strange this seems usually crosses my mind, along with the thought, "I am a Licensed Clinical Social Worker who has worked most of her professional life as a child and family therapist. And once again today, I will go through the whole work day without seeing, talking to, or directly working with a single child or family."

When I moved to Portland, Oregon in 2000, I had six years of clinical experience in a variety of settings, including community mental health agencies, schools, hospitals, homeless shelters, drug treatment centers, hospice, and private practice. I had also designed curricula and instructed graduate-level courses for professionals who work with at-risk children and adolescents. As much as I loved the work, by the time I landed in Portland I had developed several concerns about what I was doing. First, I had begun to believe that, in general, the children and families who most needed assistance were not the ones who were going to find their way into my counseling office. Second, for those who did, I felt unsure about how much of a lasting difference fifty minutes once a week for maybe ten to twelve weeks (*if* there was good insurance, and if I spent a lot of time fighting for authorization) was going to make for children from such tough environments that they would likely need at least twice that long to even begin to trust me. And finally, once I began teaching and training other child-serving professionals, I started to see that one-on-one work, even over an entire career, was never going to allow me to have an impact on the number of at-risk children I wished to reach in my lifetime.

I was in a quandary; I didn't know whether jobs that addressed my concerns even existed. And then in 2001, through a series of personal and professional connections, I discovered Friends of the Children. FOTC is the only program in the nation that provides carefully screened, full-time, paid professional mentors (called "Friends") to a community's most at-risk youth for a full twelve years, starting in kindergarten or first grade. The model is based on resiliency research, which indicates that one of the strongest protective factors for high-risk children is an ongoing relationship with a supportive, caring adult. The program selects children who are most in danger of school failure, juvenile delinquency, gang and drug involvement, and teenage pregnancy, and commits to providing them with intensive mentoring through the end of high school. Working with no more than eight children, Friends teach valuable life skills, model healthy behavior, expose children to new, positive experiences, and marshal resources to support each child's success. Founded in Portland in 1993, a national office was established in 1999. By 2001, Friends was serving over 600 children in eleven cities across the U.S.

The national office of FOTC had created a new position, Program Content Specialist, which I sought and landed. I was to begin with two primary tasks. First, the children in the Portland chapter had grown into adolescents, and FOTC wanted someone with expertise in adolescent development to look at ways the programming might need to be adjusted to accommodate the changing needs of teenagers. Second, FOTC had recently created a set of six program outcomes (Positive Identity and Personal Vision for Future, Life Skills, Social and Emotional Skills, Moral Character, Work Ethic, and Lifelong Learning), and Friends needed help incorporating these into programming. For example, what social and emotional skills should a child have by the end of second grade? Fifth grade? Eighth grade? Graduation? And if the child is not on track in that outcome area, what concrete things can a Friend do to help the child progress? These questions were addressed by developing The Milestones Project, a resource binder listing ten to fifteen developmentally-appropriate milestone goals for each of the six outcomes, in each of five developmental stages (early and late elementary, and early, middle and late adolescence). Then, for each milestone goal, the binder gave suggestions about activities Friends could do with a child to help him or her meet that particular goal.

The national office has undergone numerous changes since I signed on in 2001. As staff numbers dwindled during the recession, I was asked to take on the management of national training, and then national program evaluation, in addition to program content. In 2004, as I write this chapter, my official title is National Director of Curriculum, Training and Evaluation, and I am the longest-term employee of the national office of Friends of the Children.

8:05 a.m.—My first order of business is to check e-mail and voice mail. Four of our chapter sites are located on the east coast, and there may already be urgent messages; any needs they have must be addressed by 2:00 PST because of the time difference. There are two voice mails and about twenty e-mails, but nothing demands immediate attention. Good. I can make some progress on updating the proposal and budget for the multi-site, longitudinal study of the program model we are planning. Having obtained a grant from the Edna McConnell Clark Foundation to fund a study planning year, the national president Catherine Milton and I are now deep into not only working with our researchers and chapters to plan the study, but also attempting to obtain funding to actually launch it in the Spring of 2005. Catherine has a meeting coming up with a major foundation, and the materials (including information about the study design, costs, and justification points) will need to be ready by the end of the week. Over the course of the next hour, I update the presentation to reflect some recent design changes suggested by our researchers, and prepare a memo for Catherine listing questions she is likely to be asked about the study, and suggested answers for her to give.

9:00 a.m.—Into the conference room for the bi-weekly Executive Director Conference Call. ED's and program managers from each of our chapters dial in for an hour of information sharing and discussion; given their schedules, generally one chapter or another is missing on any given Thursday. Even so, the call is one of the few regular opportunities this community has to talk together as a group, and when chapters are geographically so far apart, concrete reminders that they are all part of a chapter network are important.

Following brief updates offered by each chapter, we launch into today's discussion topic: child selection. It is, we agree, one of the most important things we do—a program that makes a 12-year commitment to its children needs to be very sure it is enrolling the right children. To do this, each chapter partners with elementary schools in vulnerable areas (low income, high rates of violence and other crime). Program staff spend six weeks in kindergarten or first grade classrooms observing all of the children, and through observation and conversations with teachers and staff, they develop a list of the children who seem to be at the highest risk for serious trouble down the road. Extensive family outreach is then conducted to invite these children into the program.

At issue on today's call: several chapters have switched this year from selecting children in the fall of the first grade year to selecting in the spring of the kindergarten year. Chapters that select kindergarteners have found that the relationship with a Friend has seemed to help the children a great deal in making the transition into first grade. Several program managers talk about some of the mental adjustments they had to make when looking at kindergarteners, but conclude that the right children for the program are still clearly identifiable half a year earlier. I remind the group that the Milestones Project has just been revised to include developmentally-appropriate milestones for pre-schoolers (age 4-5); these should help staff doing assessments to spot kids who are lagging behind on one or more developmental pathways. We talk a bit about current research supporting the validity of kindergarten assessment and the reasons that behavioral risk assessments can be done once children have started school, but not before. In some ways, I explain, school is a child's very first "job," and failure to measure up early on leads to negative developmental pathways that can be hard to reverse. So, while a child with multiple serious risk factors might be tougher to identify prior to beginning school, she or he becomes much easier to spot upon school entry, when his or her early inability to "make the grade" is thrown into sharp relief.

The last part of the one-hour call is focused on a particular selection dilemma. One chapter's program manager reports some current tension with its school partner around selection. They have a program slot open for one boy, and have identified several good candidates, preferring one named Darius who seemed the most in need. The school principal and teachers, however, are nay-saying their pick, saying things like, "Darius is a lost cause," "It would be a waste of resources," and even "He doesn't deserve to have a Friend." They are lobbying hard for another boy named Marshall, farther down the program's list, who comes from a family with many risk factors but who has a friendly and appealing personality.

"It's a tough one," is my input. "On one hand, you need to preserve your good relationship with the school. At the same time, resiliency research says that the kids who are able to be naturally resilient are the ones with friendly, outgoing personalities who are able to recruit their own informal mentors—which is exactly what Marshall has done. He's already got most of the school staff lobbying on his behalf. But our program was specifically designed to reach the kids who *don't* have that ability—the kids like Darius, who aren't going to be able to recruit their own advocates. My view is, if there isn't anything that would make you unable to work with Darius or his family, then he's the one to take." Other staff and chapters agree, and the program manager decides to gather some more information on Darius and his family before making a final decision.

10:30 a.m., Weekly National Staff Meeting—After announcements from the President, we begin a roundtable where each national staff member offers updates on his or her current projects. I remind staff that New Friends Training, a week-long intensive required for new mentors from all chapters, begins in a week and a half. A number of staff are slated to present training sessions; I pass around the schedule as a reminder. We are expecting twelve participants, coming from Portland, Salem, Eugene, Seattle, San Francisco, and New York.

As other staff give their updates, I am struck again by the variety of backgrounds (including business and nonprofit management, law, accounting, marketing and PR, and development and fundraising) sitting around the table. I am the only social worker on staff, as well as the only staff member with direct service experience with the population of children and families we serve. And while some days being the bearer of these perspectives makes me feel as though the voice I bring adds great value, on other days it can feel like a heavy burden. I can recall staff meetings when I needed to explain to colleagues that sometimes there are other reasons our program parents can't get their children to school consistently beyond, "They don't care about their kids' future." Or to argue that describing the children we serve as "the worst of the worst" (a practice that has been discarded) isn't okay, even if it does help us raise money. During one meeting, when we were discussing the importance of mentors helping their children develop healthy cultural identities and connections, one Ivy-League-educated staff member asked, "But what are the white kids supposed to do during that time?" The social work perspective is important here.

As always, we end the staff meeting with a program child story. This week it is my turn to offer one, and I talk about a child I met on a recent training visit to our Cincinnati chapter. As part of my visit, I was invited to go on an outing with a Cincinnati Friend named

Trudy, and Michelle, age nine, who lives with her grandmother. (Her mother is drug-addicted and turns up once or twice a year, promising for a few days to clean up before disappearing again.) Michelle's grandmother is illiterate, and Michelle has had an extremely difficult time learning to read. She was held back after first grade before going on to second, and three weeks into her third grade year, the school concluded Michelle simply did not have the skills to make it and would need to go back to second. This was so embarrassing for Michelle, says Trudy, that she has been reluctant to go to school at all since.

"But," said Trudy, "there's something good about all that. For three years, I've been trying to get Grandma to try adult literacy classes, and she always said no. She says, 'You only look stupid if you try.' But after the school meeting, she called me and said, 'I know part of why Michelle can't read is because of me. I don't want her to end up like me.'" Trudy doesn't yet know if the grandmother has followed through on the classes, "but," she says, "I sure got my fingers crossed."

12:00 p.m.—I ride my purple Honda scooter 26 blocks home for lunch, as I do almost every day. In the 45 minutes I am there, I may make a sandwich, cuddle with my dog, or spend some time on my Nordic Track ski machine. As hard as it sometimes is to pull myself from my desk and do this, I believe that maintaining this boundary is one of the principle reasons I am the longest-tenured staff member in the national office.

1:00 p.m.—I return from lunch to an e-mail from Danielle, the program manager in San Francisco, who has just had a Friend named Kevin give notice of his resignation. Whenever possible, Friends are asked to give six weeks notice so a replacement can be hired and children can be smoothly transitioned from one Friend to the next, but in this case Kevin can only work four more weeks. I start an e-mail back to her, and then change my mind and pick up the phone.

She's there. I e-mail her the basic six-week Friend-to-Friend transition plan I have developed, and we talk about ways it can be shortened to four weeks. Social workers widely recognize the importance of termination in relationships, but it took solid data showing that the program lost kids when Friend-to-Friend transitions weren't handled well to get attention paid to this process. The six-week plan offers a timeline and some specific suggestions about what Friends should say (for example, how important it is for a Friend to tell children point-blank that she or he is not leaving because of something the child has done wrong, even if the child does not ask this question, and to work with each child to develop a specific way to say goodbye). We also talk briefly about ways the chapter itself can have a process for saying goodbye to Kevin.

On hanging up, there is a voice mail marked "urgent" from Leslie, one of the Eugene Friends, sounding anxious and requesting a return call. I phone her back and she explains that she has gotten a summons to testify in a case concerning a second-grader named Maya. Maya lives with her maternal grandmother, but Maya's father is seeking custody; he is an active alcoholic who has trouble keeping jobs and making rent. Once I establish that Leslie's program manager is aware of the situation, I ask how I can help. "Last week," Leslie says, "Maya's new therapist gave her a diagnosis called Adjustment Disorder with Anxiety, and I just was wondering what that means."

I explain a bit about both the process of diagnosis, and about Adjustment Disorder specifically. Leslie wants to know if this diagnosis means that Maya should not have to take responsibility for her behavior choices (she is often caught lying and stealing). I tell her absolutely not. Leslie does an excellent job of holding Maya accountable in appropriate ways, and this should continue. We talk more about testifying. I reassure her that she is not a therapist and should not have to answer any questions related to Maya's therapy or diagnosis. (She is immensely relieved to hear this.) I offer some general tips, such as being careful only to answer what she is asked, and not being afraid to take time to think about an answer, or to say "I don't know."

"Oh," Leslie says suddenly, "they're calling us all into the courtroom now—I have to go. Thanks, Catherine," and she hangs up. I realize for the first time that she was calling from just outside the courtroom, waiting to be ushered in. I'm glad I was by my phone. I leave a message for Leslie's program manager, just to let him know about the call and what suggestions I gave her. I also make another mental note that the national office ought to have a one-pager of tips and bullet points we can hand out to any mentors who are asked to testify. Another item on the "List of Things To Do When Time Allows."

2:40 p.m.—I have just settled back into work on the research proposal when the phone rings again. It's Mike, the program manager for chapters in Salem, Eugene, and Klamath Falls. He has just come out of a check-in meeting with one of his Friends, Samuel, and wants to consult. One of Samuel's boys, a third-grader named James, has a mother who is in the final stages of terminal cancer. He has never met his father, who is believed to be in prison. Mike and I have done a lot of work with Samuel over the past year to help him feel more comfortable with the situation; at first, even "going into the house, when I know this woman is dying in there" was very hard for him, as was talking openly about both the situation and James' feelings with him.

In addition to Samuel's challenges, Mike had discovered upon starting as program manager that one in every eight children served by our Klamath Falls site had had a parent commit suicide. In response, I designed and facilitated a special training for the Oregon Initiative Friends on understanding and working with grief and loss in children (with special attention paid to the issue of parental suicide). The training was a success and has since been requested by and presented at several additional chapters.

Samuel had made big strides, but now, as the mother declined, James seemed to be falling apart. Samuel had come to see Mike very upset after an outing with James. "What happened?" I ask, and Mike replies, "Well, apparently James freaked out and threw himself under the wheels of Samuel's truck." I feel momentary panic until Mike clarifies that Samuel's truck was parked at the time. We talk about the need for Samuel to acknowledge and accept James' feelings, while setting clear limits around his behavior. Samuel will also need to investigate with James whether he is really thinking about hurting himself, and we talk about ways he might approach that.

Mike also mentions that Samuel has expressed concern about the appropriateness of physical intervention in safety situations. (For example, was it okay to physically pull James out from under the truck when he refused to come out on his own? Or is that kind of response only okay when a child might be in serious and immediate danger, such as trying to run into traffic instead of diving under a parked car?) These strike me as excellent questions, on which FOTC national has no written policies. I dial our managing director, a former attorney, into the call. Our conclusion: Friends does not currently have written policies around physical intervention in safety situations, and we need to develop some. A number of phone calls to larger mentoring agencies later, we have found that none of them have such policies. We will have to start from scratch.

3:20 p.m.—I am grateful for the brief "brain rest" that copying agendas and materials for the upcoming New Friends Training allows. I copy, staple, and organize training binders while mentally going over some of the additions made to the agenda since this training was last presented six months ago. I will be piloting a workshop on "the culture of poverty," looking at what kinds of skills are required of those who live in the lowest socioeconomic brackets, as well as the belief systems they often develop. Many Friends who come from different socioeconomic circumstances have said that more help understanding the circumstances and perspectives of the families they work with would help them serve both children and parents with more empathy and less judgment.

Back at my desk, I send out e-mail reminders to the rest of the training presenters (mainly Friends and other staff from the Portland, Salem, and Eugene chapters). Then, back again to working on the research proposal. I notice I also have an e-mail from one of the ED's with questions about hiring a local third-party evaluator. Coordinating evaluation is in many ways the part of my job that is toughest for me. Not having the background working for start-ups that many national staff members do, my only jobs prior to Friends have been jobs in which I was hired to do a very specific task (or set of tasks, such as therapy, group facilitation, and crisis intervention)—all of which I could be confident I had the training and experience to do well. Never before had I been in a work situation in which my boss said, "You know, we need someone to coordinate program evaluation on a national level, and we'd like you to take it on." When it happened, I protested that I didn't have any evaluation experience, and she replied that no one on staff did, that someone was going to have to develop it, and that she had great confidence that I would do just fine.

Even so, in the same way that I would want to feel confident I had the right skills to serve a client seeking therapy (or else would refer the client elsewhere), I have days when I can't help feeling that our chapters would be better served in the evaluation realm by someone with the kind of experience in evaluation that I have in child development, facilitation, and training.

I continue working on changes to the longitudinal study proposal. For a long-term program such as Friends, which serves a relatively small number of hard-to-reach children, funding a longitudinal study presents tremendous difficulty. Funders prefer to fund "proven" programs, yet marshalling the money necessary to fund a scientific trial long enough to show significant change is tough. What if we get funding for a three- or four-year study, and by the end of that time we haven't seen enough change in our small sample size to qualify as statistically significant? Nobody would want to fund continued data collection after that, and the tremendous later changes in program children that might emerge would go untracked (and the model unproven).

5:00 p.m.—Colleagues who don't come in as early as I do are still at their desks, but it's time for me to stop for the day. I check e-mail once more, seeing nothing that can't wait until tomorrow, and power down.

As I head down the hall toward the parking lot, stretching some of the computer and telephone knots out of my shoulders, I catch snippets of conversation from the Friend and child walking just ahead of me. "You did so well today," the Friend says. "I can't believe that was the first time you've ever played kickball—you're a natural." The little girl beams up at her Friend and grabs her hand, skipping alongside her.

I feel a momentary pang—the brief sadness of someone whose hand children like this one used to hold, who now spends more work time on the phone and in front of a computer than in playrooms and kickball games. And then I remember—that computer and phone time is helping this little girl, and her mentor, and hundreds like them, get what they need to grow.

And then, walking quietly behind them, I smile.

Think About It

1. Would you have chosen Darius or Marshall for the program? What are your reasons?

2. Compare and contrast the different roles of being a "hands-on" social worker working one-on-one with clients and being a social worker who focuses on "the big picture." Would you find either particularly frustrating? What appear to be the rewards of each?

Chapter 3
Transferring Micro Experience to Macro Practice—Working at the Child Welfare League of America
● ●

by Roxana Torrico, MSW

It is a 30-minute metro ride into the city. It is usually a race to get on the train, only to be squeezed in between tons of people in business suits reading their papers, eager to begin their day. I get off at Union Station and slowly walk down North Capitol. As I look up, I am struck by the beauty of the Capitol. I am also stunned by the sight of several homeless men and women sleeping on the streets, begging for food or money. I look around and wonder: *Does anyone notice or are we so used to seeing this type of poverty that we are not affected by the sight of homelessness even on the streets of our nation's Capital?* I am always shocked at how one of the richest countries in the world does not have enough money to provide people with enough supports and affordable housing. And then I am reminded of why I have chosen this line of work.

As I walk into my office building, I remember how as a graduate student, I was certain that I wanted to work with families in a direct service capacity, not realizing how intense and challenging this work would be. After graduation, I went on to work full time with a local child welfare agency as a foster care social worker. At the time, I was also employed part time as a case manager for homeless families in a transitional housing program. In my work with homeless families, I was faced with many former foster youth who became homeless as adults. I remember wondering if there was a link between the two systems. It did not make sense to me how three out of seven of my homeless clients used to be in foster care.

After about 18 months, I recognized that direct service in a child welfare agency was not a good fit for me, and I accepted a position as a Program Manager for the Child Welfare League of America (CWLA). CWLA is the nation's oldest and largest membership-based child welfare organization. It is an association of almost 1,100 public and private nonprofit agencies that assist over 3 million abused and neglected children and their families each year. At last, I would be able to combine my professional experiences with the child welfare and homeless systems to act as a change agent. Although I knew when I accepted this position my work would be different, little did I know how different it would be!

Today is Monday. List of Things To Do: *(1) review draft for housing poster, (2) finish PowerPoint presentation, (3) schedule interviews (Utah, California, Washington, Oregon), (4) attend NPEYH.* I begin EVERY morning by checking my e-mail. I scroll through several internal and external e-mails—confirming meetings, providing policy updates, and requesting information regarding housing options for youth.

I click on the most important e-mail, a request for information. A worker from Colorado is interested in knowing what kind of housing options are available for young people in her state. I pull out my Colorado folder—I have one for almost every state. Fortunately, Colorado has a very promising housing program. I provide the worker with a contact name and send her several attachments with details about Colorado's Family Unification Program. The Family Unification Program (FUP) is the use of time-limited (18 months) Section 8 vouchers for youth aging out of the foster care system. Young people ages 18-21 who have left foster care at age 16 or older are eligible for housing assistance and aftercare services. I explain that in October 2000, Congress passed legislation that made youth aging out of the system eligible for these time-limited Section 8 vouchers. I also send her some information about other program models that are assisting youth with housing upon discharge from public systems. I make myself available for further assistance and update her on current CWLA projects relevant to housing options for young people. I click "send" and take a minute to process. I get these e-mails from workers all over the country. Usually they are surfing the Web or receive information regarding a recent presentation. I am always hopeful that they find the information useful.

After responding to the information request, I move on to the first item on my "List of Things to Do": *(1) review draft of housing poster.* One of the deliverables from my grant is to create marketing materials for youth and adults regarding housing options. In an effort to do this, I have collaborated with a national network for foster youth to create a poster to educate young people, member agencies, independent living coordinators, community based workers, policymakers, and advocates on the importance of safe, stable, and affordable housing for youth aging out of the foster care system. I have been working closely with the designers to make sure that the pictures are culturally diverse and the wording targets both young people and adults. I call the designer again to discuss some more changes in the poster—I would like one of the pictures changed. After a long conversation and yet another brainstorming session, the designer and I decide since this poster will be distributed all over the country, that we should take advantage of the space on the back. We decide to add national statistics on the cost of housing and resources on the back panels. Off to work to gather more information. Who knew how much time went into creating a poster? I have been working on this for months!

Next item on my list: *(2) finish PowerPoint presentation.* I am scheduled to attend a conference in Austin, Texas, to discuss housing for youth. I have done this presentation in the past, but I always like to add some local information when I present. I spend some time doing some research on the Internet, so I am able to incorporate housing costs for Texas in my presentation. "Found it!" According to the National Low Income Housing Coalition, the cost of a one-bedroom at the Fair Market Rate is $543 a month. The hourly wage to afford this one-bedroom is $10.44. I didn't make that much when I was 18. But here is the kicker—the number of weekly hours (at state's minimum wage) that a young person must work to afford this apartment—81! This is both powerful and shocking information that I must add. Professionals need this type of information to make change. I always incorporate a policy and practice perspective to my presentations. The people who do the work need this information to inform policymakers on the need for change. "How can we expect young people with no outside supports to afford housing on their own? How can we be surprised by the intersection of foster care with homelessness, incarceration, unemployment, and high pregnancy rates when we don't provide these young people with the tools and supports for a successful future?" I could go on and on.

I save my changes to my desktop—ready to make copies to pack up for the upcoming presentation.

On to the next item on my list: *(3) schedule interviews (Utah, California, Washington, Oregon).* I spend the afternoon making phone calls to the Independent Living (IL) Coordinators on the west coast. I am currently leading the efforts of a collaborative project with other national partner organizations aimed to improve the housing outcomes for youth aging out of the foster care system. A major component of this effort involves identifying and describing promising efforts designed to address their housing needs. As a first step, I am conducting interviews with state Independent Living Coordinators across the country. The purpose of these interviews is to gain insight into each state's discharge policy, use of funding, and housing options offered to the numerous young people as they age out of the foster care system. Unfortunately, I have to leave messages for all but one of the state Independent Living Coordinators. The IL Coordinator from Utah answers the phone! I introduce myself and give background information on CWLA and our recent initiative on youth housing. He is very interested and is willing to set up a time to do the interview. I explain that it should only take 20-40 minutes. He asks "Do I need to do any research before the interview?"

My response: "There are only two questions you need to be prepared to answer: (1) How many young people age out of your state's system every year? and (2) How much of your Chafee funding is being used for room and board services?" (In an effort to assist youth in their transitions to adulthood, the Foster Care Independence Act (FCIA) of 1999 established the John Chafee Foster Care Independence Program, allowing states more funding and flexibility to assist young people in their transitions to adulthood. States received increased funding and were permitted to extend Medicaid eligibility to former foster children up to age 21. Additionally, the Chafee program allowed states to use up to 30% of their federal funds to provide room and board services to youth 18 to 21 years of age. This includes young people who move into independent living programs, age out, and/or lose touch with the child welfare agency and then return for assistance before reaching the age of 21.) He is thankful for the opportunity to share this information. We schedule a time for the following week.

I am scheduled to spend the rest of the afternoon at a National Partnership to End Youth Homelessness (NPEYH) meeting. I take a short metro ride to the meeting. I always enjoy having meetings somewhere else—change of scenery. I arrive to the meeting just in time. The National Partnership to End Youth Homelessness, a national coalition that represents the fields of child welfare, juvenile justice, mental health, homelessness, and housing is committed to ending youth homelessness. We have a meeting about every six weeks. Today, we are having a guest speaker to discuss the issue of reentry—juveniles being discharged out of public systems without an effective discharge plan. This is an issue that the group has been interested in for some time. Our speaker is very interesting but unfortunately reinforces what NPEYH already knows—"There isn't enough research to support that juveniles coming out of detention centers are becoming homeless." We spend the last few minutes of the meeting brainstorming next steps relevant to the issue. We look up at the clock. Time to wrap up. We schedule our next meeting. On the agenda: The Issue of Reentry.

Done for the day. Off to the metro. I spend the next half hour working on my "List of Things to Do" for tomorrow.

I usually find that unless a person has worked with or knows someone who has been in public systems, it is not something that they think about. However, approximately 20,000 to 25,000 young people age out of the foster care system each year, many without familial or economic support. Not only has it been frequently reported, but I have also witnessed foster youth leaving the care of the child welfare system without the skills or support networks necessary to enable them to become self-reliant adults. My professional experiences as a trained social worker have allowed me to witness the economic losses and the emotional, physical, and psychological impact of abuse and neglect on children and families. As a result, I recognize the importance of sound practice and policies, cross-training among disciplines, and comprehensive, culturally competent wraparound services to ensure the well-being of children, youth, and families. I am thankful that I am able to combine practice and policy to make change!

Personal characteristics that are helpful in this type of position include the ability to be organized and work independently. I cannot survive without my "List of Things to Do." I am often invited to meetings and events, so it is also important that an individual in this type of position be comfortable with networking and public speaking.

This position requires that an individual have a master's degree in social work or a related field with at least two years experience in housing, homelessness, and the child welfare system. Salaries are commensurate with professional skills and experience.

Macro level social work (policy, research, program planning) is very different from micro or mezzo level practice. The most important thing to note is that there is no face-to-face delivery of services. If you enter this level of social work practice, you will serve as a change agent. Therefore, I strongly recommend that you either work part time in direct practice or volunteer, so you do not lose touch with reality. It is often easy to forget how we arrived to the social work field when we are spending so much time in meetings and writing reports.

Think About It

1. Which organizations are analyzing and influencing policies, conducting research, or providing consulting or training at a national or state level in your areas of interest?

2. Which organizations are stakeholders in housing, homelessness, family preservation, or child welfare issues?

3. Do you feel that it is important for a social worker to work "in the trenches" before working in an organization on a macro level? If so, why?

PART 2:
Program Development & Management

Chapter 4
Bringing Two Disciplines Together: Developing a Small, Groundbreaking Program
●●●●●●●●●●●●●●●●●●●●●●●●●●●●●●●

by Valerie Scott Massimo, Ph.D., MSW

C rawling downtown through typical rush-hour traffic, I wonder why I'm doing this. Then, taking my last sip of coffee, I remember some of the things I'm looking forward to today. There's that meeting with the hospital. Also, I can't wait to hear about possible new folks for our program. *Yes,* I think, as I maneuver my car into the miniscule parking lot down from the agency, *this could be an okay day.*

I swing through the glass door and greet the perpetually cheery secretary—probably the only smile in my day. People who suffer from substance abuse or developmental disabilities are seldom cheery fellows, and those unfortunate enough to fit both categories should hardly be expected to rejoice. But here I am, one year after completing my MSW, developing a program to treat such individuals. Hanging up my coat, pouring another cup of coffee, and settling into my little office, I muse on how remarkable it is to find myself here, Director of the Alcohol, Substance/Chemical Abuse Intervention Program (ASCAIP). The project was born out of my pre-MSW experience in substance abuse, one field placement in developmental disabilities (DD), a segment on grant writing in one of my administration courses, and my ongoing relationship with

Karen, who is a friend and former classmate. Over a winter break dinner last year, as the new clinical director of a DD agency, she talked about the growing problem of alcoholism among her clients. It seems people with developmental disabilities living in the community and working at "real" jobs have the same opportunity to abuse alcohol as the general public, but not the same resources to help them recover. Karen is a rare individual who can sniff out secret pockets of "start-up" money for innovative programs. Knowing I was graduating soon, she challenged me to write a grant proposal and head up a program for people like her clients if she could find a funding source. Mere months later, I'm here. My reverie is broken by the agency director, who wants to "chat" when I first come in.

Bob, nursing his fifth or tenth cup of coffee, invites me to sit across from his desk in the one chair not heaped with paper. His office, like mine, is small and windowless. (One doesn't enter this field for its posh surroundings!) No, I didn't remember I was supposed to attend the agency's board meeting this evening and give the board an update on my project. Yes, of course I will. I can leave by 9:30 if I really need to. (Oh good, not much over a 12-hour day!) Turns out someone heard from a resident that Joey, recently placed in a new apartment, was having "wild parties" on the weekends. Maybe I could drop by there? Joey's apartment is near my afternoon meeting, so here are directions if I'd like to drop in. "Drop in" is Bob's euphemism for a quick assessment, and we both know it.

Our meeting is interrupted by a phone call, and I use the opportunity to slip back to my office. I call the hospital to confirm our afternoon meeting, phone to cancel my plans for the evening so I can attend the board meeting, and begin the seemingly endless arrangements necessary to plan a conference. We're not talking a big conference here—just a day when leaders of the area's substance abuse and DD programs can meet to learn about one another's disciplines. Planning on a shoestring budget to get a few dozen very busy people together in a nice, centrally located venue where they can listen to a few speakers, share a simple lunch, and break into small groups for discussion is no small feat. What class did I take in my MSW program to prepare me for this? One of the case managers has suggested I call her uncle, who works in the food service business. Less than optimistic, I make the call. Something I learned early in graduate school was to take on my most onerous task first thing in the morning, so it doesn't weigh on me all day. Uncle is pretty sure he can help, mentioning a location that would be *perfect*, but first he must make a few calls. Nice of him, but I wish the place was tied up with ribbon and bow.

One of the things I've had to adjust to in the "real world" after school is that "semesters" never end. Everything I do leads to yet more tasks. The "paper" gets no grade; if I am extremely fortunate, it simply opens the door to more work. So why is a smile creeping over my face? This door may lead to a nearly perfect, yet affordable place to hold the conference.

Next on the agenda is a small clinical meeting with three of our case managers and Karen, the agency's clinical director, and the colleague who helped me develop this job. Four consumers (the word "client" is not used here) have been identified as possible substance abusers, purchasing alcohol on the way home from work and then drinking the night away, often fighting with roommates or causing some other kind of disturbance. There is difficulty trying to hook up consumers with Alcoholics Anonymous (AA). Public transportation is an issue, and then consumers are frustrated by not understanding what goes on at the meetings. One of the older consumers actually cried from fear of being asked to read when he attended a meeting where a book was passed around for discussion. Not only was our consumer terrified of reading, but he understood neither the passages read nor the discussions about them. A case manager in recovery himself offers to have some AA members come to our agency to run a special meeting one night a week. This seems an excellent idea, and I am given an AA name to contact, arrangements to make regarding space, transportation to arrange, and permissions to obtain from our building's landlord. As the meeting ends, one case manager says he thinks one consumer's problem is serious enough to warrant time in a detoxification center. Oh yes, I'll be sure to follow up on that when I meet with intake folks at the hospital this afternoon. No, this "paper" is never going to be finished.

Speaking of papers, I stop by the secretary's desk to see if she has found heavy paper stock for the conference. In my meetings with professionals in the substance abuse and DD fields, I have discovered many terms and acronyms known to one group and not the other. I developed an "Alphabet Soup" list of these and plan to put one in everyone's conference packet. No, the secretary (still cheery) has not really found the right paper, but she has an idea where to look when I'm in the field. Sure, I'll add this to my list. "It's a good thing you're a 'detail' person," she says as I leave her desk. I start to mention that my mother might disagree with this descriptor when I realize that, in fact, I am very much an organizer of sorts, especially when it comes to things that directly relate to issues about which I care passionately. When I can see the human faces behind the "to do" list, it becomes doable. I don't know how one tests for this capacity, but I recognize it as essential for pulling disparate pieces together to form a program, even one as small as ASCAIP.

A few more calls, and I'm off to a very late lunch (after 2:00, at least) with clinical director/friend Karen. I'm fairly bubbling with the news about a possible place for the conference (I bubble rather easily), and Karen applauds my efforts. Maybe there aren't A's to be had in this project development business, but I can go a long distance on a small amount of support like hers. Since I am going to a consumer's home this evening, she shares a sad story of a person who had been a prospect for our program. Despite AA experience to the contrary, our consumer had no trouble admitting to alcoholism. Instead, his resistance had to do with denial of his disability. Having been institutionalized as a boy, released in middle age to a transitional program, and now having "graduated" to an apartment and full time job, he *definitely* couldn't participate in a program for people with developmental disabilities! His job was in danger, as was his apartment placement, but no, this program *could not* be for him. Seeking comfort over a split dessert, Karen and I force our discussion from this to the "Alphabet Soup" handout, and we come up with the idea of playing some kind of alphabet game at the conference. As we have fun concocting bizarre possibilities, I realize that the ability to play keeps at bay the grimness and suffering that is the *raison d'etre* of work in our field. Maybe sense of humor should be measured for entrance into this kind of position.

Buttressed by lunch and play, I head for my meeting at the hospital. I find myself steered into a very formal conference room, and I rejoice that I am wearing something akin to a suit (not my usual garb). The ice is broken quickly, though, as we discuss the need for treatment for our population. Many at the table have their doubts about serving "those people" and how their presence on the unit might affect other patients. I find myself relying heavily on my group skills to steer the meeting in a more positive direction. (Thank goodness for the practice courses I had to take!) The head of the hospital's substance abuse unit expresses his hope that we can find a way to work together and volunteers Sister Mary Michael, Intake Director, to work closely with me on coordinating our efforts and developing an intake protocol appropriate to our consumers. She seems eager, and when the formal meeting concludes, takes me to her pristine office, gives me an armload of materials, promising to "get down to work" together as soon as I've read everything. As she deftly guides me through the labyrinth of hospital hallways leading to the parking lot, I can't quash the thought, "No, the semester is NEVER over!"

Now to find Joey-the-possible-alcoholic; Bob's directions are good, and I find him quickly. Unlike the projects I tromped around while deciding to go into social work, these apartments are only two stories high, not classy, but serviceable. Opening the door to me, beer bottle in hand, Joey's roommate gives me a welcoming smile. Watching a blasting, decades-old comedy show, they have the courtesy to offer me something to drink. I say I'll get it myself, knowing I can assess the kitchen if I do. This kind of snooping took me some getting used to, but caseworkers taught me the importance of assessing consumers' apartments. I note two six-packs in the refrigerator, but nothing else of concern. Nonetheless, I ask Joey to walk me back to my car during the next commercial. Coming down the stairs, I tell him about our concerns, and he gets angry, defensive. Yes, he'll come talk with someone on Thursday; he knows he needs to be "more better" if he is going to keep his apartment.

Driving away, I feel this situation could go either way. Of course, much follow-up will be needed. (Did I mention that the semester is never over?) Back at the office, there is just enough time to get through some paperwork, a few calls, most of a sandwich, and then off to the Board of Directors meeting. It is dull, only grabbing my attention when cheap shots are taken at Bob, the agency director. My own report is brief, positive, and well-received. It isn't quite like an A on a paper, but it will do. As promised, I am out by 9:30, probably leaving Bob to face more heat alone. No traffic now, I quickly reach the highway, crank up the music, and think I had a, well, *mostly* good day.

Think About It

1. What are the personal qualities that seem to suit this individual to this kind of work? Might someone with different qualities still accomplish the work and enjoy it? Why or why not?

2. In what ways did the writer's social work education prepare her for her daily work? What did she need to learn on the job? Could that be taught in your school? How?

Chapter 5
A Modern-Day Settlement House
• •

by Maureen Holland, BSW, MSW

Wednesday morning begins with its usual hectic pace. My first and second graders, Julia and Gabriella, miss the bus because we can't find Julia's gym shoes. After my 10-year-old boy walks to school with his friend, I put the girls in the car and drop them off for the day. As happens on occasion, I arrive a little late for my first event of the day, my management team meeting. One of my co-workers has brought warm bread with butter from the Puerto Rican bakery across the street. Although I am on the low carb craze like everyone else, I cannot resist a nice warm slice.

I work at New North Citizens' Council, Inc., a modern day settlement house founded in the spirit of social change and advocacy. The founder of the organization is still the leader 30 years later. She began the settlement house protesting for welfare rights on the steps of City Hall. Three decades later, she is guiding her staff in speaking out for the rights of those whose voices are not heard. Our office has an open door policy. Over 6,000 people come to our doors every year, without an appointment, looking for a helping hand. Requests usually are for food, help with the utility companies, translation, and help with learning English. Most of these clients are neighbors. They come from Puerto Rico, Guatemala, Mexico, and El Salvador. The newcomers are bewildered by the system and need a friendly neighborhood organization to help them adjust to the new culture. Welcome to the modern day settlement house.

The community-based nonprofit family service agency is in urban Massachusetts. The neighborhood is low income, and many of my friends refuse to drive in the area because of frequent drive-by shootings. For me, it is my second home. I was fortunate to have loved languages in my younger years and earned a degree in Spanish along with my social work degree. I get tired of hearing myself preach the virtues of a second language—any language. I started in the child protective service field, conducting child abuse investigations for the state. Now I work for the settlement house, which provides not only services to our neighbors, but social services for abused children and their families.

The management team meeting includes the 14 managers of the 100 person staff. I am a mid-level manager with 20 staff in my department. Today all of the managers are meeting to make some important decisions and small ones, as well. We are currently working in a run-down building that has been a home to a car dealership, a furrier, a Goodwill, and currently a social service agency. It rains inside of the building, the heat works sporadically, and there are sometimes small furry unwelcome visitors. Spread on the table in front of us are plans for a new building. I feel a little bewildered by the task of designing a building, but I get excited when we talk about alternative energy and a library. Next on the agenda is planning the Three Kings celebration for the forty children in our foster homes. Many of the foster parents were born in Puerto Rico and have fond memories of the Tres Reyes Magos bringing them a gift on January 6. We vow that we are not going to get carried away this year and will keep it simple. Somehow we end up with a hand-built manger, hay, costumes, a band, readings, and the local television station. Next year, we will keep it simple.

After the management team meeting, I meet with one of the supervisors and a home visitor. They describe the challenges in working with a teenage girl who is pregnant at age fourteen. She is engaging well with the home visitor and is expressing sadness because her mother has recently been jailed for vehicular homicide after a tragic accident that resulted in the death of an elderly couple. The home visitor is advocating for the mother to get a lawyer who will look at all angles of the case, since her punishment seems overly harsh for unclear legal violations. The mother, who has a clean history, was sober, on the right side of the road, and was exceeding the speed limit by a few miles per hour. Her three children, including her pregnant daughter, are now cared for by a hodge-podge of providers. The pregnant teen is despondent, because her mother will not be with her at the time of the baby's birth. The agency will work to find a lawyer to adequately represent her.

Now I am really behind schedule, and I arrive right on time for the meeting of the Maternal Child Health Commission, of which I am the chair. This Commission was formed by the mayor ten years ago to examine the causes of infant mortality in the city. This rate is stubbornly high and a cause of great anguish among the citizens. The 40-member Commission represents the state public health department, early intervention programs, the birth hospitals, mental health providers, Head Start, and the faith community, to name a few. The commission plans events during the year, such as the Community Baby Shower. More than 500 pregnant women and their families come to the shower to learn about topics ranging from car seat safety to post-partum depression to breastfeeding. We also discuss matters of policy, such as the lack of accessibility to birth control for undocumented residents, the need for cultural sensitivity for the Vietnamese population, and the latest training on talking to families about adoption as an option in their unplanned pregnancies.

I make a quick stop at a neighborhood restaurant and order Spanish chicken soup to go. It is overpriced but delicious. I go back to my office and spend a few minutes checking my e-mail, voice mail, and postal mail. I then sit with the manager of the Adolescent Assessment unit. It is monthly report time, and there are 80 family reports to review. The home visitor, the supervisor, and I sign each one.

All of our staff members are bilingual in English and Spanish. The majority of the families referred to us are primarily Spanish speaking. The children are teens who are abused or neglected or are having adolescent issues at home. Families are generally Hispanic, low income, with limited education, and may struggle with substance abuse or mental health issues. Most of the parents are struggling to be good parents. The home visitors model good parenting and assist the teens with their issues. The referrals always make the teen look impossible, and sometimes they are. The workers usually form a great bond with them and see improvement in the family functioning. My eyes start to get a little tired from reading so many reports. We need to finish them today, so they can be delivered to the three child protective services offices with which we contract.

My next project is to work with six other staff members to plan a retreat day for our whole agency. With a rapid growth from 20 to over 100 staff in fifteen years, there is plenty of need for team building and interaction. The HIV/AIDS staff is not clear about the child care department, while the housing advocate does not understand what the teen groups are planning. We decide to have an interactive, day-long event with food, raffle prizes, and a motivational speaker. Although staff will resist at first, we will seat them with co-workers they do not know well. It will be an opportunity to deepen our sense of mission and identity. The planning is exciting as I work with co-workers I scarcely knew before this project.

It is nearly time to go home. My husband, a high school math teacher, is at home cooking dinner for the family. We need to shuttle the children to Boy Scouts and basketball. I hope they already walked the dog. I lock up the office for an hour. Soon, a dance group will come in to practice for a neighborhood festival. I hope they remember to turn off the lights.

Think About It

1. Why might a client feel comfortable in reaching out to a settlement house rather than a state agency?

2. Identify a micro, mezzo, and macro intervention that is likely to be implemented in this organization.

Chapter 6
Coordinating a Youth Development Program

•••••••••••••••••••••••••••••

by Laura Boutwell, MSW

I have the best job in the world. I get to work *with* a group of amazing teenagers in creating meaningful opportunities for community service, creative expression, leadership development, and community building. Coordinating a leadership development program is a non-traditional but increasingly common position within the field of social work. I work for Family Service of Roanoke Valley, a nonprofit human services agency with a 100-year history of serving individuals and families in southwest Virginia. The program I coordinate was established in response to a community-wide survey, which found that only 18% of teenagers feel valued by our community and that only 23% have positive adult role models.

My work week tends to be flexible, with occasional weekend hours for various activities. As is true for many social workers, I don't have a typical day. Some days I'm in high schools, working with small groups of teenagers on service projects or teaching a class on community building and diversity. Some days I'm meeting with teenagers and adult community leaders, fashioning service projects to address community needs. Other days I'm writing grants, planning projects, or doing community outreach. Every week, I meet with teenagers to plan activities and work on projects. The common currency of my days is both the commitment to and the reality of working *with* teenagers in fashioning meaningful opportunities for leadership and service.

In thinking about my typical day, I am better able to access some of my favorite moments in the last few months. I spent one morning with Faduma, a 16-year-old from Somalia, at a cultural orientation training for Somali Bantu refugees who will be arriving in our area in the next year. Faduma was asked to provide insight into what she experienced when she first came to the United States three years ago. I spent an afternoon with a group of teenagers who had been in wheelchairs for one school day. They discussed their experiences with a person with a disability, and were able to make significant parallels between their one-day experiences and the everyday experiences of others. I spent one Saturday afternoon with a group of teenagers who were stenciling storm drains to remind area residents not to dump trash into the rivers. One evening, I spent time with teenagers and a local photographer, brainstorming a local teen arts center.

United with Youth has four main components: leadership development trainings, community building activities, creative expression projects, and community service opportunities. Leadership development trainings have included media savvy, political advocacy, public speaking, and mentoring. Training is often provided by community leaders, and following the training, participants are provided with opportunities to apply their learning. The *Keepin' It Real* program provides community building activities to a core group of teen leaders and to area high school students. This year, teens participated in an experiential training designed to provide greater awareness of the experiences of refugees and the experiences of people with disabilities.

Opportunities for meaningful creative expression are a critical and often unmet need in teenagers' lives. This year, program participants explored their creative vision in *My Community: The World Through My Eyes*, a photography project designed to showcase teen creativity and the area's often hidden refugee communities. U.S.-born and refugee teenagers were paired together and received training in photography basics, at which point the teenagers befriended newly arrived refugee families. Teens took pictures documenting their experiences, culminating in a community-wide traveling exhibition of thirty-seven black and white photographs.

Community service is a significant cornerstone of the program. Twice a week, teenagers volunteer as mentors in an after school tutoring program at the local branch of the YWCA. Every month, teenagers participate in "One-Shot" community service projects. Over the last year, volunteer projects have included the local African-American heritage festival, a candlelight vigil, a substance abuse essay contest, and an environmental project.

The United with Youth program is the area sponsor of National Youth Service Day, an annual worldwide day of service. The goals of the day are to recruit the next generation of volunteers and to show the community the value of youth. In the months leading up to NYSD, I work with teens to identify and plan meaningful service projects. At NYSD 2004, more than 650 volunteers participated in 16 projects in our area, a testament to the power of teenagers actively serving in meaningful leadership positions.

One of my favorite aspects of this job is that there isn't a typical teenager who is in the program. The teen leaders I work with are as diverse as the activities we engage in. Most of the teens are U.S.-born, although increasingly I work with teenagers who are refugees and immigrants from many countries, including Afghanistan, Bosnia, Cuba, Sudan, Columbia, Somalia, and Kosovo. I work with honor students and alternative education students. I work with teenagers who have been taught that they have potential; I work with teenagers who have never been told that they mattered. Regardless of whether the teenager is a newly arrived refugee with limited English, a GED student, or an honor student, I believe that there are overwhelming similarities and needs in all teenagers.

Teenagers know that they aren't just our tomorrow: they are also our today. The teenagers I know are committed to their community just as they are dedicated to their individual development. Teen leaders in the program run community meetings and present their projects to local government officials. They tutor younger children, write grants, and make presentations with a commitment and an enthusiasm that inspires me on a daily basis. I often tell the teens I work with that they are my boss. On the surface, it's a joke. At a deeper level, it's my reality. I believe that my best self surfaces when "my teens" are present. I admire their creativity, trust their instincts, and am energized by their commitment.

A college degree in a human service field is required for this position. Salary is dependent on the level of education attained and is commensurate with other social work salaries in the area. My specific background includes running an after school tutoring program and working with refugee children.

I work in collaboration with community agencies, universities, and individuals who understand the transformative power of positive youth leadership development. This job is perfect for social workers who are interested in proactive interventive models that shun authoritative or reactive practice philosophies. More than anything, my position is ideal for social workers who want to work *with* teenagers in fashioning meaningful opportunities for leadership and service. This job is the strengths perspective at its best.

Think About It

1. In reflecting back on your teenage years, what was the message that adults in your life gave you? What did you need to hear?

2. What are your core beliefs about working *with* teenagers?

3. How would you establish a leadership development program in your area or agency?

Chapter 7
Managing a Hospital Social Work Department

●●●●●●●●●●●●●●●●●●●●●●●●●●●

by Susan Mankita, MSW, LCSW

H ospital social work department management is wonderful work, if you can get it. While social work in
health care is still a flourishing area of practice, many of
my colleagues from around the country have fallen victim to mas-
sive restructuring efforts that eliminated social work management
positions. The good news is that many departments, like mine, remain intact, and quite a few health care social work leaders have
moved higher up the health care ladder.

For six years, I have managed the social work department at a
small long-term acute care facility. There are two kinds of days
here—the atypical and the insane. As I walk into the large building,
I wonder which kind this will be. Sometimes, the challenge of doing more with less and the severity of human need combine in just
the right way with my social work thinking, creating nothing short
of an internal explosion. There is fiery passion borne of this kind
of work, and it fuels me daily. I love my job, because I can effect
powerful and lasting changes in the lives of catastrophically ill
people, in the way other professions see their roles and, given the
right issue, in the way services are delivered in the community.

As a "working" department manager, I wear two hats. I am responsible for ensuring that the department's objectives are carried out *and* for carrying a caseload. The social workers are responsible for assessing and addressing the many psychosocial
needs of patients and their loved ones. We "follow" them during
the course of their hospitalization, which in social work-ese means
we develop and maintain supportive relationships. We work with

53

them to identify strengths, cope with crises, and adjust to loss. We help them make the transition from the hospital to a continuing care plan that maximizes their independence and quality of life. This is called discharge planning. I am ultimately responsible for ensuring that patients in our facility move through the health care continuum appropriately.

There are messages waiting for me today. I know that as soon as I listen to them, I will be off and running in response. My calendar reminds me that we have a management meeting this morning, and I have scheduled supervision for our MSW intern in the afternoon. I enter my code and the mechanized voice that greets me each morning informs me, with no apology, "You have nine new messages."

The first message is from my administrator, advising that we will need an Ethics Committee meeting today, now scheduled for 4:15. She's also wondering when the abuse policy will be ready. Next, our CFO wants a prediction of discharges for this month. The Quality Review Manager reminds me that statistics are due on Monday. Three messages are lengthy expositions from marketers hoping for an appointment this week. A physician requests help with a challenging family member, and the very family member who challenges him calls to request help with the physician. This one, from the nursing supervisor, draws my attention immediately.

"Please send someone up to see Mr. Diaz. He's a nervous wreck today."

Of course he is. His insurance company has been trying to transfer him to a nursing home all week. Each morning, he has prepared himself psychologically to go, and each afternoon, one of the social workers has told him his transfer arrangements haven't been completed.

"Perhaps tomorrow," he says each day.

I make a mental note to send someone up to see him as soon as possible.

Mr. Diaz has been through hell and survived. Far too sick to go anywhere else at first, he has been ventilator dependent and badly infected. His nightmare began after surgical removal of cancer in his gastrointestinal tract. Seems they got most of the cancer, but they weren't able to wean him from the machine that inflates his lungs with the air that keeps him alive.

Sick as he is, he is totally aware of his environment. His tracheostomy, which acts as his airway, pushing in and sucking out his breath, before it can vibrate past his vocal chords to make sounds, has forced him to become adept at mouthing words and using a letter board to make his needs known. Not unlike the game of Charades, he uses his hands wildly to make people understand him. Luckily, it is summer time, and his two teenage granddaughters hold vigil daily, playing cards and talking about boys. They serve as his voice, turn him if he gets too uncomfortable, and entertain him when boredom comes. My colleague walks in and I ask if she will run up and visit with Mr. Diaz and place a follow-up call to his insurance company to see if they have completed the steps necessary for his transfer. I relax knowing he will be attended to. I tally some of the outcome data. The 10 a.m. management meeting arrives quickly.

A Voice at the Table

Team meetings are a mixed blessing for a department manager. Hospitals hold them frequently, and there is an expectation that you will be present even if you are a vital practitioner in a three-person department, as I am. Despite this tension between addressing management issues and providing direct patient care, the opportunity for input into how the facility operates is unparalleled. My social work values have played an important role, earning me a reputation as a "voice of reason." Having a social worker on the management team is one way to make sure that no patient is labeled "difficult" without acknowledging the contribution of the hospital environment or the impact of the disease, that no family's concerns are minimized, and that the patient's needs are always primary.

Today's meeting lasts most of the morning. We are preparing for a big survey and dividing the many remaining preparations among us. We are updating our policy manuals with the latest adjustments and brainstorming about how we can best present our strengths.

Managing Risk

In this litigious day and age, criticism of health care delivery runs high. Social workers can be critical players in managing risk, by observing for indicators that might lead to a lawsuit and starting the facility to work to correct problems and undo damage, if possible, before they intensify.

As I make rounds on the medical floor, before heading down to lunch, I see Katie, Mrs. Johnson's daughter. I know Mrs. Johnson will probably be medically stable for discharge soon and stop in to make sure the family has no new questions about her impending transfer. I soon realize that Katie's responses to me are not her usual friendly ones.

"Are you OK?" I ask.

"Just fine," she responds with a controlled voice that at once confirms my suspicions that she is extremely angry about something.

Because I know Katie from the family support meetings, I take a chance and reach in.

"I can see whatever it is, you're trying hard to keep it inside. I care about you and your mother and I'm here to listen and help if I can."

"Maybe a lawyer can help," she blurts out, her anger finding expression before a willing audience.

Floodgates open, and as her anger finds a voice, she starts to cry. She is angry with everyone right now, especially Dr. Salerno. No phone calls for over a week and she found out about her mother's new infection by accident. Everyone has "written her mother off" with discharge pending. She'd hoped her mother would be better when it was time to leave the hospital. She feels helpless and no one seems to care.

We agree that one way of improving the situation will involve the communication among her, the doctor, and the staff. A meeting with our Interdisciplinary Team is set for tomorrow. I advise my administrator of Katie's distress, and she calls the physician herself. Several staff members rally, making empathetic, information-filled visits to the room. Tomorrow, I will engage team members, family members, and physician in a problem-solving session that will satisfy Katie's concerns. Another crisis soon averted...for now.

Preparing the Next Generation of Leaders

The bulk of the caseload is divided among social work staff, consisting of a full-time MSW and a social work intern. When I am sitting at meetings, they are rushing between patient rooms, juggling phone calls. I count my blessings daily for my coworker, Maria, whose skills are sharp and whose competence makes my job that much easier. She is a fairly new social worker, and I provide her with clinical supervision she can apply toward her license. In my view, it is a manager's responsibility to prepare social workers for professional advancement. I momentarily fantasize about leaving work to finish my oft-neglected Ph.D. How well-prepared is she to run the department in my absence? Quite prepared, I decide. She has participated in the management team during my occasional absences and in the supervision of our intern. When she began working here, I encouraged her to participate in one of the many quality improvement teams, and she joined the Information Management Team. She quickly rose to a leadership position on the team and has earned respect. She is organized, compassionate, has great communication skills, and has shown flexibility in situations requiring it. It's delightful to watch her blossom.

Our intern from the university, Ana, has some natural gifts and insights that make supervising her a delight. At 3:00, we meet for her individual supervision, and she shares her anxiety about one client on her caseload. The spouse of a patient in ICU seems unwilling to bare his soul to her; in fact, she believes he actually finds her annoying. She recounts multiple efforts to engage him in a discussion of his feelings, all to no avail. It becomes apparent to her that her desire to please him has superseded his needs, and that leads to a productive discussion yielding additional insights and a plan to make another try. She saw her first dead person this week. She had ample opportunity to leave the room, but chose to stay and support the grieving new widow, a woman in her eighties whose relatives live in Argentina. Ana will be an excellent social worker.

At lunch, my mind returns to Mr. Diaz. If he *is* going to leave, we should get him a cake. He is one of our success stories.

The team worked with him throughout the summer. The speech therapist helped him practice his swallow so he could once again eat the Cuban rice and beans that made him salivate, instead of relying on the tube feeding that the dietitian monitored for adequate intake. The skin and wound care nurse taught his teenage granddaughters how to care for his skin so it wouldn't become red and raw or break down into ulcers. Nurses hung IV bags, checked the sites through which medication goes in, gave him his medication, and continually reassessed his condition. The respiratory therapists managed his airway, making sure that he got enough support, while at the same time, advancing the balancing act called weaning—learning to breathe on his own to avoid being attached to the ventilator for the remainder of his life. A physical therapist worked with him twice a day and strengthened his muscles, so now, he can walk around the nurse's station with assistance, tubes and all. It has been a long road, but even *he* has begun to experience brief moments of optimism... perhaps, *perhaps*... he WILL live through this.

End of Life Decisions

Ana and I sit with members of a family who have requested that their loved one be removed from life support. Our ethics committee considers all cases that involve "end of life" decisions, offering ethical guidance to patients, families, and physicians. This family has come to believe there is no chance of a meaningful recovery.

We explore with the family what "meaningful" would be from the patient's perspective, if he could tell us. We help the family identify benefits and burdens of continued treatment. They say the patient was a proud and independent man who disliked doctors, hospitals, and pain. His wife is convinced that he would not want to live like this. His daughters sob softly in the background and agree. I am crying a little, too, but inside so no one else sees.

Challenges to Balance and Perspective

When I finally get the call from Mr. Diaz's insurance company, I am sitting in the office rewriting the hospital's abuse policies. This is a priority, because the Joint Commission on Accreditation of Healthcare Organizations (JCAHO) will make its visit soon, and failing the survey is too horrible to imagine. I know Mr. Diaz's insurance company is anxious for him to leave the hospital. Hospital care is extremely costly. He has, in fact, been ready to go since last week, from his physician's perspective. Though I have had several pleasant chats with Monique, the nurse case manager who's been monitoring his progress, the woman who calls me today is Monique's boss. We have a manager-to-manager chat about Mr. Diaz's benefits. She wants to be completely sure that I know that as soon as she resolves a paperwork glut, she will be sending an ambulance to transport him to a nursing home.

He has been waiting for them to finalize his transfer arrangements all week, and now it's Friday. She advises me that her final approval may not come until evening. I request that if the approval comes down from her higher ups after 7:00 or 8:00 p.m., they send the ambulance the next day. She informs me that she will send him at 8:00, if the paperwork comes through at 8:00, 11:00 p.m. if it comes through at 11:00 p.m., or 2:00 in the morning if she decides she wants to. Unless, of course, I want to keep him in the hospital for free.

My blood is boiling… I am ready to say something extremely un-manager like when she says…

"…and I don't have the time now to debate this with you," and hangs up.

Have you ever looked straight at a phone, cradled in the receiver and yelled "YOU'RE SICK" at the top of your lungs? You now know that I have.

Fuming, I run half-crazed into administration, ready to pounce on my bosses for all the woes of the health care system. Relating this story, skin and face burning, I ask them to back me up on this. We cannot possibly release this man under these circumstances, regardless of cost to the facility. I prepare for the worst.

"Of course, we won't [release him]," she says. "We are responsible for this man's well-being. He is not going anywhere until you tell me it is safe."

I feel the adrenaline rush slipping away, and my heart rate goes back to near normal. Somewhere in the back of my mind, I remember saying something similar about safe transfers at a Monday morning management meeting.

"What are you going to do about this?" asks the Assistant Administrator, who has overheard. He knows me well enough to know that I won't let this slide.

Making Health Care Humane, One Policy at a Time

At day's end, I drive home, deliberately avoiding the radio so thoughts of the day can settle in, some finding resolutions, and some inscribing a mental note amidst the rubble that is my brain for tomorrow's attention. I remember my boss's question. That case manager needs education, for sure. I wonder if she is the only person so jaded by the bottom line focus of today's health care environment that she sees people as assets to be moved between accounts. First thing Monday morning, I will write a letter to the company's president questioning the transfer policy. Certainly no publicity-conscious managed care company would dare admit to transferring patients during late evening hours, I realize. I smile victoriously as I think about how I will have an impact on safe transfers throughout the community by writing to all the managed care companies, showcasing the offender's statement that they would never put one of their enrollees at risk in that way. Tonight, revenge is rich for the hospital social work department manager, but only because it can improve access to safe, appropriate care for people who cannot advocate for themselves.

Think About It

1. How effective do you think you can be in channeling your rage about injustices rather than saying or doing something that you would regret later?

2. Why is it inappropriate to discharge a patient at a late hour?

3. What are some advantages of having a job in which you have a mix of management and direct service duties? Disadvantages?

PART 3: Advocacy & Organizing

Chapter 8
Doing Political Social Work: My Sojourn
● ●

by Mitchell Kahn, MSW

I have three distinct memories of my life before the age of four. First was my mother bringing home my new baby brother, and second was my subsequent enrollment in nursery school. The third recollection is of a teacher at that nursery school hiding my Black playmate in a closet when a prospective white couple came to view the premises before enrolling their child. I don't think I ever got over my agitation at seeing my friend's fear and bewilderment. I guess this was my first experience with racism and injustice. My complaining about this incident led my parents and others to protest and withdraw their children from the school. Some of you clinicians may argue that this was a clever and politically correct way for me to get back home with Mommy. Well, it didn't work, and I soon found myself in a different nursery school. But as a four-year-old, I gained my first organizing lesson: open your mouth when you see something wrong. It's the first step to being an actor for social change. The next is taking action. And that is what good social work is all about. It's not just the talking, it's the doing.

Ragtag Radical to Trained Organizer

My early years were spent growing up in Newark, NJ, where I witnessed the endemic racism and poverty that was to lead that city to violent upheaval in the summer of 1967. I wanted to do something, anything really, that would help address these problems. In college, I was a founder and activist in the Students for a Democratic Society (SDS) chapter at the University of Bridgeport, organized demonstrations, and worked for a while in an Office of Economic Opportunity (OEO) community action program on the Lower East Side in New York City. I brought intensity and passion to scores of "actions" but had little in the way of what we might call concrete skills. In 1969, I entered the University of Chicago's School of Social Service Administration (SSA). I was full of radical vision and high energy but also had a lot to learn.

My first year's field placement involved helping to plan and organize the emerging Near-North-Lincoln Park Community Mental Health Center. I spent my spare time working with the citywide Alliance to End Repression, a coalition that campaigned against the abuses of the Chicago police establishment following the killings of Black Panther leaders Fred Hampton and Mark Clark. I had also organized the Hyde Park Bail Reform Project, which raised money for the National Welfare Rights Organization (NWRO) to post bail for members who were arrested at demonstrations.

My second-year placement was with the Alliance for Labor Action. My job was to coordinate regional community support for the bitter 1970 United Auto Workers strike at the LaGrange, Illinois GM locomotive plant. The organizing dynamic from union hall, to picket lines, to community meetings was an intense and exhilarating experience. And my field instructor, Paul Booth, was a great teacher. He is now a national leader with the American Federation of State, County and Municipal Employees (AFSCME). Trained in the Alinsky tradition, Paul schooled me well and taught me the skills and discipline that were necessary for successful organizing campaigns. His wife Heather, also a wonderful organizer, gave me useful criticism over coffee in their Hyde Park apartment. Heather went on to found the Midwest Academy, the National Citizen/Labor Energy Coalition, and National Citizen Action. This influential period in my life set the stage for my future work as a political social worker.

Integrating Practice and Teaching

After leaving Chicago I returned to New Jersey, where I continued to work as a community organizer and began my teaching career at Ramapo College. As a teacher, I want to bring students to the ongoing struggle for progressive social change, and to show them how they can be change agents who can make a difference. When development of Ramapo College's BSW program began in the mid-1970s, I insisted that there be a separate macro practice course and field placement to accentuate the importance of community organization and political advocacy.

Outside of college teaching, I was involved with several organizations where my students were able to work side by side with me. The first was the New Jersey Tenants Organization (NJTO), where I have worked for the past 30 years as Organizing Vice-President. Over the years, scores of my social work students have completed their macro practice field internships there. They have been involved in direct action organizing, drafting, and lobbying for tenant protective legislation; conducting research on public policies such as rent control and taxation; and working in electoral campaigns. They have been part of an organizing process that has yielded the strongest statewide landlord-tenant law code in the nation, the enactment of rent control in 120 municipalities, and the development of an influential organization for social change.

My students also worked with me at the New Jersey Federation of Senior Citizens, where they were responsible for researching, helping to draft, and securing passage of three major pieces of state legislation, most significantly the New Jersey Generic Drug Act. The generic drug campaign was an intense and successful battle that pitted the Federation against a coalition of the world's largest drug manufacturers who had their corporate headquarters in New Jersey. Other students conducted a significant community research project on bank redlining in the state's six poorest cities. Their findings were used in the national effort to win congressional support and passage of the federal Home Mortgage Disclosure Act and the Community Reinvestment Act, an important source of community economic development funds.

In 1982, I was one of the founders of New Jersey Citizen Action (NJCA), a statewide coalition of labor unions and community organizations dedicated to promoting a broad social welfare agenda. Since then, many of my students completed field placements there. They have played key roles in countless political and legislative campaigns, including passage of the state Worker and Community Right to Know Act concerning toxic substances, the Health Care Bill of Rights, Medicaid expansion, and tax reform legislation. Recently, students have been working on campaigns and legislation dealing with lead paint poisoning, predatory lending, racial profiling, family leave, and campaign finance reform. I am also director of the Bergen County Housing Coalition, which has been a source of fieldwork for students working in the area of homelessness prevention.

Relevant macro practice dictates involvement in electoral politics. It takes the ability to influence and control government to create and maintain the vital programs and social policies that promote the social work profession's vision of a humane society. I have worked in scores of political campaigns on the state and local levels, and have been involved in legislative and lobbying work on a regular basis. Most recently, I helped manage my wife Joanne Atlas' and her running mates' winning election campaign for the Ringwood, NJ Borough Council. I encourage students to get involved in electoral politics, as well. During the past two years, my students worked in the NJCA Transit Voter Campaign, where they registered 5,000 new voters, conducted voter education, and did Get Out the Vote (GOTV) work.

A Day in My Life: June 14, 2004

6:00 a.m. This day begins at 6:00 a.m. when I have my two cups of coffee and go out for my daily 5-mile run. I have done this religiously for 26 years. I do this not just for reasons of physical health or my competitive race schedule, but as the foundation for my work day. I consider it disciplined work, not fun or particularly enjoyable, but it gives me the time to think about each day's tasks and how best to handle them. I find it essential to get "centered" early, especially on long days that require multi-tasking. Following the run, I shower, shave, and shove an assortment of 40 vitamin and mineral tablets down my throat with a bowl of oatmeal. With heart disease and diabetes on both sides of my family, I dare to battle the Fates in any way I can.

8:00 a.m. I'm out the door. So what do I do on this two-hour drive to Trenton, where I am scheduled to testify before the State Assembly and Senate Appropriation Committees? In a few weeks it will be illegal to make cell phone calls while driving in New Jersey, so here go my last few. I check my voice mail at the college to see if there are any urgent messages. A few agency field instructors left messages about next year's macro placements. Nothing urgent. Good. I can make those call backs in spare moments later on today or tomorrow. I call the Bergen County Housing Coalition, where I leave a good morning message on the answering machine for my staff with instructions to run the *Client Satisfaction Survey* data on

SPSS. We need to include this data in the next quarterly report to our funders, who want greater accountability in terms of outcomes.

8:15 a.m. I do a quick run through in my head on my testimony and all the arguments I have to use with the legislators. I make a quick mental note of the legislative committee members who I have to buttonhole before and after the hearings.

8:30 a.m. Another hour and a half or so of driving to go. I listen to the news on NPR for 15 minutes and then it's time to catch up on my reading.

8:45 a.m. In addition to my regular commutes, I've been logging more than 10,000 miles a year driving to and from meetings. Book tapes keep me thinking and help make recreational use of this down time. My wife Joanne brushes up on her Hungarian this way. I'm not always so academic, and a good mystery will do the trick at times. I pop in Tape One of Alice Sebold's *The Lovely Bones.* This haunting novel temporarily puts me in a more transcendent mood and makes the ride tolerable.

9:50 a.m. I enter the Capital Building and by chance bump into Adam "AJ" Sabath coming out of the Senate Majority office. "AJ" graduated from our social work program in 1993 and went into "politics." He currently serves as a chief assistant to NJ Senate President Richard Cody but will be going on leave in a few weeks to run the Kerry for President Campaign in New Jersey. While it is now the case of the protégé superceding the tutor, we have always been close, and I can always rely on him for useful information and advice. We have a quick cup of coffee, and he gives me the heads-up on which legislators are holding the cards. He claims the bill I'm testifying on is a done deal as is, and not to be too optimistic about amending it in ways to better serve tenants. I tell him he forgot his Alinsky, and "it ain't over until it's over." While leaving, I shrug off his pessimism as best I can. I've got dozens of tenants waiting at the hearing room and I've got to keep them pumped up and thinking positive.

10:15 a.m. I gravitate to the room where the Assembly Appropriations Committee will be meeting at 11: 00 a.m. The Senate Committee will be hearing the same bill at 2:00 p.m. The issue at hand is final discussion on a bill that will create the "Millionaires Tax," a state income tax increase on incomes over $500,000, which will be rebated to lower income groups as part of a property tax reform measure. The "Fairness Coalition" is pushing for this bill. Two groups I represent, the New Jersey Tenants Organization (NJTO) and New Jersey Citizen Action (NJCA), are key members of the coalition. Unfortunately, as the bill is currently constructed, the state's poorest residents will benefit least. I will be testifying on behalf of the NJTO, which is seeking to have tenants included in the rebate proposal. Governor James McGreevey, who claimed he was the tenants' best friend when he campaigned for his office, has been resisting including tenants in the bill, focusing all his efforts at shoring up his declining support from middle-class homeowners. Many Democratic legislators who also won with tenant support are refusing to buck the governor on this issue. There is an important lesson here: Be vigilant, especially with those politicians claiming to be your allies. Don't take their loyalty for granted, and make them accountable when they vacillate.

Scores of tenants begin to show up at the hearing room. They're all wearing buttons that read "I'm a Tenant and I Vote" and some come waving large signs, which are quickly confiscated by security guards. I speak with those tenants who will testify, going over key points: the lack of fairness and second-class status placed on tenants; the plight of poor and senior tenants; and the exclusion of 70% of the state's Black and Latino populations, who happen to be tenants. This latter point is crucial to emphasize, especially since the chairs of the committees in both houses are African American. The room is soon packed to the gills. I am hoping that this strong showing—in addition to our barraging committee members with hundreds of phone calls in the days leading up to this hearing—will yield results. After listening to my group's testimony (and the responsive cheering of our supporters), Committee Chairwoman Bonnie Watson Coleman states, "We'll take care of you." But the hearing ends without our proposed amendment being introduced or a vote taken on the bill. However, Coleman is one of the most powerful Democrats in the state, and her words are encouraging.

12:30 p.m. NJTO President Matt Shapiro and I meet and decide that it is absolutely crucial that we get the bill amended today at the Senate hearing. We instruct our members to get a quick lunch and then head to the Senate hearing room for more battle. Matt and I decide to do some intense face-to-face lobbying with Senate committee members wherever we can find them in the State House. I am able to speak to Senators Joe Coniglio and Paul Sarlo beforehand. Both of these guys won close, bruising election campaigns with strong tenant support, and I mince no words in telling them what we expect from them. I also touch base with Senator Bernie Kenny, the sponsor of the bill. Kenny comes from Hudson County, the only one in the state with a tenant majority. I have Monsignor John Gilchrist with me at this meeting. An important ally, Gilchrist is a very popular priest from Hudson who must be respected by any rational politician.

2:00 p.m. After meeting with these senators, I have the sense that they got the message and will be speaking to each other about our concerns. An hour later, the hearing confirms this. Committee Chairman Wayne Bryant rolls out the red carpet for us, not only treating us with respect, but effusively thanking us for the leadership we have shown on tenant and housing issues in the past. Senator Sharpe James, who is also the Mayor of Newark, apologizes for keeping us waiting. By the hearings' end, a majority of committee members are talking about the tax rebate for tenants as if it had always been in the bill with their strong support. Fine, everybody wins.

4:00 p.m. Matt and I touch base before leaving. Matt will go over the amendment tonight and fax the exact wording we want to Senator Bryant. We will follow up with Chairwoman Coleman to make sure that the Assembly bill contains the same amendment. (Note: The amended "Millionaires Tax" passed both houses and was signed into law during the next few weeks.)

4:30 p.m. I check my voice mail at the college and make the necessary call-backs. On my way out, I stop by the Senate Majority office and catch "AJ" before he leaves. I'm not one to gloat, but I can't resist letting him know that his old mentor still has something left in the tank.

5:00 p.m. Time to catch my breath, grab a bite to eat, and get back to my book tape on the ride up to Elizabeth.

7:00 p.m. As Director of Organizing for the NJTO, it has been my job to build the organization and state tenant movement by organizing new groups. The NJTO has 130 local affiliates throughout the state, but we need to organize twenty new ones each year just to keep that number constant. There's a fairly predictable ebb and flow to the lifespan of tenant organizations. Once they succeed (or fail) in helping tenants solve their problems, they outlive their usefulness and gradually disappear. But there is no end to the need for them somewhere in New Jersey, so I'm generally out one or two nights a week tending to this task.

I arrive at the North Avenue building where the tenant meeting is going to take place in a half hour. Elizabeth is an old multi-ethnic, working class, industrial city. The low-income African American and new immigrant population from Latin America inhabit much of the city's marginal housing stock and this building fits the description, "once decent, going bad fast." The landlord is contemptuous of his tenants and intent on doing as little as possible to maintain the building. A few brave individual tenants have been unsuccessful with their one-on-one battles with the landlord and have called me in to help them organize.

My first job as organizer is to convince the larger mass of tenants that the way to best solve their problems is through the creation of a strong, united organization. I also want them to see that their quest for decent housing is part of an ongoing social justice movement for tenants' rights in New Jersey. I have to be prepared to answer their doubts and fears, and gain their commitment toward collective action. Without this commitment to act collectively, even a high degree of technical legal knowledge and the NJTO's strategic expertise would be virtually useless in bringing their landlord to heel. Once I can get them to have faith in themselves and each other, everything else will fall into place.

7:30 p.m. The meeting begins right on time and it's a positive sign that Dawn and Regina, the initiators of this meeting, have done their homework and followed the game plan outlined in my organizing manual. They've gotten a small steering committee together and informed the city's mayor and their city councilman of the building's problems. In addition, they have gotten a commitment from the Cable TV news channel to run a piece on the tenants' problems. Also, they have decided to work with our larger affiliate in the city, the United Tenants of Elizabeth. A good start, but a majority of their tenants are still sitting on the sidelines.

Once the meeting begins, I sense that some of the tenants are cynical. Others who are receiving rent subsidies fear that joining will lead to landlord retaliation. We have to work through these issues. I go over the laws protecting them from landlord reprisals and the loss of their subsidies. I deal with their cynicism by discussing the cases of buildings similar to theirs in the city where the tenants were able to beat even tougher landlords. This process often takes longer than I'd like. Often, there are one or two people who will give you a dozen reasons why they can't win. Another will have more complaints about fellow tenants than with the landlord. I have been through these stumbling blocks hundreds of times and almost instinctively know how to respond. I've got to be firm and remind them why most people came to this meeting, and that was to learn how they could win, not lose. It is crucial to draw a line in the sand separating the splitters from the committed joiners. If they don't want to progress, there's always the TV waiting for them back in their apartment. One loud tenant who knows all the answers leaves, but unity is essential. By 8:30, there is a consensus to proceed in formalizing the organization.

I then lead the tenants in a discussion of their particular problems and possible strategies that can be employed. I give them some homework to do: documenting every problem in the building, arranging to have the city building inspectors come out to the building, researching the landlord and his business interests, and outlining specific assignments for floor captains. I don't want them to get too far ahead of themselves, so I urge them to postpone deciding on more militant action until the organization is solidified. They need time to build up membership and do more preparatory work. I emphasize that successful organizing is a careful and sometimes painstaking process. I wrote the *New Jersey Tenant Organizing Handbook* like a cookbook. Miss a step or ingredient, and the whole thing goes awry.

At 9:00, I tell them I am leaving but they should use the next half hour to elect officers, set up a dues structure, and establish an effective communication process. We agree to meet in two weeks to choose and implement a specific course of action.

9:10 p.m. I leave this meeting feeling optimistic about the group. The core group is energized. Most of the tenants get the "vision" of what it takes to solve their problems, and they seem ready to go for it.

9:15 p.m. It's been a long day, I'm exhausted, and my voice is shot. Can't wait to get home and end the day with a slice of reheated pizza and glass or two of wine with Joanne. Back in my car this tired body gets back to *The Lovely Bones.*

Think About It

1. What element in the lobbying process for the "Millionaires Tax" Amendment did you see as crucial for its successful outcome?

2. What organizing principles are emphasized in the case of the North Avenue Tenants Association?

Chapter 9
Life as a Policy Associate

● ●

by Theresa Hancock, BSW

My day begins with triage. A child advocate's workflow is never clear-cut. I am working on at least five projects, each with at least twenty tasks and assignments. Of the hundred things I need to do today, which comes first, second, third? Each one is important and urgent. Priorities depend on deadlines, both mine and my colleagues', as well as schedules, meetings, and the ultimate wild card—the outside world. I know the contents of my list and their order will probably change dramatically during the day, but it helps to start somewhere.

Today, writing testimony is at the top. It is late April and the state legislature is in full swing. A voicemail message lets me know that my agency's executive director got a call from the local child-hood lead poisoning advocacy group. The hearing on their bill has been moved up to today and they want us to testify. As the state's only comprehensive source of data on the well-being of children, our support for the legislation is very valuable. I have worked on lead poisoning with the advocacy group for two years. Since I am responsible for health issues, I am the logical choice to write the testimony and speak at the hearing this afternoon.

At moments like this, I am incredibly proud of my work and my colleagues. All of the hard work we do here at KIDS COUNT, triple-checking our data calculations, getting input from the gamut of stakeholders, keeping current on national research and trends, seems very worthwhile. We have earned our reputation by giving the extra effort to ensure that everything we publish or advocate for is informed and accurate. That often means working late or reading research reports during lunch instead of my current novel, but it is worth it.

In the abstract, the testimony needs to do two things: establish the problem and support the proposed solution. In practical terms, that means borrowing text from our *Factbook* about the effects of childhood lead poisoning and its prevalence in Rhode Island. The *Factbook* is our annual report, which includes 52 indicators of child well-being across health, education, safety, and economic issues. I write, "Lead poisoning occurs when young children eat lead paint dust or chips in older houses that are not well-maintained. Lead poisoning can kill children, but more frequently causes lifelong developmental delays and behavioral problems. In Rhode Island, lead poisoning has decreased by more than half over the past ten years, but poor children are still much more likely to be poisoned." I also write, "The proposed legislation, a tax credit for property owners who remove lead from their housing, will create more safe housing for children and reduce the rates of lead poisoning." It is just another example of the connections among all of the areas that we work on: health depends on housing, which is related to economics.

People I work with, from community providers to state department officials, are surprised when I tell them my degree is in social work. They fail to see its connection to policy analysis and assume I went to school for political science or sociology. In my opinion, my background in social work is the perfect preparation for what I do. My generalist education taught me about all of the issues that people deal with in their daily lives and about the services that try to help them. More importantly, I learned to think in terms of systems. I did not start my social work education knowing that I would work in policy, but I did know that I was interested in systems. Volunteer work I had done on the micro level showed me how interesting and complex systems are, from families to communities to services. The work I have done since college deals with systems from many angles: analyzing how policies affect the larger systems that children and families interact with, as well as connecting the dots of various policies and services to create better functioning systems. Learning to think of individuals in the context of their families and communities is critical to what I do.

Switching gears from lead paint and testimony, I move on to another project. For the past two years, we have been working with a group of seventeen states on school readiness. The latest research indicates that children's experiences from birth to age five, either positive or negative, determine whether they are ready to learn when they enter kindergarten. The goal of the project is to help states measure how well they are providing the positive experiences that children need during the early years. At the end of the project, each state will have a list of indicators that measure the ingredients children need for school readiness: health insurance, quality child care, mental health services, full-day kindergarten, and so forth. Each list will look different, because it will connect to the policy successes and challenges in a particular state. When states start to measure the effectiveness of their policies, they will see where they need to invest to improve the school readiness of their children.

The next step in the process is getting the states together to work on a particularly difficult area to measure: children ages birth to three. There is a gap in the data we have on young children. We know a lot about them when they are born (low birth-weight, infant mortality, births to teens) and when they enter kindergarten (preschool experience, immunizations, beginning reading skills), but not much in between.

I have already sent out the meeting invitations, contacted speakers, and booked a hotel. My task today is to figure out how to get everyone who is coming to the same starting point, so the meeting can be productive. I need to develop a read-ahead packet that includes the current research on child development from birth to three, indicators that have been developed, and services that are particularly important to children ages birth to three and their families. I start with the usual suspects, national research organizations including Child Trends, Zero to Three, and the Ounce of Prevention Fund. Fortunately, I find what I need right away and download the reports. After a quick check to ensure that the materials address some specific groups (low-income children, children with special needs, racial/ethnic minorities), I give the packet to our Deputy Director for approval.

Consulting my list, which has remained fairly intact today, I find that the next item involves crunching some numbers. I am working with a group from South County made up of child care providers, housing advocates, teachers, mental health professionals, child abuse experts, and pediatricians. The group formed to improve the well-being of children in their county. They want to develop a strategic plan and have asked me to help them assess where they are doing well and where they need work.

They already have information on the county's individual cities and towns, but I can aggregate the information into county-wide figures and compare them to averages for the state. Using an

Excel spreadsheet, I take city and town data on health, education, safety, and economic well-being from the *Factbook* and combine it to get South County numbers. When I compare them to the state numbers, I find that South County is above average in many areas, but below in a few. The children in this county would benefit from more full-day kindergarten, improved food stamp outreach, and more child care. These are issues that the group may want to include it its plan.

I convert the data into a handout for this afternoon's meeting, so the group can analyze it for themselves. Going to meetings like this is one of the best parts of my job. It is incredibly interesting to get out in local communities and work with the people on the front lines. It keeps me grounded in the issues and educates me on how the policies I analyze at the state level affect real people at the local level. I try to continually make these connections so that the research and writing I do will be relevant and useful.

Along with the county data, I will hand out some information on strategies other communities have used to work on the problems South County faces. Learning from the work of others is incredibly important. It provides excellent ideas that can be adapted, but more importantly, it provides a sense of possibility. When communities identify problems, solving them can seem overwhelming. Knowing that someone else has succeeded is very encouraging.

When people ask me about my job, I describe it as a labor of love. The hours are long and the work is difficult. I could be making more money doing something else. The work to be done is so vast that I could spend every hour of every day working to improve lives of Rhode Island's children. Sometimes it seems we are fighting a tidal wave, but I believe in the cause and I know every effort I make brings us one step closer to our goal. Even small things, like providing data that helps a community program get a grant, make a difference in the lives of children. I do not do this work for myself. The reward is knowing that, however small the steps, change is being made and children are better off with my efforts than without them.

It is 4:00 and I am off to the State House to discuss the lead poisoning bill in the Senate Finance Committee. Most people I know are terrified of public speaking, but I actually enjoy this part of my job. It is extremely gratifying to see my work come full circle. I got the raw lead poisoning data from the Health Department, did my calculations to make it succinct and powerful, and now I get to present it to people who can use it to improve kids' lives. I expect to wait for an hour or so until my bill comes up.

When I get to the State House, I meet up with my colleagues from the local childhood lead poisoning advocacy group to discuss strategy before the hearing. I also spend a few minutes using preparatory empathy, something I learned in social work school, to put myself in the legislators' shoes and imagine what they might ask me. When my name is called, I stand in front of the ten lawmakers on the committee and read my testimony. They ask me a question about the connection between poverty and lead poisoning, one I thought they might ask. I answer easily, because I anticipated the question and thought through my response. Even if some members of the committee do not give me their full attention, which happens often to people testifying on all sorts of bills, I know that being there has had an impact on them. Now, we wait and see if they vote our way on the bill.

Think About It

1. How do different areas of social work advocacy (health, economic well-being, education, safety) connect in the lives of children and families?

2. How is a generalist social work perspective useful in policy analysis?

Chapter 10
Representing the Faith Community in the Policy Arena
● ● ● ● ● ● ● ● ● ● ● ● ● ● ● ●

by Mary Dunne Stewart, MSW

As I download 28 new e-mail messages, I chuckle thinking "this is the beginning of our slow season." We are just winding down from the most contentious General Assembly session in recent history. Since the state legislators could not agree on the budget, the eight-week session turned into a 17-week fiasco. As an advocate representing Jewish, Christian, and Muslim values before state government, I have been swamped for the past four months. As the Associate Director of the Virginia Interfaith Center for Public Policy (VICPP), an interfaith, membership-based non-profit, non-partisan advocacy and education organization, I focus on children's and healthcare issues. Since we only have two full-time staff and two interns, my duties encompass many aspects of nonprofit administration, legislative advocacy, community organizing, and education. As I filter through my inbox, I read and respond to urgent messages, while saving other informational messages for later. Each morning, I receive an e-mail with all the headlines and articles related to health and human services from the major newspapers in Virginia. This morning, I scan the headlines and read three articles—one related to monetary donations made to state delegates and senators, another about the veto session next week, and a final message about the inadequacy of the child protective services system in Virginia.

My top priority this morning is preparing a presentation that I will deliver tomorrow to a group of about 65 people of faith at a local church. Members of a particular denomination will be gathering in Richmond for an eight-hour advocacy training. I have two hours on the agenda to discuss the work of VICPP, the role of the faith community in the political process, the nuts and bolts of advocacy, and results of this year's General Assembly session. Typically, when I present to groups, I have about 45 minutes to an hour, so I need to prepare to ensure that I have enough material for the two-hour session. I'm actually rather nervous. Although I've never had a problem filling time before, I've never been allotted two hours. It just seems so long! Usually, I don't really need to prepare much for a presentation, but at our recent media training, my Executive Director and I created a new catchphrase for our collateral materials—"Learn. Pray. Act. The Common Wealth Depends on Us." I take a little extra time this morning to incorporate this new message into my usual presentation. While I'm preparing notes, I bounce a few ideas off Doug, VICPP's executive director. He is an accomplished and very experienced public speaker and is rather helpful in assisting me with presentation preparations.

After I finish making an outline for my presentation, I gather all the materials I need for the seminar—membership brochures, our legislative agenda, a prayer pamphlet, a handout about the legislative process in Virginia, and "purple papers." With every presentation, one of my goals is to leave having inspired some of the participants to join VICPP. Since we are a membership organization, our strength before legislators is partly in numbers. The more Virginians we represent, the stronger our voice. So, while I don't spend a great deal of time pushing membership, I do distribute membership brochures at speaking engagements. The legislative agenda details our priorities for the year, which are determined by balloting the membership. This year the priorities are poverty and the working poor, healthcare, at risk children and youth, tax equity, abolition of the death penalty, and housing and homelessness. The prayer pamphlet is a leaflet we distribute to every state legislator on the first day of the General Assembly session. It includes scripture related to justice from the three sacred texts of VICPP—the Old Testament, the New Testament, and the Koran. The handout regarding the legislative process in Virginia provides individuals with a glossary of legislative terms and important phone numbers and Web sites. The "purple papers" is my favorite handout. Each Monday, Wednesday, and Friday during the legislative session, we distribute a brief quote, statistic, or scripture passage to all legislators on purple paper. At the end of the session, we create a one-page compilation of all of the purple papers from throughout the session. This document helps members to see one of the ways we strive to provide a spiritual presence at the legislature.

As I'm gathering the materials, I realize that I have about twenty minutes before a task force meeting that I'm hosting at our office.

Our office, by the way, is located about four blocks from the state Capitol on the third floor of Centenary United Methodist Church. The church has some extra space and donates offices to VICPP and to a faith-based shelter and feeding program. My executive director, his seminary student, my MSW student, and I share a Sunday School room that has been converted into an office. I don't have any privacy, which can be difficult when on the phone, but the location is prime and the price is right.

The task force I'm convening today is working on planning "poverty diet" public forums in ten to twelve communities across the Commonwealth in November. My MSW intern and I conducted research and compiled many statistics and personal stories of individuals utilizing food stamps in Virginia. Our purpose is to sensitize members of the legislature and people of faith to the plight of low-income citizens in Virginia. So, we devised a curriculum whereby participants are asked to spend no more than $2.55 (the average food stamp benefit in VA) per person per day on food and beverage items. The task force members begin arriving. We are working with one legislator from Charlottesville, his legislative aide, the Director of the Office of Justice and Peace with the Catholic Diocese of Richmond, the Director of the Virginia Community Action Partnership, and a policy analyst from Voices for Virginia's Children.

We don't have central air conditioning, and in early June in Richmond, it is quite hot. I turn on the window units, but the drone of the machines makes discussion rather difficult. About five minutes into the meeting, I turn off the AC units and feel terrible as colleagues remove their suit coats and sweat through the meeting. Luckily, our agenda is rather short. Our goal today is to finalize the curriculum. Each member gives feedback on the eight-page document while I furiously write notes. I agree to send each member the updated packet in about two weeks, along with a project plan with a timeline—including setting dates and locations across the state, contacting local partners such as food banks and other hunger programs, coordinating the invitations to legislators, and making contacts with the media. Coordinating these events will be hectic, but our new social work and seminary interns starting in August will be able to step in and assist with the planning and logistics.

By the time we finish the meeting, it's past lunchtime and I'm starving. I eat at my computer while scanning new e-mails and checking the news headlines of the day online. When working in advocacy, it's important to be knowledgeable of current affairs—

for me, health, human services, and state level politics are particularly important. When I'm finished with lunch, I take a few moments to return phone calls. Our machine had two messages—one from a pastor in Roanoke, Virginia, a small city about three hours from Richmond, who is requesting a speaker on faith-based advocacy for an adult education class, and another from a member of the Board of Directors inquiring about our most recent membership drive.

Every Wednesday, I deposit funds received during the past week. The majority of our funding is from membership dues and grants. We have a blend of various types of memberships, including individuals, congregations, organizations, and judicatories (denominational groups such as dioceses, synods, conferences, or presbyteries). Our membership includes Muslim, Jewish, Presbyterian, Roman Catholic, Lutheran, United Methodist, United Church of Christ, Religious Society of Friends, Disciples of Christ, Episcopal, Church of the Brethren, and Baptist representation.

I was drawn to VICPP because of the interfaith nature and diversity of membership. Incorporating the faith-based dimension of peace and justice into the social justice philosophy, planning, and administration skills that I learned in social work school is very fulfilling. In graduate school at Virginia Commonwealth University, I participated in a "Planning and Administration" track focused on macro practice. Because I am also interested in clinical practice, I took the "clinical track" requirements as my electives, thereby giving me the educational background in both clinical and macro practice. After graduation, I leapt directly into macro practice with the Virginia Interfaith Center. In my position, I draw on several skills that I learned and sharpened in graduate school, such as program planning and social justice advocacy, but I have had to learn new skills that were not included in the MSW curriculum at my alma mater, such as community organizing, fundraising, and media relations.

Working for a small nonprofit has enormous advantages and a few disadvantages. While I personally enjoy working on a very small staff in a grassroots organization, I yearn for more administrative support. I am reminded of this as I enter contributions into our database, endorse and make copies of the checks, create a fund report, walk the deposit to the bank across the street, and prepare thank you letters. Today, it only takes about thirty minutes, but during membership renewal, it can be quite a tedious process. While I dislike the administrative aspects of my job, I am grateful for all of the amazing opportunities afforded to me. I am gaining experience in project management, media relations, advocacy, fund raising, coalition building, grassroots organizing, community education, public speaking, nonprofit management, and office administration. The benefits certainly outweigh the drawbacks.

Upon completing the deposit, I notice that Doug, my executive director, seems to have a few minutes, so I ask him if he has some time to discuss some of my other projects. We take a few moments to review the job description I've created for the new MSW intern starting in August. We are going to dedicate most of his time to working on worker justice issues—increasing the minimum wage and ensuring localities have the right to enact living wage ordinances. He will represent VICPP on a worker justice coalition, track related legislation, post information to our Web site, write action alerts, and help prepare Doug's testimony regarding specific bills before the General Assembly. I would also like the student to get experience working with the Board of Directors. I am considering having him act as the staff liaison with Board members, keeping communication open regarding their role in the implementation of the organizational strategic plan and calling on members when we need assistance in our advocacy, education, and fundraising efforts. After Doug and I finalize the student's work plan, I briefly update him on the poverty diet meeting that he was unable to attend because he was preaching at a nearby church's Wednesday noon service. Since Doug is an ordained minister, he is frequently asked to preach at churches across the state.

After updating Doug, I return to my desk to complete our final edition of *LegisLink* for this year. During the legislative session, we publish a weekly newsletter to inform members about the status of important legislation and how they can be involved in the process. In our final edition, I am creating a table to summarize the major outcomes of legislation with which we were concerned. I have been working on the newsletter for the past few days and take about twenty minutes to proofread and make a few minor changes to the summary. As I finalize our legislative summary, I am reminded of our major successes and failures of this past session. One of our principal accomplishments was our advocacy in coalition to revise the state tax structure. We worked with many secular and religious partners to encourage the legislature to overhaul the tax code to make the system more fair and adequate to meet the needs of the Commonwealth. While some modifications made the system somewhat less regressive, the tax structure remains unfair because the poor still pay a greater percentage of their income in taxes than the wealthy. However, the legislature did address the adequacy issue by increasing some taxes and user fees to increase funding for education and public safety. Other accomplishments included maintaining the ability of localities to enact living wage ordinances, providing parenting classes to incarcerated individuals, and repealing the sunset provision from the mental health parity law. We did have defeats of several bills we were supporting, including one mandating clergy to report suspected child abuse and neglect, and another that would have abolished the death penalty.

It's 4:15 p.m. and time for me to go. During the summer months, we work somewhat shorter hours, because of the demanding schedule during the late fall and winter. I love getting out a bit early in the summer, because I can run to daycare, pick up my baby, and enjoy the sunshine.

Think About It

1. What is the role of social justice in social work practice? How is social justice important to clinical practitioners?

2. Discuss some of the implications for social work practice in a faith-based organization.

3. What might be some challenges in working with a coalition representing diverse religious interests?

Chapter 11

It Takes a Village: Reclaiming Our Youth Through Community Partnerships

•••••••••••••

by Scott P. Sells, Ph.D., MSW, LCSW

I will never forget the statements that changed my life and how I viewed the world: "Children and teenagers live in families and families live in communities," and "We must strive for academic excellence with the students we teach." These statements were made by different people within the space of a single month during August of 1997. These statements would eventually intertwine with one another and change my life and those of my students forever.

The first statement, *"Children and teenagers live in families and families live in communities,"* came from the dean of my university, Dr. Otis Johnson. When he made this statement, it was as if a light bulb went off inside my head. All my life, I had been a micro practitioner and believed that I would be more effective treating one family at a time. I thought that macro community practice should be left up to the administrators and child welfare policy professionals, not direct practice social workers. Besides, I thought, how can one individual make a difference? The problems at a community level were so vast that I was afraid to try. However, Dr. Johnson's statement made be rethink my position. I suddenly realized that I was only able to treat the multitude of child and adolescent problems as they came thundering out of the lip of a giant faucet. To be more effective, I needed to treat the faucet or where the source of the problems emerged on a community level. My current practice of one family at a time would have only limited impact. Only two questions remained: how and by what means would I implement these ideas? These questions would soon be answered.

The second statement, *"We must strive for academic excellence with the students we teach,"* came from the university president, Dr. Carlton Brown, during faculty orientation. During his presentation, Dr. Brown said that faculty must do more than just lecture in the classroom. Faculty have a responsibility to demonstrate "academic excellence" to their students by integrating concepts from a textbook into the real world. A "town meets gown" process would move faculty out of the comfort of their ivory towers and into the community. Students would then become involved in projects that improved the lives of residents in the community. As I listened, it was as if God were hitting me over the head with a 2x4.

The statements by Dr. Brown and Dr. Johnson came together into one idea. I could strive for academic excellence by forming a bridge from the classroom to the community. In the process, I would learn from my students and find a way to reach children and adolescents from a community perspective.

It was a leap of faith, but the next day, I went to the director of my social work department and made the following request:

Dr. Jackson, I realize that I have been hired to teach micro clinical practice courses, and that I have no experience teaching macro community organization classes. In fact, if someone had told me that I would be making such a request even a month ago, I would have thought they were crazy. However, crazy or not, I want the opportunity to teach a course in community organization and, together with my students, find a community in trouble. I want to teach a concept from the textbook one day, and transform that same concept into real life practice the next. I am not yet sure how this transformation will occur, but I want to try.

At first, Dr. Jackson thought I was joking. However, I told her I was very serious. Dr. Jackson eventually agreed to my request. For the next week, I poured over everything I could read concerning community practice. During my readings, two main principles stood out.

First, a thorough needs assessment had to be accomplished before attempting any changes or interventions. Never assume to know what the community wants or needs based on statistics from a book or a quick drive through the community. One must interview the residents in the community and let them tell what they need and how the problems should be solved. Any proposed programs must fit their stated needs, not yours. In the process, one must move slowly and gain trust before making any sudden changes or movements.

Second, residents within the community must have shared ownership of the project and help run the programs that will solve their own problems. If programs are agency-based and agency-driven, the chances of long-term sustainability are "slim to none." In fact, the risk is great that these agency programs will help create a "learned helplessness" mentality. Residents will learn to become dependent on these services, rather than struggle to find their own solutions. In time, a mindset of helplessness may set in and result in an inability to solve one's own problems. This helplessness and dependency can then trickle down from the parents and be passed on to the children, creating a potential vicious cycle of poverty and emotional problems.

With these two cardinal principles intact, I met my first class of undergraduate social work students in a class entitled "Community Organization." Only four students showed up and all of them were equally skeptical and cynical about making a difference in any community. I was not prepared for such resistance, and I began to second guess my choice to teach this class. However, I refused to give up. For the next five weeks, the students and I attempted to find a community that would allow us to work with them. Just when it looked hopeless, the president of the Midtown Neighborhood Association responded to our call, and invited us to set up and conduct a town meeting. We could then do a needs assessment from a resident's perspective.

This invitation became the pivotal turning point in the project. Students suddenly became excited and less skeptical as we started our preparations for the town meeting. From the textbook, we learned how to construct a well-written press release to draw both newspapers and television stations to the event. The textbook also showed us how to prepare for and conduct a successful town meeting. Students got excited when they found out that our project was newsworthy and that the press wanted to interview them.

We also realized the importance of our work after we walked through the Midtown neighborhood and witnessed the high number of abandoned buildings. Our perceptions were confirmed when we obtained the following statistics:

- The Midtown Community consisted of 3,952 people — 97% African-American — with an average household income of only $17,096, compared to $28,000 citywide.

- Only six communities out of 89 possible communities in Savannah, GA had higher crime rates than Midtown.

- 65% of children under six lived in poverty, as did 48% of those under 18.

- Midtown had the third highest rate of substandard housing, with 38% of all residential homes abandoned or in need of one or more major repairs.

At the town meeting and beyond, miracles started happening, and the students began to change right before my eyes. I also began to change right along with them. The following is a summary of these miracles through the course of only one year.

On December 10, 1997, residents told students that they were tired of talk and that it was time for action. Residents stated that they were no longer a community and that most people stayed locked up in their houses, too afraid to leave. To solve this problem, they needed a highly visible symbol, a community center, that they could build with their own sweat labor. The act of building the center could bring the community back together.

The original four students were so affected by the town meeting that they stayed with the project even after the course was completed. They presented their experiences to the next community organization class and outlined the next series of steps.

Students heard about this class through the grapevine, and the enrollment suddenly jumped to 16 students. These students decided to invite Midtown residents to their next class and conduct focus groups to brainstorm ways to locate and rehabilitate an existing abandoned building.

On February 8, 1998, a miracle happened. While the students and residents were making their presentations, an elderly Midtown resident, grandmother of 23 and great grandmother of five, stood up and donated a building she had purchased with her life savings to be used as the Midtown Community Center.

On June 10, 1998, the students worked collaboratively with the community to solicit the help of key business leaders. They raised $55,000 in private money from several corporate sponsors. Architects agreed to donate their services to design the center, and contractors agreed to build the center.

On July 17, 1998, the residents and students met to design two essential programs for the community center. The first program would feature a community family counseling clinic where residents and their children would receive counseling and support services at no charge. It would be called "community" counseling, because an entire family's network (friends, neighbors, ministers) would be assembled in one room to support the parents in efforts to solve their child or teenager's behavior problem. Social work students would conduct an internship rotation on-site under the supervision of a faculty member. The second program would feature a senior center, owned and operated by Midtown resident seniors. The program would feature a greenhouse to teach children horticulture and a mentorship and after-school program.

On September 1, 1998, residents, students, and I wrote a grant to receive funding from the Department of Housing and Urban Development. We received the second highest score out of all the applicants and were awarded $361,000.

On September 28, 1998, residents and students were so empowered by these efforts that they joined forces with the local police force to organize a peaceful march at 1:00 a.m. The goal was to close a sports bar that served as a magnet for crime and drugs before the new Community Center was built. More than 200 residents showed up to march. On December 17, 1998, the city revoked the owner's liquor license, and the bar was closed down.

On March 1, 1999, the ground-breaking ceremony took place.

Reflections

The spiritual component within this community has really been incredible to witness. It has changed my life in the process. I now see the world through a different pair of glasses. I see how the empowerment of one community has had a ripple effect on so many more lives than one person can possibly make. It truly does take a village to change a community and in the process change the life of an individual child.

These changes can best be summed up in a recent paper written by one of my students:

Before I began the project, I thought the Midtown community was hopeless. I am a Savannahian, and every time I drove through that community, I looked and thanked God that I did not live there. However, after taking part in many of the activities, I have a new outlook on things. I no longer see the Midtown community as hopeless. I saw people who were needing a hand up and who were willing to give a hand. They may not be out of their houses yet, but that day is coming and I helped make that happen.

Academic excellence and community practice are now alive and well at Savannah State University. We successfully followed the two cardinal community principles of a thorough needs assessment and community ownership from a grassroots level. As a result, things have begun to change in a small community known as Midtown.

If you come to Savannah, we invite you to drive by the corner of 35th and Reynolds. But I must warn you. You will not recognize the place as a community in need. Children will be outside playing, and the homes will look like new.

Think About It

1. Do you think it is truly possible for one person to "make a difference"?

2. What are some interpersonal skills someone like Scott Sells had to have to convince the Midtown residents that he was not simply a "do gooder" but someone who could turn his vision into a reality?

3. What could make you continue to participate in a school project once the school year has ended?

PART 4:
Policy From the Inside

Chapter 12
Policy Supervisor in a State Government Setting

• •

by Karen Kimsey Lawson, BSW, MSW

I am a supervisor of a unit that provides policy support for long-term care services of a state Medicaid agency. The atmosphere is challenging, as my division oversees the operation of services that cost almost $2 billion annually and serve 46,000 individuals throughout the state. With eight years of policy experience, I am the most skilled analyst on staff and work with the other analysts to enable them to perform their jobs. This includes listening to any concerns they may have about their job responsibilities and providing support. Generally, individuals who enter these positions are highly independent, motivated, and perform their jobs with little supervision. They also love to conduct research.

I stumbled into this profession nine years ago when I was in the middle of pursuing my master's degree in social work. I was placed in the Medicaid agency as part of a Governor's Fellowship that introduced me to the world of long-term care services in a policy environment. I immediately fell in love with the work setting and the promise it held to advocate for those who received these services. This was a shocking revelation for me, because I trained as a clinical social worker and had planned to provide direct services to my clients when I graduated. When I received my MSW, I applied for and was hired as a policy analyst with my starting salary in the low $30,000 range.

The policy issues that affect this position are numerous and frequently change. In many cases, this agency's policy adjusts according to the desires of the federal government, state legislature, and the Governor. As policy practitioners, social workers need to keep abreast of the latest policy developments and understand that the focus of their work can change frequently. The ability to be open-minded and adapt to change is very important here! Examples of laws that have a heavy influence in this agency include the Americans with Disabilities Act and the Health Insurance Portability and Accountability Act, or HIPAA. HIPAA is so important that all employees of this agency have to complete an online course about this law, take a test, and pass it in order to work here.

I am responsible for facilitating workgroup meetings for one large workgroup. Whenever the group meets, it is my responsibility to arrange for meeting locations, provide accommodations as needed for attendees, prepare the agenda, provide research for the group, and ensure all documentation is copied and ready for the meeting. Strong organizational skills and the ability to facilitate groups are a must in this setting, because the stakeholders are often very diverse and can be at odds with each other. It is my responsibility to lead these groups and, understanding the dynamics of the stakeholders, create a non-threatening environment in which thoughts and ideas are shared and decisions are made. Sometimes the group cannot reach consensus, and we have to make decisions at the agency level. These groups are very rewarding, and I find leading them puts many of my social work skills to good use.

Policy analysts often are responsible for creating and revising laws, regulations, and policies for programs. I spend a lot of time working on state regulations for our programs. Regulations are a set of policies that have the strength of law and guide the operations of our long-term care services. Some regulations are only a few pages in length, and others are more than 100 pages. As a policy supervisor, I am responsible for making changes to any regulations for programs I oversee and providing supervision to my staff as they revise or create regulations. Regulations are highly technical and require a significant amount of concentration to revise. There have been many days when I spent the entire time in front of my computer, revising regulations! An individual must enjoy attention to detail in order to successfully revise or create policies of any nature.

Sometimes my position brings me into legal situations I had never considered would be a part of my professional experience. For two years, I supervised two home- and community-based waivers that provided services for persons with developmental disabilities. Even though I changed positions to supervise long-term care policy, a provider that I had audited requested a formal appeal to protest the overpayment amount we told him he owed the agency. To prepare for this appeal, I spent several hours working with our attorney to become aware of how to act as a proper witness. I spent the night before the hearing mentally rehearsing for the appeal, because my answers have a heavy impact on the hearing officer's decisions. To our surprise, the provider canceled the appeal at the last minute, and we did not have to defend our decision. While I did not have to participate in this appeal, this experience reminds me how important it is that social workers need to keep abreast of legal issues and know how to respond in these situations.

While I do spend much time working as a policy analyst, I also have supervisory responsibilities. For example, I recently met with one of my analysts to brainstorm about an upcoming workgroup meeting. She is new at facilitating groups on a topic she is not very familiar with, so we bounced off strategies about handling questions they may ask and what information to take to the meeting. She is gaining more confidence with each meeting she leads, and I can see that she is becoming more certain of her abilities. This is the joyful part of supervision. I am currently recruiting for a vacant analyst position, and I will spend much time with the new analyst to acclimate the successful candidate to the world of Medicaid policy.

Recently, I have found myself improving on my grant writing skills. I am responsible for the oversight of two grants to promote systems change in long-term care services. This state's administration is keenly interested in applying for grant opportunities, and I am in the process of developing a grant application. Grant writing skills are very beneficial to policy practitioners, and I encourage individuals who are interested in this level of practice to obtain these skills.

Some of my time is spent presenting before stakeholders. Examples include traveling to statewide conferences to present on Medicaid-funded services. I love presenting in front of individuals with disabilities, their families, advocates, and providers, as this gives me the opportunity to inform them about available Medicaid services and their rights to access them. They ask many thoughtful questions and my presentations always seem to run past the allotted time, because individuals ask so many questions. After the presentation, I give them my business card and encourage them to call if they have additional questions. I love this part of my job, because it allows direct interaction with people and I have the chance to help individuals understand a very complicated and often intimidating service system.

Much of my time is devoted to providing technical assistance on Medicaid services to individuals in and outside of our agency. I receive many calls, but these days most requests come in the form of e-mail. Some are calls from legislators, inquiring on the status of policies; others are inquiries from agency staff requesting assistance on a variety of subjects. While I enjoy the busy pace of this position, I have learned to use a day planner to keep track of daily activities. I find the ability to multitask is critical in this position.

I also have the opportunity to work on legislative studies and monitor legislative action. Recently, I spent several days on drafting a report on an issue my agency has been studying all summer with stakeholders. Once completed, stakeholders and the agency will use this report to influence policy decisions made by the Governor and by the state legislature. I have written several reports of this nature and I find writing them to be fun! The ability to provide in-depth analysis and excellent writing skills are critical to complete these reports. My training as a social worker prepared me for these requirements, and I feel very confident in my abilities in these areas.

There are challenges in this level of work. Sometimes efforts of social workers in macro level practice can be met with resistance, even by other social work professionals. One of the more difficult situations I faced had to do with developing a program that some social workers felt would place waiver recipients at risk of fraud, abuse, or neglect. The proposed program would have given Medicaid beneficiaries more control by allowing them to hire, train, supervise, and fire their own personal care assistants. This program was highly controversial because individuals with disabilities wanted this level of responsibility, and the professionals who cared for them felt they were not capable of handling it.

There were many attempts by those opposed to the program to "kill" its development by protesting to their legislators, at public hearings, and by writing letters of complaint to the Governor and my agency. I responded to many letters of concern expressed by professionals that this program was inappropriate for individuals with disabilities. I even received letters at home from a local social work health care organization (of which I was a member) asking for me to oppose the development of this program. Despite all of this protest, I knew in my heart that this program was the right thing to do, because it would empower persons with disabilities. We were successful in developing this Medicaid program, and the service was embraced by individuals with disabilities. The program's success led to expanding consumer-directed services to four out of six of our waiver programs. Over 1,000 Medicaid beneficiaries now choose this option.

A common misconception of macro practice is that social workers at this level of practice do not have much opportunity to make a difference on an individual basis. In fact, I love this level of policymaking because it allows social workers to make a difference on a larger scale, but it allows them to see the impact on individuals and their lives. An example that will always remain with me involves a waiver program I helped to create that provides home- and community-based services for persons with developmental disabilities. When the first person was enrolled, an advocate called and to tell me how much the program meant to the child and her family. They had planned to institutionalize the child because of a lack of community supports, but her enrollment in the program provided them with the supports needed to keep her at home. The advocate's voice cracked with emotion as she described how this program was the answer to their prayers, and she thanked us for our efforts to develop the program.

The days as a policy supervisor are long and busy, but are extremely rewarding. I enter each new day with the chance to influence state policy that affects thousands of individuals, to assist them during the twilight of their lives or to empower others to assimilate into everyday life that we "able-bodied" folks often take for granted. Whenever it gets tough and I think about another job that would be less stressful, I think about the wonderful individuals I have met and helped. My heart swells with joy and I am ready for the next series of challenges that await me.

Think About It

1. What are some social work skills that are valuable to social work practitioners in this setting?

2. Can you think of examples of situations in this setting that might challenge a social worker's ethical boundaries? How would you address them?

3. What aspects of this work setting would be challenging and rewarding to you?

Chapter 13
Interning on Capitol Hill

● ●

by Carmela Isabella, BSW

When people hear the words "social worker," very seldom will they associate these words with politics. In the fall of 2003, during my senior year at Elms College, I decided that I wanted to do my social work field placement in Washington, D.C. in a congressional office. I was able to make this possible by enrolling in a program called the Washington Center for Internships and Academic Seminars, which placed me in a senator's office, as well as provided me credits and housing. While Senate interns typically do not receive monetary compensation for their work, some paid intern positions are available within the House of Representatives.

Upon my acceptance to a senator's office, everyone asked me, "Carmela, what does politics have to do with social work?" My initial response prior to my experience in Washington was, "I am interested in promoting legislative initiatives that would increase education for minority communities." I wanted to become involved in developing and advocating policy. By the time my internship in the Senate was over, I was awestruck not only by how much more the social work profession is influenced by politics, but also how much I was able to make a difference for the social work profession.

During my time on Capitol Hill, I assisted the correspondence office and the legislative staff. My day typically began at about 9:15 a.m. and ended about 6:15 p.m. My responsibilities included, but were not limited to, attending hearings, researching and summarizing related literature, working with constituents, attending meetings, and monitoring how the members of the Senate voted. In the four months of my placement, I dealt with many issues.

One of the first things I did each morning was to look in *Roll Call* and *The Hill,* newspapers that are solely dedicated to Capitol Hill, to see what public hearings were taking place that day. I would then tell the appropriate legislative staff member the whereabouts of the hearings. It was not unusual to find many hearings occurring simultaneously during the day. In these situations, I was called upon to represent the legislative staff at these hearings, where I would take detailed notes concerning the issues being presented.

Public hearings are usually the first step in the legislative process. During a public hearing, committee members hear witnesses (specialists, government officials, and spokespeople for individuals or entities affected by the bill) representing various viewpoints. I became aware that social workers need to know that they should not just wait until a vote is about to occur to lobby or advocate a cause. Social workers need to start early on in the political process, so that their cause can get a hearing.

Since the beginning of the social work profession, research and social policy have always been an integral part of all social work practice. The agenda of federal, state, and local policymaking bodies is social service and welfare policies. Instead of focusing on the issues on a micro level, I dealt with issues politically on a macro level. Although there were many issues to work on, I specifically assisted a legislative correspondent who worked on issues pertaining to Education and Section 8—Affordable Housing. After seeing what public hearings were taking place for the day, I would research electronically, looking for articles and related literature regarding Education and Section 8—Affordable Housing. I would then summarize the information and put it into a binder. Once the binder was complete, I would give it to the legislative correspondent who, after reviewing it, would then pass the information to the Senator. Once these daily tasks were completed, I was free to work on other issues.

Another part of my job, one that was very important and an activity I always enjoyed, was meeting with constituents, organizations, and lobbyists. They are the reason the political process exists. A law is created or altered because there is a need for change. Senate staff members frequently meet with constituents, lobbyists, and organizations because the senators spend a great deal of time in committee hearings and on the floor of the Senate. As an intern, I was privileged to observe some of the meetings. On one occasion, I attended a meeting with two lobbyists who had concerns about child welfare. They brought to our attention *S.*1704, the *Keeping Families Together Act.* This was a bill in the Senate to amend the Public Health Service Act to establish a state family support grant program. The program would end the practice of parents giving legal custody of their seriously emotionally disturbed children to state agencies for the purpose of obtaining mental health services for those children. The lobbyists were in favor of the bill and wanted our senator to co-sponsor the bill. Every social worker needs to know about this bill, especially those who work with children and families. Child welfare is the largest primary practice area for social workers, so this bill would affect many social workers who are dealing directly with families and children. This bill could single-handedly change their policies and ways of operation.

Another of my responsibilities was to give Capitol tours to constituents. Since the attack on September 11, 2001, the only way to see the inside of the Capitol Building is to contact the Capitol Building directly or through the offices of your members of Congress. These tours lasted about forty-five minutes. I immensely enjoyed leading these tours. Touring is an informal way for constituents to meet with the Senator's staff, and because I represented the senator, the constituents were able to talk to me about issues that concerned them. At the same time, not only was I able to teach and show the constituents the history of the Capitol, but I also had the opportunity to show them live debates and voting by the members of Congress.

Elected officials receive hundreds of letters on a daily basis on a wide variety of issues. As an intern, one of my tasks was to select and research some of the issues found in constituents' letters. I chose those that pertained to the social work profession, such as health care, Medicare, agriculture, homeland security, environment, and Veterans, to name a few. Among the many issues I worked on, Medicare was the biggest concern among constituents. Many social workers are working directly with clients who are in homes, facilities, and hospitals, as well as clients who have HIV/AIDS, who have disabilities, who are members of state prescription plans, and who are dually on Medicare and Medicaid. At the same time, here I was in Washington, D.C., taking calls and reading letters from very concerned constituents who were worried about the future of their prescription drugs benefits. I was working in Congress during the Medicare debates and the passage of the new Medicare bill. The bill passed in both the House of Representatives and the Senate, and President George W. Bush then signed it. This new law, once it goes into effect, will affect social workers all over our country, changing their policies and ways of operation drastically.

I felt my social work skills gave me an advantage over other interns. Social workers have "hands on" experience with social services. The skills of social workers are exactly what politicians need. We are trained as clinicians and active listeners, which enables us to reframe and translate what people say—whether intervening with angry individuals or meeting with constituents, lobbyists, or organizations. Social workers are able to assess individuals and groups and define the nature of the problem. We understand social systems and how they work, and we understand social service policy and the consequences of various choices.

I have always been an activist, lobbying for social justice. However, this time, I was on the receiving end of different styles of lobbyists and organizations, which is where I learned what to do and what not to do. I found that setting up meetings and forming business relationships with the staff of elected officials is one of the most effective ways of lobbying. Oftentimes, people take a defensive approach, contacting their members' offices in outrage. I noticed that those individuals' messages are often unheard; all you need to do is encourage your elected officials to vote "yes" or "no" on a particular bill. I understand the anger and frustrations people feel about issues close to their hearts, but to be successful as lobbyists or advocates, they have to do it in a civil manner.

This internship had a profound impact on what kind of social worker I want to be. Originally, I wanted to work in an inner-city high school. I went to Washington with questions concerning educational policies and left pursuing a career as a social worker in the political arena. I want to change policy, campaign for elected officials, and educate social workers about how the political process affects the work and working conditions of social workers.

I assisted in the making of the law, whereas most social workers follow an existing law. Many social workers work in systems and agencies funded by the government. The government decides whether social workers should be licensed. Our government is also responsible for making and funding policy, whether it is for clinics, programs, communities, facilities, education, schools, or health. There has been a tremendous reduction of funds for human and social services as a result of current difficult times in our country. Whatever field you work in, your limitations and policies will be affected and frustrate you. In political social work practice, we try to make the job of social workers in a nonpolitical atmosphere less stressful by providing laws that will help the profession and preventing passage of laws that will hurt it. This is why every social worker in every field of practice needs to know basic information about politics and the political process. Know your issues and, instead of getting frustrated, get involved.

Think About It

1. What public policy issues currently concern you and why?
2. How would you change these issues?
3. What are some of the issues on the public policy agenda facing the social work profession?

PART 5:
Training & Consultation

Chapter 14
Training in Eastern Europe

● ●

by Mona C. S. Schatz, MSW, DSW

My international travels began in 1992, through the invitation of the Institute for International Connections (IIC), an organization that teaches family therapy and a range of family intervention techniques in the newly emerging democracies of the former Soviet Union. IIC began through the work of Virginia Satir, the founder of family systems theory and family therapy in the late 1960s. Satir spent her entire social work career teaching other professionals how to improve family life through her special techniques. After many years front-and-center both in the United States and throughout the world, Ms. Satir was aware of how precious and precarious our globe is and how vital it is to teach peace to others. According to Dodson (1991), finding peace in family life held an important focus for Ms. Satir, and fostered her belief in the importance of efforts extended to foster global peace. She cherished a phrase known by her students and colleagues: *Peace within, peace between, and peace among.*

I provide that brief introduction to express how important it is that we build upon the work of those who precede us, so we are not re-inventing the wheel, so to speak. As I have been a part of training teams who are teaching family intervention in countries such as the Ukraine, Russia, Romania, Albania, and Azerbaijan, I am always amazed at how Satir's approach to working with families is so successful. In these next few pages, I want to give you a sense of how we can work with other professionals around the globe, providing exciting training experiences in which we are all involved in a rich learning process. This work is very exciting and challenging.

Social Worker as Trainer

My first human services/social work position was in a youth agency serving pre-adolescent and adolescent girls. Among my varied responsibilities, I was responsible for co-training the volunteers who worked with our young girls. Since I had not been taught how to do training, I was mentored by several special people who had learned to do training through their own trials and errors. From these wonderful mentors, I learned how to create experiential training experiences and how to make training programs meaningful for those involved.

Since those early training experiences, I have been able to provide different training programs in many different settings over many years now. In general, training programs serve to add knowledge and skills to audiences of professionals throughout their careers. University education cannot give social workers more than a basic preparation. Training programs may serve as pre-practice experiences in some organizations, as well as in-service learning experiences, occurring at different intervals. Training programs are often provided either under the aegis of an agency, under umbrella or coalition structures, or through special organizations that offer packaged training programs.

There is no university degree program for trainers; we usually emerge because training was needed and our job descriptions indicated that this was part of our work load, or we volunteered for the job or volunteered ourselves. There are some good books and articles that can help a trainer become really competent (see Additional Reading, in Appendix B). This chapter, however, is not about teaching anyone to be a trainer. Rather, I want to provide a composite snapshot of my recent training experiences in Eastern Europe.

Family Training Program

I was excited to go to a conference in Russia and help with one of the IIC conferences. Many of IIC's training experiences are done with a team of professionals, and this was the case as I went to Russia. We were working with a "sister organization" in Russia that was equally responsible for helping to design and implement the training programs. IIC trainers were not attempting to bring in a training experience where we set ourselves up as the "U.S. experts."

No. We designed a conference experience with East Europeans, Russians, *and* Westerners (U.S. participants, Europeans, Australians, Irish, in particular). The conference development process, as well as the hands-on learning, were two-way processes. Working to improve our work with families was the basis for our coming together, but we had different starting points. For the new countries emerging from the former Soviet Union (now 22 countries), working with families at risk was new. Under the former Communist lifestyle, family and community programs—as well as social workers—were banned. Only after the fall of the Soviet Union was it possible to re-introduce programs that would help families cope with the range of problems that face families everywhere. For the Westerners attending these conferences, the learning was equally challenging since the Cold War mentality had left us ignorant of a huge portion of the globe's population. We were ignorant of the history and culture(s) and had no real understanding of family life, no less personal development issues.

Each of these IIC multinational conferences is several weeks in length. We use a retreat setting that provides lodging, food, and conference facilities. Only recently have I been doing some training in which we are working with East Europeans exclusively. In these cases, I am providing training to an entirely foreign audience. Because I am unable to speak Russian or any of the languages of these new countries, we use translators. I have come to appreciate the translation process, because I am able to slow my presentation down and review what I have been doing, make changes, or provide clarification when needed.

Talking About Crisis...

At one of our conferences, we were using two professionals as co-leaders, a U.S.-based therapist and an East European/Russian, to work with groups of about eight to ten participants. The groups had both Westerners and East Europeans and we were meeting in these groups both in the morning and in the afternoon. At times, we would have sessions of the entire conference group of about 80 people. At these large sessions, we would present some key ideas for everyone's consideration, and then we would use our small groups to expand on these ideas and concepts.

About the third or fourth day of this conference, we were met with a tragedy. The teenage son of one of our organizers died in a nearby lake. The young boy had been helping to care for the younger children, playing with them, and organizing different out-ings. His death stopped us cold in our tracks. The events that took place after the drowning taught all of us about scarcity as well as tragedy. The city where we were meeting had only one person who could dive for the lost body to recover it from the lake, and the city had only one coroner who could transport the body to the morgue. We could not move the body once it was recovered; we just had to wait until we knew what it would take for the family to take their son home for burial. Everyone was shocked by this event and the trainers met to discuss what we should do. Should we cancel the rest of the conference or continue?

We did continue. We decided that we would take time, how-ever, to help everyone with the grieving process. Some participants had brought their family members to this late summer conference, and there were spouses and children who needed to talk about what had happened, in addition to the attending conferees. One of the participants worked with the children and teens, doing cre-ative drawing and poetry to foster their expressions. Those of us who were working with the adult participant groups began our group time talking about crisis intervention and grief. To my sur-prise, the Ukrainians in my group were very aware of crisis and grief and they wanted to tell those of us who were Westerners about their own experience during Chernobyl.

Mara (name changed), married and a mother of a young child (maybe two or three years of age), recounted her experience when she and her school mates were transported to Odessa during the Chernobyl crisis. Mara was a teen of about 15 at that time. She talked about every aspect of that horrible day—the day when loud-speakers were blaring out instructions and information that she could hardly understand. She remembered how the bus that took them to Odessa stopped along the way, and all of them were hosed down (because they may have had radiation poisoning). Most of the children on the bus were much younger, and everyone was scared. No one knew what was really happening. She wondered if the world had blown up. She had no idea if her parents were alive or dead. It would be weeks, she recounted, before she was told that her parents were alive. It would be months before she saw her parents and eventually was able to return home.

The group listened intently to this re-telling of the first days after the accident at Chernobyl. We were being given an inside look at how scared Ukrainian children and adolescents were in the early days and weeks of this nuclear horror. Each person in the group heard how Mara felt as she was whisked away from her school. Each of us heard the uncertainty she faced, not just as the bus left the city, but as they traveled to Odessa and then lived in a closed compound for months thereafter.

Mara's story was told and we all needed a break. The intensity of her experience was shared among all of us. We needed to move around; we needed to get some air. We needed time to relax ourselves and consider what Mara's experience meant, personally. When we came back together, we were able to express how important her experience was and what it meant to each of us. We felt much closer to her and to our Ukrainian colleagues, and we became more open with our own sense of vulnerability.

Using a Miracle Question

At a more recent training session for potential supervisors in Azerbaijan, I offered the group a technique that I have used from time to time in family, group, and individual work. This is the miracle question attributed to de Shazer, one of the founders of the solution-focused approach to therapy. It goes something like, "If you woke up tomorrow and found that there was a miracle, that things were different, what would have changed?" There are variations on this question that all try to help the person or family look at what they really want to be different in their lives. I hoped that the supervisors who were in this small group training would see that this type of question offers clients a great deal of latitude and creativity, and puts the solution in the client's own hands. In the newly emerging democracies, so much is changing that at times, flexibility and creativity are key ingredients to maintaining one's sanity.

One of the group members really got frustrated with this question and challenged me to tell him why I thought this question would work for anyone. I asked him to think about what his response would be if he were to be given a chance to respond to such a question. His response was quick. He said, "Lots of money! Maybe, a million dollars!" I said, "Okay," and asked him to continue thinking about what he would do with that money and how he might come to earn that kind of income. He laughed, of course. But, he was also frustrated because he saw his response as another sign of the hopelessness that he felt every day. At the time, he had no place to live and no income from a job. I invited the others in the group training to contribute their insights.

Fortunately, I was able to take some more time with this male participant after the session. Ivan (not his real name) took this opportunity to tell me about his family and his years on his own. I learned that both of his parents had died when Ivan was seven or eight years old. He went to live with other family members, but that family situation did not work out well, and Ivan ended up on the streets as a pre-adolescent. He was now in his early twenties and was still on the streets.

As Ivan talked, I felt that he was telling his family story, probably for the first time. He was being given the time to tell me about his memories of his mother and his father. He loved both of them very much. He connected with those good feelings about himself. He also told me some things about his life on the streets, though this was much harder. He had had to do whatever it took to get food and a place to sleep. He was ashamed of some of his decisions and choices. I was deeply moved by what he shared with me. I felt as if I had gained some new insights into how a small child, lost and alone, tried to survive under the Soviet regime, where supposedly everyone had a home and food. Supposedly, no one was starving and abandoned.

I left after my training program was completed. I was, however, able to return several months later for a larger conference being held in the region. Fortunately, I saw Ivan again when I returned. We had a big hug for each other and we were truly relieved that we had another chance to connect, even if for just a few minutes. As we caught up on our months since we talked, I learned that Ivan had finally gotten a job and had a place to live for the first time. He was appreciative that we had spent so much time talking when I was there before. I wondered if our talk had maybe opened him up to the goodness that was part of who he really was… his mother and his father who loved him.

Final Thoughts

Even though I spend a great deal of each year in the classroom, my international training work in the emerging democratic countries has allowed me to be intimately involved in social work practice by providing training to people who are the trailblazers for newly emerging human services and social work practice. IIC has provided an excellent vehicle for cross-national social work, educating professionals through a very innovative training program.

I hope that by recounting these events, I have given you a small window through which you can see how someone can take social work expertise and share it with others, especially colleagues halfway around the globe. I appreciate sharing with you how my heart always gets touched by those who are part of training programs everywhere I am!

Think About It

1. What might be some challenges when working with professionals in different countries, particularly where the culture is non-Westernized?

2. When you reflect on the two individuals who tell about their own personal challenges, how important is the family for these people? What might be some attributes that families provide their own members that could be considered true regardless of one's nation or culture of origin?

Chapter 15
Entrepreneurship and the Mezzo/ Macro Social Worker

• • • • • • • • • • • • • • • • • • •

by Diane Strock-Lynskey, MSW

I'm sorry," the Director of Outpatient Geriatric Mental Health Services stated, "but we don't do home-based assessments. You will have to bring your client in to the mental health clinic." As a BSW practitioner working for almost five years as a Probation Officer in family court, I had just been assigned a 13-year-old girl who had been truant from school for over 180 days.

During my first home visit to meet with "Heidi" and her father, the reasons became apparent. When Heidi was 12, her mother died from cancer. At the beginning of the school year, Heidi's father, age 59, had had a severe stroke. After six weeks of inpatient rehabilitation, Mr. W. had returned home and was receiving occupational and physical therapies via a home health agency. He refused all other services. Heidi became responsible for cleaning, meals, and other aspects of her father's daily care.

During the visit, Mr. W. seemed very withdrawn. At one point, he noted, "I'm really not sure why I'm still alive. Sometimes I think Heidi would be better off if I were dead." No wonder Heidi was not in school—she was afraid that her father would take his life and she would be left alone. I asked Mr. W. if he might be willing to talk to a mental health worker about his feelings and offered to set up an appointment and provide transportation. He said he would be willing to talk but was adamant about not leaving the house, fearful that he might fall and further injure himself.

That day, I resolved to find a way to get the mental health system to change its position on home-based assessments. Since the current Director's position on this seemed fixed, I knew that whatever I did had to influence him from a different vantage point. I went immediately to my supervisor and explained the situation and what actions I wanted to take. Ray was a staunch advocate and told me to go ahead and do what I had proposed.

First, I went to our agency's executive director, explained the situation, and asked him to contact the Commissioner of Mental Health and advocate for a home visit from a social worker. Next, I contacted the school district superintendent and asked her to do the same. Both parties agreed to make the call. One week later, Mr. W. was assessed at home and found to be clinically depressed and at high risk for a suicide attempt. He agreed to medication and counseling. He also agreed to receive Meals on Wheels and to attend a support group for stroke patients. Heidi returned to school and after receiving tutoring and attending summer school, was able to graduate from eighth grade and enter high school. The last thing I did was to ask the executive director to set up a meeting to work on revising the clinic policy on home-based assessment. Two months later, this was revised to allow for home visits under extenuating circumstances.

I can trace my decision to get my MSW, with a specialization in management, planning, policy development, and community organization, directly to this situation.

All in a Day's Work

It is 8:30 a.m. on Tuesday, my day to work in my home-based office and make some progress on my private practice work. I am just settling down to continue writing a student curriculum on human rights and diversity for a local college when the phone rings. The person calling turns out to be the executive director of a small nonprofit agency representing art galleries, artists, and other crafts persons across the state. She received my name by "word of mouth" and is seeking a consultant to work with her, the staff, and the Board of Directors on developing a three-year strategic plan.

I am President and CEO of S-L Associates, a woman- and minority-owned (I am partly of Native American heritage) and certified (by the State of New York) firm and practice that I founded in 1987. I have a master's degree in social work and I concentrate on working with groups, organizations, and communities in the development, implementation, and management of change efforts, the promotion of work, organizational, and community quality of life, and the attainment of social and economic equity. Some of the activities I engage in include qualitative research, strategic planning, team building, conflict management, curriculum development, group facilitation, training, and crisis intervention. The caller notes that she had "no idea that you can also get a social work degree that focuses on management" and is "intrigued that a social worker could be doing what you are doing."

I ask her to share some background about her organization, how the board is structured, and what she hopes to accomplish. She raises concerns about staffing, fiscal resources, and the need to strengthen the board structure. We talk for a bit about the benefits, as well as work involved, in setting up a regional system of board representation.

She asks me to discuss some of my thoughts on strategic planning. I draw from several strategic planning models. How I use these models is tailored to the needs of each organization and linked with an assessment process. I draw from the values of my professional training and education as well as from my own cultural background. These include a strong emphasis on collaboration, equity, collective involvement, personal ownership and responsibility, and building a sense of community.

She asks some questions about how I approach needs assessment. By the end of the conversation, she is very excited about what we have discussed and requests that I send her, as soon as possible, a written proposal outlining the steps that would be involved and a budget. She notes that the Board meets in two weeks and will make a decision at that time.

After getting off the phone, I look at the clock and realize that it is now mid-morning. It's time to review my date book and plan for what lies ahead over the next month. The first thing listed is four phone interviews that I will be conducting over the next week for a strategic planning project. These interviewees include the CEO of a major insurance company, a local County Clerk, a middle school teacher, and a local historian.

The next item listed is a training session on sexual harassment prevention and intervention that I will be conducting next week for a large, state government agency. After this is a focus group session that I will be facilitating involving leaders from Hispanic Catholic communities located in a major metropolitan area. The session will identify what these leaders would consider the most important historical documents to collect and preserve from within their communities. In the middle of the month, there is an "Executive Summary" that I need to finish for a major corporation. I have just completed an organizational assessment, and the management wants to know what my recommendations are regarding follow-up interventions that may be needed.

The last item listed is a problem-solving session scheduled for the end of the month. This session involves a conflict among executive management, supervisory staff, and line staff within a small government agency. During a recent consolidation of work space and functions, two units within the agency have been merged into one. Pressured into moving before the new work space was ready, line staff have been working in an area that has water leakages, hanging wires, and an insufficient number of computer work stations.

There have been major layoffs and a hastily put-together reorganization resulting in confusion over roles and responsibilities. The line staff have threatened to file an OSHA (Occupational Safety and Health Administration) complaint against the agency, and the supervisory staff have threatened to file a union grievance against management. My role will be to: (1) assist each group in more clearly defining its concerns, (2) identify what each group considers workable solutions, and (3) develop and implement a process to bring all three groups together and work with them to create an environment conducive to developing workable strategies that everyone can agree on.

Next, I review my date book to determine where I am in the semester and what needs to be done in relation to course development, preparation and delivery, grading, department meetings and projects, division meetings, committee work, advisement, letters of recommendation, participation in college community activities, and a host of other responsibilities. Since 1990, I have worked as a full-time faculty member of a BSW program. Over the years, I have served as Coordinator of Field Education (1½ years) and Director of the Program (8 years). Working through the ranks, I am now a tenured, full Professor of Social Work. I have taught most of the courses within the department over the years. However, my specialty areas include Human Behavior and the Social Environment; Mezzo and Macro Practice; Field Education; and Death, the Dying Process, Loss and Grief.

After getting my MSW, I worked for about ten months in the continuing education unit of a school of social welfare at a local university. My job was to develop and conduct training for child protective and child welfare workers. I then moved into training supervisors of income maintenance, medical assistance, and foster care units. While I enjoyed this work and learned a great deal, I was interested in broadening and advancing my skills.

After being in this setting for two years, I received a call from a friend—a social worker who had recently taken a position as the training director for a new center being developed under another area of the university. The purpose of this center would be to promote employment equity for women in state government. The new executive director, also a social worker, envisioned an organization that would integrate research, training, and advocacy into one unified approach "to bring about substantive change efforts." They were looking to fill a position that would involve 50% time as a community organizer and 50% time as a trainer. With much excitement and anxiety, I applied for the position. Two months later, I was hired.

For the next five years, I worked with women's advocacy groups on employment equity issues and assisted them in organizing to bring about changes in employment policies, developed and conducted training on sexual harassment prevention and intervention, served as chair of a task force on women in blue collar jobs, acted as a public speaker on women's employment issues at conferences, and worked with labor unions to advance quality of work life issues. It was an incredible opportunity and experience. Looking back, it was also the very necessary "grounding" I needed in direct mezzo and macro practice that set the stage for my future private practice work.

When the President of the university left and the center narrowed its focus to that of primarily research and mentoring projects, I decided to leave and start my own practice full time. With over ten years of experience but no immediate work in sight, I put two of my major life philosophies to the test: "trust in the universe" and "belief in the principle of abundance." One week later, I received a phone call from the Dean of the local Master of Social Work program. He was going on sabbatical. Would I be interested in covering one of his graduate-level management courses? Three weeks later, I received a second call. Would I be interested in developing training for the affirmative action office of a state agency? One month later, I signed a three-year consulting contract.

Three years later, I received another phone call. The BSW program (which also happened to be my alma mater) had an unexpected full-time teaching vacancy. I had been recommended by one of the school's professors, after having served as a guest speaker in her class. Would I consider interviewing?

Rewards, Challenges, and Opportunities

Even after all these years, it is sometimes hard to believe that I have been fortunate enough to have the opportunity to prepare future social workers to enter the field. I view BSW practice as the heart and soul of the social work profession. I believe it is my responsibility to keep my practice knowledge and skills current so I can, in turn, ensure that the students enter the field as prepared as possible. My consulting work has enabled me to effectively bridge the world between teaching and the realities of direct practice. One continually feeds into the other. The outcome, I believe, is that I am a much better teacher and a much better practitioner because of this continual exchange process.

After reviewing what lies ahead over the next month, I glance down at my watch. It is now noon. I quickly calculate that in the time remaining, I might be able to get most of my prep work done for tomorrow's teaching and the phone interview with the CEO.

My husband calls—he has a meeting at 7:00 tonight and will be coming by to pick up our son for a doctor's appointment. Our three children will be home from school by 3:00 p.m. Based on my teaching schedule, I am able to be there to greet them 2-3 days a week. I love the stability and sense of security that this has provided for us over the years. Fortunately, I am a "night" person and do some of my best work between 9:00 p.m. and midnight. Project work will be done in intervals over the next month.

The balance between teaching and consulting will continually shift, depending on deadlines and priorities, along with the inevitable "glitches" that arise. While the "roller coaster" nature of this can be stressful, the built-in reprieves of breaks and the summer, as well as the ability to be selective about what consulting projects I take, offer enough fluidity to make it all manageable. The opportunity to work with others to effect meaningful, constructive change within the context of groups and larger systems such as organizations and communities continues to be incredibly exciting and rewarding. I thrive on the spontaneity, creativity, and growth that come from each experience.

Think About It

1. What are some skills needed when providing consultation to organizations?

2. What are some skills needed to start and run a consulting practice?

PART 6:
Research & Funding

Chapter 16
Doing Social Work Research

• •

by Suzanne Bushfield, Ph.D., MSW

I wake up early to the sound of rain—a rare occurrence in the desert southwest. I'm in the habit of making a quick mental list of the day's activities in preparation for the multi-tasking that I know will be demanded of me today. Once at work, I check my computer-based planner, which really helps me monitor my progress on several projects. This week, my top priority is the book chapter I am authoring on pain and the family. While I have not conducted original research in this area, the chapter is for a large medical textbook on pain, and my chapter will emphasize the evidence in support of social work's focus on the family as a part of pain management. It is reassuring to know that research and building evidence is valued, and that new practitioners in the field of medicine might be learning about social workers and the family as important partners in addressing pain. I remind myself that change sometimes comes slowly—the book will come out next year, and it will be read and used by medical students in the following few years. I hope the chapter will result in changes in how physicians and social workers work together. Realistically, it is a lot like the results of social work practice—we often don't see them; we are merely "planting the seeds" of change.

My research assistant (an MSW student) has spent long hours in the library obtaining copies of articles that we have selected for my review and discussion. I have organized this literature by important themes. This is the part of the research process that really takes a long time—longer than I want, since I am eager to proceed. My outline for the chapter, submitted many weeks ago, suggested that I would first establish a framework for thinking about pain and the family. Then, since I believe that different theoretical perspectives suggest different interventions, I want to review the evidence of the effectiveness of specific interventions for pain. In particular, I hope to establish that interventions that include the family are most effective. Today, I will have coffee with two colleagues, whose input I value, and once again discuss with them the conceptualization I am trying to write about in this chapter. For me, this is a key component of the research process. Ideas and concepts are worked out initially "in my head," but ultimately, I need to check out whether these ideas translate into understandable conversations. My colleagues will tell me if my concepts are making sense and offer additional insights that might not have occurred to me. My goal is to weave what others have done with some of my own original research regarding risk and resiliency, and the importance of hope and a strengths perspective in addressing families and pain. As we talk over a variety of topics, my colleagues indicate that my ideas are making sense. I'm glad to have that reassurance! When you work very independently, it still helps to have someone else to consult with, to validate your work.

As I prepare to teach my undergraduate research course, I notice that reflecting on my own work as a researcher helps to make the research process come alive for my students. I often tell my students that research is "a whole lot of thinking, followed by a little bit of writing." The time it takes to conceptualize a worthwhile research project is time well spent; when I have tried to rush that process, it yields disappointing results. This morning, I read in the newspaper about the process of dieting. The suggestion was that one has to spend time thinking about the change one wants to make, and then planning the steps to begin to approach that change. Research, I remind myself, is a lot like that.

My next stop is the campus Research Consulting Center. This is a wonderful resource for students and faculty. Here, I can talk over the design of my qualitative study, and get help and guidance with SPSS and data entry for statistics. Yes, I do teach research, and I should know all this! But, just like my students, I get rusty when I don't use the skills. And the computer program for data analysis is such a time saver! Back in the "dark ages" when I took statistics, everything had to be done by hand. I'm reminded how much technology has changed how we do business as social workers and researchers. I'm glad that I can go back as often as needed to the stats lab for a "refresher" on some of the statistical tests, and clarification of exactly what I am trying to find out. It's a good idea to use the tools and resources available—and not be embarrassed to ask for help. In that way, I have empathy for students and clients: it's not always easy to ask for help, but it does help to keep research a more interactive process, rather than working in isolation. I spend the next two hours in a necessary task, but not at all my favorite one: entering data I have collected. Even though this is not, for me, a welcome task, I keep reminding myself that it is a necessary part of discovering what my research will reveal. I have learned to dedicate short intensive periods of time for this task, so that I am accurate. Then I reward myself with a break! Before leaving the stats lab, I notice that the consulting center has put together a great new Web site with resources on how to create questionnaires and how to conduct interviews. I will link this to my own class Web site for research, since I know my students could always use the help.

Today there is a faculty electronic poster session on campus. I always learn something here—people from other disciplines are using technology in their teaching and research, and I can borrow their great ideas and adapt them to my content area. Isn't it great to have access to such collaborative relationships? I wonder if social work departments don't benefit from being organized into colleges and schools with other disciplines, so we can share the common threads in interdisciplinary collaboration. I guess it is a good example of networking. As a social work researcher, I am using the same skills I needed in social work practice. As I talk over the course that my colleague has designed, I realize that there are many ways to build evaluation components into an electronic course format. That final step of evaluation sometimes gets overlooked, but it really completes the problem solving (and research) processes.

I return to my office to work on another project. I am busy with data analysis of a qualitative study. I have videotaped interviews with young adults who have demonstrated exceptional resiliency. Their stories need to be told, to help social workers recognize and support the strengths that have helped these individuals overcome a life surrounded by poverty, crime, abuse, violence, and absence of family support. Some people think that research is a very dry subject, but there are ways to make the stories of my research subjects come alive and inform us with the richness of detail gleaned from qualitative research. For this project, it was particularly important to gain approval for the use of human subjects in my research. It took a lot of extra time to describe the purpose of my study, the risks and benefits of participation, and my plan for obtaining informed consent. But protecting the confidentiality of my participants is critical. When I look at the NASW *Code of Ethics,* I am reminded that research is included there, with specific guidelines for social workers. And now, there are very explicit federal guidelines. I'm glad my institution is very conscientious, and that the Institutional Review Board provides review and oversight of research, so as to protect people who participate in research. The motto I repeat to my students (and myself) is: never assume your research is so unimportant that it does not require human subjects review. My study was approved, but I must pay special attention to how I protect the videotapes. I keep them in a locked cabinet and take care to review them with my door closed.

Checking my e-mail once again, I notice a Call for Papers. This one has come from the Society for Social Work Research, a professional organization that supports research. The announcement really excites me, because the conference is in England. I immediately call two of my colleagues, and we brainstorm about projects that we might submit, or new ones that we might undertake together. It would be fun to travel to England to present our research in an international forum and to learn what others are doing around the world.

It has been a busy day. I think I enjoy research because it fits with many of my personal qualities: I am very self-directed and enjoy a variety of tasks. I also need to keep my ideas and creative energies focused on the reality of the needs of the larger community in which I work. Research demands an ability to look ahead and imagine what could be, as well as a firm grounding in what is.

I never really set out to be a researcher. But the longer I practiced social work, the more I wanted to know about what works, and why. I developed an appreciation for building evidence and theory, in order to contribute to my profession. There is a lot of hard work in research, but there are rewards, as well. When others read my work and it helps them create new projects, I feel very gratified to have helped in some way. An example is the e-mail I received from a graduate student across the country. She is working on her dissertation and has come across my work on the efficacy of early and frequent social work intervention in hospice. She contacts me to clarify the citation of my work in her study.

Pursuing research presents some big challenges. Funding is very competitive, and many researchers like myself are connected with universities, where they have teaching, advising, and service duties, as well as research. Sometimes research activities are punctuated with frequent interruptions, and it is easy to lose your focus. Another challenge as a researcher is to pay attention to the big picture. Some research demands an attention to very small details, but those details always exist within the context of the larger social environment, including diverse policies, theories, and realities of practice. To advocate effectively for underserved groups, we need research to build the evidence to make effective arguments for policy and programmatic change.

As a researcher, I have made the choice: rather than try to change the world, one person at a time, I will work for macro level change through my research.

The day is coming to an end, and now it is my favorite time of day: reflection time. As I arrive home, I relax, have a glass of ice water, and gaze around my desert garden. I watch the hummingbird and my dog's ridiculous attempts to scare the bird away. This "down time," I have come to recognize, is a chance to renew myself spiritually, physically, emotionally, and mentally. I review two conversations I had today: one with my elderly parents, who both experience chronic pain from arthritis and other ailments; and the other with a student who is dealing with pain, accessing a pain clinic, and many frustrations that come with trying to get effective treatment. The conversations bring my day to a full circle. I am reminded once again of how important it is to link research and practice. How can I help to ensure that new evidence is available to practitioners?

I guess that is why social work teachers are expected to be social work researchers, so the next wave of social work practitioners can have all the knowledge and skills they need to deal with the changing environment. (And, so those suffering with pain may find the hope they need for relief.)

Think About It

1. How are research and practice linked? Can you identify a problem in your own social work practice (or the area in which you plan to practice) that could benefit from research?

2. How does your agency (or an agency in your community, if you are not employed or in field placement in an agency) use research to inform or support its programs and practices? What kinds of data does the agency collect?

3. Do you know the steps in the research process? How are these steps similar to or different from the problem solving process used in practice?

Chapter 17
A Day's Work at the Institute for the Advancement of Social Work Research
● ●

by Barbara Solt, Ph.D., LICSW, ACSW

I*s anybody interested in a short-term job filling in for a maternity leave at a social work organization downtown? It's about 20 hours per week for about six weeks.* This passing remark made by Professor Joe Shields at a holiday party was how I heard about the position.

"Sure," I said. "I am only taking three courses next semester (my last in the doctoral program after taking four courses in each of the previous three semesters), so I should be able to handle that, in addition to the ten hours I'm working as a research assistant." I figured it might be a good networking opportunity for moving back into the world of work as I reached the final stages of my doctoral program at Catholic University of America's National Catholic School of Social Service.

Four years later, I am still here. As so often happens, new positions derive from networking, from being in the right place at the right time, and deciding to "go for it." The woman headed for maternity leave for six weeks decided post-delivery to return only part time, and a short time later to stay home full time to care for her infant and pre-schooler. Also, the director left within a month after I started work, and two months later the third staff person of this small organization also moved on to another position. What I thought would be a short-term, part-time diversion from academics and a toe-dip into still another part of social work practice turned into something a bit more "exciting" than I had envisioned. My years of social work experience in a range of settings, both nontraditional and traditional, guided me as I found myself in uncharted territory. Not only do new jobs come via networking and passing remarks, but they always bring surprises—the kind that aren't on job descriptions or what you thought you heard during the hiring interviews. The phrase "other duties as required" is the part of most job descriptions that really should be seen as a big alert signal—"an adventure lurks here."

Some History, Before Getting to Now

Here begins the "person-in-the-environment" part of this day in the life of a senior program associate, a very unique position that combines social work practice, education, and research. The "person" I was at the time was a seasoned developer and manager of community based services, who 31 years post-master's degree decided to retool by entering a doctoral program. I decided that I should devote myself full time to the effort so that I would finish before retirement, so I had concentrated fully on finishing coursework before easing back into employment or consultation.

My work history was unique in that I had worked in large public agencies, small nonprofits, higher education, a national church office, and as a regional branch leadership trainer for a fraternal benefit organization. Most of these jobs were "startup ventures," in which the position I filled was a new one and/or the service in which I worked was in its infancy. I found that I liked the challenge of organizational development, and that once the staff was hired, the policies formulated, and the operation up and running fairly smoothly, I was ready for a new adventure. (I was also often exhausted from working long hours and weekends, and needed to take a break before plunging in again.) I was a classic workaholic. Single and devoted to a life of service, the boundary between my volunteer work and employment was often blurred, as I moved into a new community and began to network and find social supports.

Thus, I now looked to find work as a consultant or "worker for hire" in a place where I could limit my time commitment and move into a more balanced work and personal life. I had done a number of consultancies that allowed me to experience an even wider array of organizations and afforded me the opportunity to learn even more about human resources, volunteer management, policy-setting, fundraising, and organizational behavior. So I was not totally surprised when I found myself the only holdover staff during a time of organizational restructuring.

The "environment" part of this story is a relatively new, small organization, but one with ties to much of the leadership of the social work profession. The Institute for the Advancement of Social Work Research (IASWR) was formed in 1993 to "strengthen practice and policy through social work research." A task force of social work academics, researchers, and practitioners with support from the National Institute of Mental Health recommended the creation of a new organization devoted to developing social work research capacity, so as to strengthen the knowledge base for social work practice and policy. The National Association of Social Workers (NASW), the Council on Social Work Education (CSWE), the Association of Baccalaureate Social Work Program Directors (BPD), the National Association of Deans and Directors of Schools of Social Work (NADD), and the Group for the Advancement of Doctoral Education (GADE) became the founding and financially supporting organizations of this new venture. The National Institute of Mental Health provided significant funding for the first four years, followed by the Ford Foundation's support for the next several years. The Society for Social Work Research (SSWR), formed shortly after IASWR to serve as a membership organization for social work researchers, began providing financial support in 2000. Each supporting social work organization is represented on the IASWR board of 13 members, along with three officers and two at-large members.

A full history of IASWR and its purpose is presented in the journal *Research in Social Work Practice* (Zlotnik, Biegel, & Solt, 2002). The IASWR Web site *(http://www.iaswresearch.org)* also includes an overview of the organization's history, mission, and strategic plan, as well as an array of archived examples of the work done in fulfillment of its mission. Briefly, IASWR serves as an arm of the profession and a forum for practitioner, educator, and research leaders to meet to formulate partnerships and to work together to assure that social work research and researchers are developed, and that social work education programs are equipped with research-oriented faculty, so future practitioners emerge grounded in evidence based and tested theory-driven practice to benefit consumers of social work services and to advance effective social policies.

To this end, IASWR's work is focused inward to the profession, as well as outward to other disciplines and to private and governmental organizations focused on developing and using science to promote the public health and national safety and well-being. The staff currently consists of an executive director (Joan Levy Zlotnik, PhD, ACSW), myself, and an administrative assistant (Brenda

Bustos). IASWR is a field placement for master's level students and has hosted the BPD Policy Fellow during the summers. IASWR rents space from the national office of NASW, and its proximity allows for ready informal exchange with staff there. In addition, IASWR sponsors CSWE, BPD, GADE, NADD, and SSWR conference-related workshops aimed at developing researchers and educators through sharing research findings and/or through facilitating linkages to organizations who support research and advanced education and by providing technical assistance. In 2003, IASWR began sponsoring summer research methods workshops for doctoral students and faculty who want to learn more about methodological advances. In addition, through issue-targeted funding from foundations and the federal government, IASWR has conducted a number of literature reviews and convocations of researchers to share their findings on such issues as injury prevention, child welfare, social work and public health, substance abuse and HIV/AIDS, cancer, and aging. Reports on these projects are available on the IASWR Web site.

So What Is It You Do?

Some years ago a friend asked me, "Barbara, why is it you always work at something I can't understand?" While said in good humor, it succinctly states the difficulty of translating to the general public what social workers do. We have our own language, and we do things that sometimes take some time to become visible. Indeed, at times process is our product, and this is very true for the work of IASWR. Whether, at the time my friend made the statement, I was working as a "fraternal coordinator" or as an "urban ministry strategy developer," the sentiment serves as well for "senior program associate for an organization advancing social work research."

Since I completed my doctorate, a number of friends and colleagues have asked, "What are you going to do now? Are you interested in teaching? Are you going to do research?" My usual response is, "Why do I have to do anything different from what I'm doing?" I'm not interested in traditional classroom teaching. While I'm not conducting research, I think I am contributing to the research world by assisting in the process of translation and dissemination of research findings, through the training of advanced methodologists, and through facilitating the relationships between researchers and funders so that research projects can move from nascent inquiries to full-blown studies.

The first project on which I worked for IASWR was coordinating the development of a workshop curriculum funded by the National Institute on Drug Abuse (NIDA) to acquaint social work researchers with the process of securing funding by this National Institutes of Health component. The workshop would cover how to use the standard application forms (PHS-398), how to formulate a research design and consult with NIDA project staff before sending in a full proposal, and what to expect from proposal reviews. This task involved relating to social work faculty from around the country I had never met, who had no idea who I was, and each of whom had very specific sets of knowledge to integrate into the design. Having worked for a national organization, I was familiar with the vagaries of communication that is not face-to-face. but the world of conference call planning sessions and editing of PowerPoint presentations via e-mail round-robins was another challenge altogether. The experience resulted in numerous "your mailbox is full" messages, until I learned that I needed to archive any e-mails with attachments very quickly. The experience also showed that my initial interest in computers almost 20 years prior was standing me in good stead.

While the technology of social work practice is the relationship, the conscious use of self, and the use of theory to guide one's actions, the technology required for this work also requires a knowledge of PowerPoint editing and preparation for translation to print, as well as use of desktop publishing software. Over the years, I had ventured into the computer world and become fairly conversant with current software. So, here I was, a lone ranger with a computer and a phone, and a job to be done. The curriculum got done, thanks to the hard work of the consultants, the NIDA project staff, and the then IASWR board president, Lynn Videka. As I studied for my comprehensive exams, I realized that the schedule flexibility working for IASWR offered, as well as the opportunity to learn more about the world of social work research, was of real interest. And so, when the new interim and later permanent director, Joan Zlotnik, was hired by IASWR, we charted a new position that moved me from consultant to senior program associate.

The Portfolio

At the beginning, much of my work was of an administrative nature—fielding e-mails and phone messages, handling communication with funding entities, preparing reports, and drafting written materials to help tell the IASWR story to our constituents and to the public. I helped draft the 2000-2003 Strategic Plan, based on the planning task force's work. I created brochures. I reviewed the IASWR archives to pull together the story of the early years, so it could be used in demonstrating our capacity in proposals. In addition, I began attending meetings of collaboratives with other behavioral and social science professions, as well as public meetings of the major federal research funding organizations. It became clear that most of the social work world was not aware of IASWR, and most of the public we encountered had little awareness of the research function of our profession. Having long ago recognized that "it doesn't exist until it's documented," I began to develop the documentation portion of IASWR's work. I set about systematizing some written resources aimed at our constituents and others, to help demonstrate to others what we do. One of those resources is the IASWR LISTSERV® Announcements.

IASWR Electronic Mailing List Announcements

Increasingly, organizations turn to electronic mailing lists as a cost-effective way to disseminate information in a very timely way, in this case, virtually instantly, or at least as soon as the subscribers read their e-mail. Different from electronic bulletin boards or chat rooms where one must take a specific action to get to the information exchange, the LISTSERV® mailing list is essentially an e-mail-delivered resource. One subscribes to the list, which is managed as a database through which messages sent to the list are distributed to all subscribers. Some mailing lists are "open" in that any subscriber may address a message to the list. The IASWR list is "closed," so only the "owner" can post messages, which are then sent to all subscribers, who can read them, but cannot reply.

The IASWR announcements subscribership was at about 600 subscribers in 2000. Announcements about conferences, training sessions, and grants available were sent out sporadically, perhaps semi-monthly. Being a veteran newsletter editor, I decided to format and formalize the IASWR Listserv Announcements so they were sent out weekly, usually on Wednesday or Thursday, and were formatted so the reader could know that sections would be in a consistent order and easily scannable.

The format is not high-tech. Headings include: Calls for Abstracts or Papers, Conferences, Funding, News and Notices, Online Resources, and Research Findings. Current issues run about ten pages, single spaced. Subscribership passed 1,600 in April 2004, for a net increase of some 1,000 since I began editing it. There is no charge to subscribe, and all issues are archived on the IASWR Web site.

Feedback from readers at conferences, and via a formal electronic feedback evaluation form, have shown that this is a valued service that helps social workers not only through the information they receive but also as a "branding product" for IASWR. Many who do not know about IASWR or its purpose know about "the listserv" as subscribers, and they forward it on to others, highlighting particular items of interest. Gradually, I began introducing myself at social work conferences as "the IASWR LISTSERV® Lady." Others have introduced me as "the IASWR LISTSERV® Honcho" or some similar label.

Assembling the Announcements

While there are now many electronic newsletters and announcements, this one is uniquely focused on information of interest to the social work research community. Items regarding policy advocacy are included occasionally, especially when the policy relates to research or involves research-based practice issues. Each item includes a brief narrative and the URL or hyperlink, which can be "clicked" to go to the source for fuller information. The information is not merely by or about social work researchers, but rather is culled from a variety of information sources that may be of interest to the wide array of foci of social work research, such as aging, child welfare, mental health, substance abuse, housing, and community development.

Rather than depend only on what comes across our desk, as before, I now subscribe to more than a dozen news sources and scan them for items of interest or importance and timeliness. Each day, I scan some 20 e-mails. The assembly of each issue takes one to two days each week, or about half of the 30 hours I work for IASWR. I group information in each section so that it is listed either in order of deadline dates, or contiguous by issue area. I try to include not only the specifics of what, where, and when, but also information that guides the reader or provides information useful in either teaching research or providing information about resources that can be used in research or teaching. I hope that regular readers may learn more about how to conduct, translate, and disseminate research by reading the conference notices and requests for proposals, and other items.

Increasingly, we receive requests to include notices of workshops and special journals. Then, too, we receive hard copy newsletters and journals, which we scan for information. Fortunately, more and more of these hard copy sources also have a Web site, so more cutting and pasting and less typing is involved.

Other Days, Other Publications

In 2001, I initiated a hard-copy semi-annual newsletter called *IASWResearch...Reports...Resources* for dissemination at conference exhibits and other workshops, as well as to send to deans of schools of social work and others on the IASWR mailing lists. This publication, of some six pages, includes more information on resources and research issues than can be included in the Listserv Announcements. Known as "The 3Rs," this instrument also includes information on what IASWR staff is doing to develop and strengthen relationships with key individuals or organizations involved in the national research enterprise. The publication reports on Capitol Hill briefings conducted by coalitions in which IASWR participates, meetings with NIH Directors and attendance at Advisory Councils, news of forthcoming IASWR-sponsored workshops and trainings, as well as selected resources where the social work researcher can find more information useful to the conduct and teaching of research. The "3Rs" is assembled using desktop publishing software, and some 1,500 copies of each issue are distributed.

In 2002, as a result of a joint task force, IASWR, SSWR, and the World Wide Web Resources for Social Work (WWWRSW) initiated a jointly sponsored monthly collection of Web-linked resources, including journals, Congressional reports, and other items of interest to the research practitioners. This newsletter is assembled and distributed by Gary Holden and colleagues at New York University, but I maintain liaison with Gary, share information to be considered for inclusion, and regularly include news related to research from new issues in the IASWR Listserv Announcements.

IASWR recently began providing the content for the new NASW Web site research page. A different research area is presented each month, with information highlighting recent research findings conducted by social work researchers. The page includes a "What is Social Work Research?" piece for the practitioner and general public, who may not know that social workers not only use research in our practice, but also conduct research, which is useful to other disciplines and to policy-setters. These research Web pages are not meant to be exhaustive sources of information on the subject, but highlight and call attention to the types of research being conducted and include literature citations for additional information. I coordinate this project and serve as liaison to the NASW Web design and editing staff.

Training and Meetings

The year 2003 began a new venture in providing training in research methods. Dubbed "Rigorous and Relevant" by the faculty who conducted the initial workshop on qualitative research, this phrase is now being used to signify the title for subsequent training offerings by IASWR. My day's work on this project includes handling the planning of schedule design (usually via conference calls and e-mail), coordinating consultants' contracts, producing publicity about the workshops, and answering questions from interested participants.

IASWR coordinates workshops and symposia in conjunction with our sponsoring organizations' conferences. For example, I coordinated the day-long symposium funded by NIDA at the 2004 SSWR conference, in which six researchers presented research findings related to cultural issues, drug abuse, and HIV/AIDS.

I enjoy attending the many meetings, workshops, and conferences conducted by national research-supporting organizations, such as the NIH, AHRQ, CDC, NSF, NAS, and IOM, as well as some significant foundations as they either seek input from research constituents or provide opportunities to develop working relationships between the social work research community and others. On these occasions, research agendas are formulated, interdisciplinary collaborations are strengthened, and IASWR represents the social work profession and its research interests. A highlight is when we are able to contribute our profession's unique and integrative perspective to the topic at hand.

Round-Up

Today when I reply to people's question, "What do you do?" I say, "I am a social worker." Then they ask, "What kind?" and I tell them that I work in an area about as far afield from frontline social work practice as one can get. This is true, in the traditional sense.

Yet it is not true, in that what I do is a real example of the wide-ranging work that social workers perform. We marshal resources, communicate, advocate, document, network, and develop organizations. We use our relationship skills, our knowledge of human and organizational behavior, of systems, practice modalities, and influencing policies.

That is what this senior program associate does. Each day presents very unique and interesting opportunities to serve our profession.

Think About It

1. How has mass communication via the Internet changed the way social workers do their jobs?

2. How relevant do you feel the research in the social sciences is to your work or your career goals?

3. Subscribe to the IASWR LISTSERV® Announcements. How can the information in this publication be used in your work? By other social workers?

Chapter 18
A Life-Altering Experience as a Social Work Researcher

●●

by Denise Travis, Ph.D.

It is a necessary requirement that students of social work take research classes. Over the years, it has been my perception that students and faculty alike have experienced the following scenario. *Instructor:* Where do you feel you need to start? *Student:* From the beginning.

The role of researcher in the field of social work is important for several reasons. On a micro level, it is direct practice social workers, by virtue of their contact with clients, who are most aware of their needs and how policies will affect them. On a macro level, program evaluation helps document best practice and make recommendations to close gaps in service.

Inherent in the scholarship of research education are the principles and dynamics involved in protecting the research respondents. History provides evidence of these important principles dating back at least to the infamous Tuskegee syphilis experiment. To that end, the following information must be given to research respondents in writing and their signature obtained before they can be included in a study: purpose of the study, procedures, possible benefits to the respondent, possible risks to the respondent, monetary compensation, confidentiality, and right of refusal. Much care is given to protect the research respondents. What was not covered, in my academic studies, was the risk to the researcher.

Receipt of Grant

In 1999, I applied for and received a grant from the Indiana State Board of Health to conduct a Ryan White Title III Needs Assessment entitled *HIV/AIDS Needs Assessment of Lake County Indiana's Communities of Color*. My interest in applying for this grant was initiated by the loss of two friends to AIDS. The first was a 40-year-old self-identified gay male and the second a 43-year-old heterosexual female who acquired the disease from her bisexual fiancé.

Together with three MSW students acting in the role of research assistants, I developed eight instruments designed to elicit answers on knowledge, attitude, and behavior of HIV and condom use from many different populations, including HIV-positive African-American males, HIV-positive Latino Males, African-American females, Latino females, clergy, intravenous drug users, service providers, and family members of HIV-positive people. This was a very powerful experience. The students were assigned populations according to their skill and practice experience. For example, one of the students had practiced in the substance abuse field for several years, so she was assigned to the intravenous drug users.

Prior to the commencement of the research project, I took the students through a research workshop that was designed to help them differentiate between factual observations and assumptions, develop the research instruments and the Consent to Participate document, and be prepared for the data analysis process. I saw this research project as an opportunity for me to (1) share the knowledge I acquired during a research training workshop delivered by the Center for Disease Control with the research assistants, (2) increase the dissemination of knowledge regarding HIV/AIDS in communities of color in Lake County, Indiana, and (3) add to my knowledge base as I continue to improve my capacity to teach and practice social work.

There were 80 respondents in the study. As we completed the data analysis, the research findings were both expected and surprising. The respondents who were HIV-positive were practicing safe sex more than the respondents who were not HIV-positive. Contrary to what was anticipated, the respondents who were members of the clergy were very receptive to acknowledging that HIV/AIDS was an illness that had affected their various congregations. However, they felt inadequate in addressing the problem. The most alarming finding came from the female respondents. We hypothesized that limited access to medical care or transportation were barriers to HIV prevention. The findings documented that it was in fact self-esteem that was the largest barrier for the respondents involved in this study. That is to say that if the male partner had an issue with condom use, the female tended to acquiesce. The data were presented at two professional seminars, one sponsored by the Northwest Indiana HIV/AIDS Community Planning Group and the other sponsored by the Indiana State Board of health.

Life-Long Learning

In the course of this study, I learned something that had not been taught to me during all of my academic studies—that is, the risk to the researcher. While interviewing the ten family members of people who were HIV-positive, a pattern arose. In all of the first six interviews, the respondents began crying when asked the following question: *What is your greatest fear for your loved one who is HIV-positive?* Without exception, the answer was death. In fact, all of these respondents' family members had already died. On an intellectual level, I was aware that the content of the interview might cause emotional distress to the respondent, and stated the same in the Consent to Participate form. On a human level, however, I was unprepared.

I was relieved to find out that the respondent in the seventh interview was a 6-foot 4-inch male who was hefty in size. As I arrived at his office, I relaxed and told myself, "Surely he is not going to cry." And then we arrived at "the question." Initially, he teared up, and then he let loose as he told of his fear for his sister, who was still alive, and her young daughter. He went on to express his anger at his sister's husband, whom he reported was bisexual and intentionally infected her because he thought she was too independent.

When the interview was over and the tape recorder was turned off, the respondent asked me, "So, how did you become interested in studying HIV?" Almost immediately, I burst into tears. Perhaps in an attempt to soften the moment, he stated, "Oh, Dr. Travis is crying. Let's turn the tape recorder back on!" I chuckled, and the respondent put on his pastoral hat and began to pray for those we had already lost to AIDS and those we would lose in the future.

As I left his office, I was completely disoriented. Although my office was only four blocks away, I got lost twice. To make matters worse, my next appointment was my eighth interview for the study. The only thing I could do was rely on my social work skills, center myself, and do what I had to do. This was an invaluable experience for me and an example I have shared with my students in multiple classes—that is, attention must be given not only to the effects on the respondent, but to the effects on the researcher.

Conclusion

Typically, social work researchers attach themselves to projects about which they are passionate. Given this, there are certain questions that we must ask ourselves. *Is there a potential for countertransference to interfere with the research process? Can we remain objective in the data analysis phase? Do we have the patience and fortitude to allow the process to evolve? Can we accept that it is more important to complete the study in an ethical and valid manner than to validate the research hypothesis?*

Social work research is a noble profession. According to the National Association of Social Workers, the mean starting salary for master's level social workers is $40,000. It should be noted, however, that the salary for researchers generally depends on the amount awarded in the research grant.

As a social worker with concentrations in both clinical practice and social policy, I am committed to continuing my own education, as well as increasing the academic research level of the students under my domain.

There are several organizations that are available to support social work research. The National Association of Social Workers and the Council on Social Work Education have research information available on their Web sites. More information on social work research can be obtained from the Society for Social Work Research.

Think About It

1. Should social work research scholars include a chapter on "Risk to the Researcher" (including the possibility of secondary or vicarious trauma) in their textbooks?

2. A question of reflection: What would you do if you found yourself in the same position as the author—that is, eliciting tears from the respondents involved in the research? Or breaking down in tears yourself during research interviews?

3. Do social work researchers have a responsibility to research respondents who have an emotional reaction to their research?

Chapter 19
FUNd Writing: Working as a Grant Writer

● ●

by Donna McIntosh, MSW

Hi Donna—it's out. When can we get together?" That was the message on my voicemail when I got home one day in April. I teach full time in a BSW program. I have been a grant-writing consultant for a number of years. What I feared most in that message was the due date of the grant. Sure enough, when I called the agency back, they told me May 8. Almost the last day of classes! Could I pull this off? I felt strongly about this particular grant and wanted to be part of it. I scheduled an appointment for two days later to meet with key agency staff.

In the meantime, I was able to go to the federal funding source Web site and download the RFP (Request for Proposal). When I first started writing grants, I used a typewriter. Today, grant writing is made so much easier by technology, from online posting of the RFP to downloading the complete application forms. Cutting and pasting on the computer is a more efficient use of time and energy than retyping several times on a dinosaur typewriter.

Two days later I was in the agency office. This wasn't just a consulting job for me. I believed in the mental health philosophies of this agency. I had been on the board of directors in the past. I felt a part of the team rather than the "hired pen." We had worked on other grants, many of which had been funded.

"Let's get started," said John Sampson, CEO of the mental health agency. In anticipation of the RFP coming out, John had been talking with key stakeholders in the county of choice for this grant. While there was some skepticism, it appeared that the primary stakeholders who could make this happen were in support of applying for the grant.

"Will we have letters of support from them? Will they want to see and review the grant before it goes out?" I asked. These were critical grant development questions. If you can't demonstrate support from key stakeholders in your application, forget writing it. Also, I worried about "too many cooks in the kitchen"—too many people reviewing the grant slows the process. Kathy Davis, the Associate Director, replied, "Yes, they will write letters of support. We will send them a copy of the grant but won't need to run it past them as long as we agree on the concept." John, Kathy, and other key agency staff had been conceptualizing the model for a while.

This was a federal SAMHSA (Substance Abuse Mental Health Services Administration) grant for systems change. What SAMHSA was looking for was a consensus building process in communities to adopt exemplary models of mental health practice. What John wanted to see happen was a jail diversion exemplary model adopted in the community of choice. Over several decades, since deinstitutionalization, the mentally ill population was slowly shifting to the criminal justice system. They were housed in jails and prisons. In the year or two prior to this RFP, a person with mental illness had died in the local jail. That case propelled the issue into the spotlight and brought professionals from the criminal justice and mental health systems to the table together. The timing of this RFP could not have been better. John had also spent some time with his staff researching some of those jail diversion models and had selected two from other states that appeared to most closely fit the legal and mental health systems in our state.

Organizing the Effort

"The first thing we all need to make sure of is the deadline for the grant. Is the grant to be received by May 8 or postmarked by May 8?" I joked with John and Kathy. We have to have it correct in our heads as we develop the timeline for completion of the grant. For any grant I have ever done, it always means FedEx overnight delivery!

The next area we examined were all of the supporting documents. What do we already have from other grants that can be used for this one? Because we had written SAMHSA grants before, we knew that some of the forms and attachments were standard. I had created a checklist for supporting documents. Kathy and John would have staff begin to assemble the many pages. We also had to review the RFP to see if there were any limits on the number of pages for the supporting documents section. There were standard federal forms to complete. There were also directions for other supporting documentation, such as one-page résumés and job descriptions of key personnel for the project. If the RFP says one page, then it has to be one page. This meant staff time reworking wordy résumés or job descriptions to be condensed to one page, but in a manner that still captured the totality of that person's experience and responsibilities. Also, it is not wise to reduce documents to a small size to fit one page by either changing the font to a smaller size or reducing it on the copier. Most RFPs detail the font size and margins to be used, as well.

Moving on efficiently, we developed a list of stakeholders. We assigned the drafting of a letter requesting support to be sent to stakeholders. The letter included a return date for letters of support. We weren't going to have time in the final hours of the grant to track down stakeholders for letters. An early return date would allow John and Kathy time to follow up with certain key stakeholders if they hadn't received a letter by the deadline.

"When are you going to start the budget development for this with your fiscal director?" I asked John. John and his fiscal director, Tom, had already started developing the budget. "I am going to need a copy of your budget as soon as possible, because we know from past grants that the budget justification section in the grant narrative has to support line-by-line the proposed budget," I said. The grant narrative also had to reflect the staffing pattern proposed, as well as integration of budget items into rationales for how goals and objectives would be met with the funds requested.

The next area we addressed was grant research. Because John had a staff person already doing jail diversion and criminal justice programming around the state, the agency had a well-organized library of resource materials, including major research on jail diversion programs. John was making it a priority for that staff person to give me whatever research time I needed for the grant. I requested that the staff person, Colleen, provide me with national, state, and local statistics from the county of choice. It is important in the statement of needs section for the grant to demonstrate any national and state trends that clearly establish the need. However, for a grant for a local community, we needed the statistics to show that this community had a documented need significant enough to warrant an award of funding.

The final aspects I needed that day included a date for me to be in their offices to edit the grant narrative, and the target date for final assembly of the grant. In the meantime, as I finished sections of the narrative, I would send them to John and Kathy for review. They would also be sending me updates of supporting documents completed and a copy of the budget. Again, technology is wonderful. Without e-mail and the Internet, I would have had to camp out at their offices almost on a full-time basis.

And the First Line of the Grant Reads...

After the first line it just flows for me, but until I get that first line in my head, there is no point in trying to write. What I have learned over the years is that I need to walk, drive, and sit and think about the grant. I push words and concepts around in my head. Mindful of the deadline, I then sit at the computer and it all starts to flow from my head to my fingertips. Of course, I keep the RFP right beside me while the fingertips are flying.

First, I typed up the headings and subheading structure as laid out in the RFP. Most grants will have a similar structure—the abstract, a statement of need, proposed project description, target population, goals, objectives and outcomes, work plan, staffing, diversity, organizational capability, evaluation methods, funding request and sustainability plan, a budget and budget justification, and supporting documents and forms. Different RFPs don't always have them in this order, but these are the common sections for most grants.

Over the next two weeks, it took me about 30-40 hours to write, edit, and re-edit the grant narrative. Some days I worked on it only a little bit and other days I spent a good six to eight hours writing. This particular RFP had a requirement of 25 pages of narrative. When a grant says total pages not to exceed a certain number, don't exceed it. I have seen funding sources throw out proposals because they exceeded the page limit. In fact, part of a good grant application is demonstrating that you can follow the directions precisely. Was I able to confine my words and address all of the requirements of the narrative into 25 pages? Not on the first few drafts! I don't work that way. I sit down and type on the computer whatever thoughts and concepts come to mind that respond to the RFP, highlighting the unique aspects of this grant application that will make it worthy enough for funding. I don't fix grammar or spelling in those first drafts. I simply let everything spill onto the page. Once I have everything answered and there are no more words left in me, then I start to pare down the document. It's a method that works for me every time. The first grant narrative draft for this grant was 40 pages long. I certainly had my work cut out for me to edit it down to the required 25 pages.

Edit, Edit, and Re-Edit

Believe it or not, the greatest amount of time for the grant was not the first draft but all the redrafts. I probably edited this grant narrative about five to seven times before it was finalized. The first redraft pared down the pages and cleaned up the grammatical accuracy. On the following drafts, I continued to look for typos, but the focus was to ensure that what was left still gave enough detail and answered all of the requirements of the grant guidelines. The funding source grant reviewers will read each section to ensure that it addresses all of the requirements for that section. Critical points are lost if the narrative lacks substance or clarity. I know this to be true, as I have served as a federal grant reviewer for Health and Human Services grants. Every point lost is a potential step away from getting funded. If the funding source asks for the same information in three different places, then give them the same information in three different places.

There are two areas that are potential points of friction in grant writing. One occurs when the agency staff that has contracted with you to write a grant wants something in the grant, either wording or a service concept, with which you don't agree. It didn't happen on this grant, but on others I had worked on, even with this same agency, we had to have some discussion about language or concepts. I have found it's important to have those discussions and work it out. Fortunately, with this agency, I have had a long working relationship and feel like a part of the agency. They respect my input as a seasoned grant writer. But I do remind myself that I am only writing the grant, and they have to live with the grant if it gets funded.

The other area that can sometimes be difficult is leaving your ego at the door about your writing! At least three to four people edited this grant, and they all had different writing styles. They tried to edit from a perspective of not changing the style but checking for grammatical accuracy and accuracy of information about their agency. They trust my experience and instincts as a grant writer. It is important, however, that those people most responsible for implementing the funded grant read and edit the grant. I always make sure I have the last draft responsibility. I hold that privilege not only because I am paid to do so, but also because I read the grant yet one more time to make sure that it meets all of the grant application requirements. I am also the person who makes all of the suggested changes, so we are all working off a master document and don't have multiple versions circulating.

The last edit day of the narrative was a full eight to nine hours just for the narrative. I spent that day in their offices. There was tension from the looming deadline, but the synergy and creativity made for a very positive team atmosphere. We work well together on grants. I don't take that for granted (no pun intended), and neither do they.

The Final Assembly—Following the Rules and Double Checking

It is May 7, and the final day for assembling the grant is upon us. We have finished the narrative. We are now converging in the conference room for assembly. I read through the checklist from beginning to end and Kathy says, "check" to each page. We also check to make sure original signatures are signed in the required color ink (black or blue) for each page requiring a signature and date. It's done. One copy is fully assembled. We run the grant through the printer for page numbering. Again, it's important to follow the directions. If the RFP says to start with the cover administrative form as page 1 and go from there, that is how it needs to be paginated. So of course, the table of contents for this grant is the last page completed after the full grant has been paginated. I then pull out the partially completed table of contents page and type the page numbers on the table of contents for each major heading. It's then inserted back into the document complete. Once we have a full grant application, we make the 15 copies we need. The original and two copies go to the funding source. The remaining copies are for project staff. One complete copy is also given to me for my records.

The secretary has called the closest FedEx office to see how late we can send it out on this date for delivery on May 8. We have until 6 p.m. It's now about 4:30. We have to refer back to the RFP to find out if the original and copies to the funding source are to be left unbound, stapled, or clipped. That small detail, seemingly trivial, is also very important. It feels like a highly pressurized treasure hunt to find that small detail in the RFP. Once found, we discover we aren't to bind the applications to the funding sources. The staff person assigned with by far the greatest responsibility—

getting the grant out through FedEx—is just now leaving with the grant.

Did We Get the Grant?

When that grant goes out the door, there is a collective sigh and a noticeable change in the air. We sit together in the conference room for a moment. We feel good about the work we have done. But it's not quite over. We now will wait for months for the verdict. Did we get funded or not? We would like to think that with all of that work and commitment, it will get funded, but the competition is fierce. Only ten grants will be awarded nationally. I have learned it's not always about the concept or program as much as how well the grant is written. That surely increases the pressure and feelings of responsibility for me, as the author of the document. But for today, John, Kathy, Colleen, and I sit in the conference room smiling at each other. It's "in the mail."

Think About It

1. Should a grant writer have worked in the fields of practice for which he or she is writing grants as a paid consultant? What are the pros and cons of the grant writer having worked in the applicable field of practice for which the grant is written?

2. What are the considerations in having a paid grant writer for an agency rather than having full-time staff write grants for their own program areas?

3. How would you, as a consulting grant writer for this grant, determine a consulting fee? Consider the amount of time given to writing, editing, and assembling the grant.

4. Should a consulting grant writer, who is not a regular employee of the agency, have a say in the contents of the grant (i.e., the conceptualized program proposed)?

PART 7:
Higher Education

Chapter 20
The Field Office: Teaching and Supervising Student Internships

• •

by David V. Henton, LCSW, BA, MSSW

My day begins late today. One of the great things about my job is the high degree of autonomy I have. This includes flexibility with scheduling. Because I know my day will not end until late this evening in Victoria, Texas (over a hundred miles away), I don't leave for the university until after 9:00 this morning.

Upon arrival at my office, I respond to e-mail and phone messages. I return a student's call about a written assignment due at tonight's field seminar in Victoria. Several agency-based field instructors have returned my phone calls as we try to coordinate interviews for next semester's BSW interns. After returning calls and responding to e-mails, I go upstairs to the main social work office, where I greet and visit briefly with our administrative assistants and student workers. Hortencia Hernandez, one of our efficient and highly organized staff in the School of Social Work, reminds me that I will need to deliver course catalogs, supplies, and mail to our satellite program in Victoria when I leave campus this afternoon.

After visiting with Hortencia, I have appointments with two students who will be entering field in the fall. It is late Spring now, and the field office has begun interviewing the twenty-five students who are completing their final courses and will be entering professional internships in the fall. My 10:00 a.m. appointment is with Maricela Ramirez, a student who was in my "Intro to Social Work" course several years ago. Although my primary teaching responsibility is in the field office, I am periodically asked to teach in the classroom, as well. I remember Maricela well and am delighted to be discussing her internship with her. Maricela informs me that she is only interested in interviewing at Child Protective Services (CPS) at this point. I review her academic record and note that she is qualified for competitive stipends we are able to offer our CPS interns. She is bilingual/bicultural (English and Spanish), has taken our child welfare elective, is an excellent student academically, and has written a powerful essay outlining her interest in and commitment to a career in child welfare. I agree with Maricela that she is exactly the type of student who will excel at CPS—a quick learner, able to think on her feet, exhibiting unusually strong assessment skills for an entry level practitioner, culturally competent, ethical, and passionate about children and families. I call Angela Ausbrooks, the agency-based Child Welfare Grant Specialist at CPS in Austin, and we arrange an interview for Maricela.

My 10:30 appointment is with Dana Osbourne. Dana is unsure of where she would like to interview, but she has expressed an interest in either school-aged children or older adults. After further discussion about the type of supervisor she would like and experiences she hopes to have in her internship, I make several phone calls to area agencies on her behalf. By 11:00, she has two interviews set up for potential placements. One is with a Communities-In-Schools (CIS) dropout prevention program at a nearby middle school. The other is with the Area Council on Aging's day program for older adults. I wish Dana good luck on her interviews and remind her to follow up with me after she has completed them.

I then check in with the Field Director, Dr. Karen Knox, who has called me during my interview with Dana. Karen reminds me of a commitment the field office made to provide some agency-based continuing education to a large AIDS Services Organization (ASO) in a nearby city. Because of my previous practice background in mental health, Karen asks me if I would be willing to provide training on working with people with AIDS/HIV who also have a mental illness. I agree and promise to call the ASO's Director of Client Services to discuss dates and times for a workshop on mental illness.

As she always does when she sees me, Karen asks how my current students in field are doing, and if there are any problems we need to discuss. Discovering that we both have time for lunch, we decide to leave the university, get a bite to eat, and do some catching up. Although Karen is readily available to me in an emergency, we often go a week or more without touching base on routine issues. It is nice to discuss field matters and our students' progress over a relatively leisurely lunch. We discuss the incoming students for the fall. Karen shares concerns she has about "goodness of fit" issues with several students. In the field office, we take our professional gatekeeping responsibilities seriously, and while it is rare for us to encounter students who are inappropriate candidates for social work, we do occasionally have students who are not suited for a particular setting. Today, Karen is concerned about Martina Sanchez, an excellent student who is interested in working in hospice. Karen tells me that Martina has recently lost a beloved *tia*, and that she has concerns about Martina interviewing with hospice at this point. We agree that when I meet with Martina for her initial field placement interview, I will gently explore her recent experiences with the loss of her aunt, and help her determine whether or not hospice is an appropriate setting for her internship at this time.

Karen also updates me about some additional field sites that have recently become available. These include the constituency service office of a state representative and a therapeutic foster care program. She reminds me that several alumni now serving as field instructors are particularly interested in interviewing this group of students.

We arrive back at the university in time for my 12:30 meeting of the University Insurance Committee. A huge part of working for a university is service, and like the classroom faculty, I am expected to serve on school, college, university, and community committees. The Insurance Committee is the University Senate committee responsible for quality assurance and evaluation of the university's various health insurance programs for faculty and staff. The meeting lasts about an hour, at the end of which we have finalized the plans for our annual consumer satisfaction survey.

At 2:00 p.m., I have a field conference meeting with my colleague Sonya Lopez and two current BSW students at Casa Esperanza. An MSW with significant experience in children's mental health, Sonya is the founder and executive director of this child and family services agency, which exists primarily to train our university's students in social work, family and consumer sciences, applied sociology, and educational psychology. Today, Sonya and I are having our final three-way conference with each of the two BSW students she has supervised this semester. Both students began the semester with considerable difficulties. One had appeared unusually timid and fearful of client contact. The other had been overly assertive. Earlier in the semester, we had had several additional three-way conferences together, in which we had clarified expectations and developed plans for improved support, supervision, and communication. Both students have subsequently excelled in their internships, and the back-to-back final evaluation meetings are celebratory in tone. Both students will graduate shortly with their BSW degrees and can expect positive references from both Sonya and me as they enter the job market as professional social workers.

After the meetings at Casa Esperanza, I return briefly to the main social work office to pick up the supplies I will be delivering to Victoria. I then set out on my weekly drive. It is spring in the Texas Hill Country, and the warm sun and beautiful wildflowers have a peaceful and renewing effect on me. As usual, I enjoy the pastoral scenery and the light traffic, and the drive is a nice respite from a hectic day.

I arrive at 4:30, an hour before our integrative field seminar is to begin. I deliver the supplies to Cheryl Robbins, the able half-time administrative assistant at this, our distance education site. I visit with Cheryl about an upcoming open house we are planning to publicize our social work program in this rural, under-served area of the state. Then I make myself available to students, should any need to see me individually prior to our seminar.

The seminar begins promptly at 5:30. The twelve students, all current social work interns, have driven from five to 150 miles to be at this, their fortnightly integrative field seminar. However, I make this trip every week because in addition to working as their faculty field liaison, I directly supervise three interns in agencies without social workers. When the Field Seminar ends at 8:00, I meet with these three students for group supervision (or "Group Soup" as we call it). Although we also meet for individual supervision, I have learned that group supervision provides rich and synergistic opportunities for the students to learn from and support each other. It is also an exciting learning opportunity for me. In almost twenty years in social work, this is my first experience facilitating group supervision, and I am loving it!

Tonight's "Group Soup" is an interesting one. I marvel at the different ways in which the students use the group. Juanita Escobar is doing her internship at a local junior high school through the family service agency that employs her. She frequently uses "Group Soup" for problem solving, and tonight is no different. She is concerned about several students whose self-injurious behaviors (cutting on themselves) have gotten progressively more serious. She also shares the ethical dilemma she encounters routinely regarding potential weapons. The school district in her community has a "zero tolerance" policy on weapons, and children can be expelled for possessing them in school. However, she wants to encourage children who may have brought knives to school to know that they can be relinquished in her office. We talk at length about her role as an employee of the family service organization vs. the role of school employees, even though both occupy the same campus.

Celina Garcia, another direct supervisee of mine, interns in a faith-based transitional housing program serving women recently released from prison. Tonight Celina shares how working with a young mother has suddenly raised unresolved issues about life in her own family of origin. Celina's colleagues in the group and I listen empathically and commend her for her self-awareness and her ability to use the group appropriately as a place to process what she is experiencing in field.

The third student in the group, Maggie O'Rourke, frequently uses the group as a place to vent, and tonight is not unusual. Maggie is a non-traditional student with a long career in the business world who is entering social work in her mid-50s. She is organized, confident, capable, and sure of herself. Her internship is in a nursing home in a rural community outside of Victoria. The administrator, a new college graduate in her early 20s, does not understand the role of a social worker in Long Term Care, and Maggie is working valiantly to educate the administrator as part of her internship. It is not easy, and Maggie often complains in "Group Soup." However, as I have seen firsthand during my visits to her nursing home, Maggie is consistently professional, positive, and appropriate in her interactions with the administrator. Only in "Group Soup" does she have the safe luxury of venting her frustrations. She thanks us for listening, and shares that we have been able to help her maintain a positive attitude in her determined efforts to educate the administrator before her internship is over.

Supervision ends shortly before 10:00 p.m., and we all go our separate ways. For me, the two-hour trip home means windows rolled down, loud rock and roll on the radio, and several brief stops to stretch and perhaps have a cup of coffee to ensure my ability to drive safely. The university will reimburse me for overnight accommodations on the evenings we have seminar, but I sleep better in my own home, in my own bed, with my dogs by my side. Besides, these students and this job are energizing for me, and (even with the loud rock and roll) I often find myself reviewing the day's events with satisfaction and with gratitude.

When I went into social work almost 20 years ago, I never intended to teach. My last job with the state mental health department entailed significant staff development activity, and I discovered that I loved working with adult learners and I had gifts and talents as an educator. Although I enjoyed all of my social work practice jobs, supervising interns was always my favorite aspect of each job. I consider myself blessed beyond measure to now teach social work, and to work full-time in the field office of a School of Social Work.

Think About It

1. Social work is a stressful field in which burnout is a serious problem. How is this job more stressful and how is it less stressful than most social work positions?

2. What personal and professional attributes might lead a social worker to work in the field office of a School of Social Work?

3. From the supervisor's and the student's point of view, what are some advantages and disadvantages of group supervision?

Chapter 21
Carving Out a Career: Academic and Community Collaboration

●●●●●●●●●●●●●●●●●●●●●●●●

by Stephen C. Burke, Ph.D., MSW

I wrote, and subsequently responded to, the following "Help Wanted" ad: "Looking for an individual who is a self–starter and enjoys working a flexible schedule. The successful candidate will possess the following attributes and skills: the courage and ability to help empower individuals, groups, and communities to discover their personal and collective strengths; and, the skills required to communicate ideas that inspire individuals, groups, and communities to make life-changing decisions." It can be perplexing attempting to pigeonhole the job that I carved out for myself.

Am I an educator? Most certainly! As the Bachelor of Social Work (BSW) Program Director at Marywood University School of Social Work, I work with students new to the social work profession. Employing teaching strategies that encourage students to reflect upon their values, as well as gently challenging their present belief systems, my intention is to create an atmosphere where they can make informed decisions about social work as a major and as a possible career. I teach the first two courses, as well as the last two courses, that students take in our BSW Program. I purposely arrange my teaching schedule that way, because I want to witness the effects that our BSW program may have on the personal and professional growth of our students.

As a Doctoral Program faculty member, I advise experienced practitioners who are new to the scholarship side of the profession as to possible research directions for their dissertations. Having an ability to envision where a student's area of interest could lead in terms of dissertation research is crucial. Additionally, being knowledgeable about methodology, or how to collect the data one needs to do research, is very important at this level of scholarship. My objective with doctoral students is to somehow inspire them to take risks to create social work knowledge that will benefit the profession as a whole. Besides advising students on their dissertation research interests, I also teach two doctoral level courses, one focused on social policy and the other focused on the effects of social and economic factors on human development.

Am I a community practitioner? Definitely. Working in agencies in the role of a field instructor one day a week, I assist MSW level students in refining and honing their assessment and intervention skills. From creating a program that assists families transitioning from welfare to work, to helping a nonprofit housing agency to develop needed lobbying skills, my efforts with graduate students are exemplars of school and community partnerships. Being a guest in the agency, a university-based field instructor must at times walk a fine line between suggesting possible changes in that agency's program or policy and at the same time maintaining one's welcome. Besides being adept at relationship-building, community practitioners—and all social workers regardless of their practice setting—must operate from the values and principles delineated in the profession's *Code of Ethics*.

I enjoy practicing in agencies because it keeps me "fresh" with what is happening in the social work world. My collaborations with graduate students in the community provide me an opportunity to meld theory with practice—thus benefitting the agency, the practicum student, and the students I teach in the BSW and doctoral programs.

Am I an author? Indeed! Aspects of my classroom and community work have been communicated to peers in articles written for professional publications. For example, a colleague and I co-authored an article that informs our academic peers about the advantages of introducing a variety of viewpoints when teaching doctoral students. Another article describes active class assignments to instructors teaching introductory courses in BSW programs. An article that a former student and I completed sheds light on the operation of faith-based organizations. The ability to communicate ideas and experiences in print and electronic media requires the development of writing and editing skills.

Am I an administrator? Of course. As BSW Program Director, it is my responsibility to ensure that the curriculum helps students to acquire the knowledge, values, and skills necessary for beginning social work practice. That only happens if I can recruit qualified students and faculty and create instructive and challenging courses. In order to accomplish those objectives, the job requires me to exercise team-building and budgetary skills. Additionally, I must be knowledgeable about how to apply the accreditation standards of the Council on Social Work Education to the curriculum and administration of the BSW program. To be honest, some of my least favorite aspects of this job are related to administration. However, when I witness the professional and personal growth of senior year students, the administrative tasks that I have performed in support of their educational experiences are well worth it. Again, one reason I purposely teach first-year and senior-level courses is to validate the effects of the administrative, teaching, and advisory work I do with students throughout their tenure in the BSW program.

To be successful at this job, whether in the role of an educator, a practitioner, an author, or as an administrator, I rely on my communication skills and ability to facilitate empowerment stances of individuals, groups, and communities.

I Have Never Been Bored in This Job. I Have Been Fatigued and Frazzled, But Never Bored.

7:45 a.m. It is just my habit, being a morning person, that I get to work early. Unless I start my day in an agency supervising a graduate student, which I do one day a week, I am usually in my office by 7:45 a.m. If the truth be known, I could do much of my writing and course preparation work at home—but I like my office, and I enjoy being around colleagues and students.

Most people would find my office too small for their liking. I find my work space both comfortable and comforting. Everything I require, in terms of office and creature comforts, is within easy reach. The office walls are full up, from top to bottom, with posters, photographs, and paintings. My office is a welcoming place for students, colleagues, or an occasional family member to drop by and talk.

I like to reserve the first two hours of my work day for writing. Mornings are when I am the freshest. Mornings are also the time when I can best put together ideas that may have come to me during the previous afternoon or evening concerning the writing project at hand. My present project is an extension of work I have done on a new generation of nonprofit agencies that provide services to families transitioning off of welfare. Generally speaking, the only interruptions to my writing time are those that are self-inflicted. Indeed, I have a quiet and very comfortable office.

10:00 a.m. I have a Senior Seminar today from 11:00 a.m. to 12:15 p.m. I will use the next hour to re-visit my planned-for activities and opening remarks. During today's seminar, students will have an opportunity to express aspects of their personal and/or professional selves through a piece of literature or art. Last week's seminar, using this same format of self-expression, was laden with emotions—tears were shed and shared by all. I am using my anticipatory skills to prepare for today's seminar as I plan to make connections between group process and aspects of reflection. My group worker skills will be in evidence today. I am very excited for today's seminar to begin.

12:30 p.m. A poem and a song were used in today's seminar to discuss issues of grief, hope, and resilience. As was the case last week, the students and this instructor were teary-eyed during parts of today's seminar. Unlike last week, I think we were successful in making connections between the students' narratives and the underlying emotional content. The ability to set a tone that encourages expression and risk-taking is a skill that I learned in graduate school and I use in classes and in work group settings. Today I received feedback from a number of students indicating that they thought the seminar went well. An idiosyncrasy of college-level teaching is that one often receives immediate feedback regarding one's efforts. This can be both a frightening and an affirming prospect!

12:40 p.m. It is registration time for next semester's courses. A student drops by unexpectedly to discuss what she has to do to declare a second major. Luckily, I have a colleague who is well-versed in such subjects and I give him a call. Both the student and I, demonstrating a solid confidence in the response received, wish each other a good afternoon and offer mutual good-byes. This transaction lasts a total of eight minutes. Without the assistance of my friend, the student's request for information could have developed into a major vision quest for me. I have resigned myself to the fact that I simply do not function adequately in certain areas of academia without the help of key colleagues. It does take a village. Time for lunch and getting caught up on CNN headlines.

1:15 p.m. For the next hour, the Executive Committee of Caritas, the BSW student service club, is scheduled to meet. As Program Director, I function as faculty advisor to the club. Staffed by BSW students elected by peers, the Executive Committee will be discussing the specifics of a fundraiser to be held next week. Caritas is raising money to charter a bus for a Globalization Against the War march in New York City. I cannot stay for the entire meeting, as I have a Dissertation Committee meeting at 2:00.

These students have evidenced their leadership skills throughout the year. There is not much for me to do at this point but be proud of the way they conduct Caritas business. In the beginning of the school year, I did put in a lot of work with this committee around issues of team-building, the "how-tos" of running meetings, and the construction of meeting agendas. For the past six months, I watched one student in particular struggle with the mantle of responsibility that elective office can bring. She has matured to the point that her peers are urging her to run again next year for a leadership position. The most difficult thing for me to learn was that I had to "let go" of the committee and empower the students to make their own decisions. There were a couple of instances during the past months when I debated about stepping in. To my credit, I held back that urge, and the club leadership worked things out. I make my apologies about leaving early but I simply must not be late for this next committee meeting—nothing like chairing a committee to make one feel responsible for setting an example of being prompt.

2:00 p.m. I convene the Dissertation Committee with all committee members present. This is a key meeting in which we share suggestions for modifications to my doctoral student's dissertation document—in essence, the committee is assisting the student in preparing for her dissertation defense, which is scheduled for five weeks from today. At this point, the committee's questions and concerns center around the student's interpretation of data as they relate to the findings. No major modifications are suggested—just some fine-tuning.

In the role of Chair, I find the experience of facilitating the dissertation process not unlike "herding cats." As Chair, I have some special responsibility to see that the dissertation meets scholarship standards and is actually completed within certain time parameters. But dealing with three other faculty members, each with his or her own ideas concerning this piece of research, has tested my group skills and in particular my ability to keep the committee on task.

This committee meeting lasts until about 3:30 p.m. Having taken notes as to the suggested modifications, the student thanks the committee members for our efforts and support over the past three years. Three years! I recall meeting with this student, almost four years ago, when she could barely put into words her ideas about what she wanted to research. Now, before me is this 200+ page document, her dissertation, that shines a light into a dark corner and illuminates an area of knowledge for the entire social work profession to see. As a committee, we all did our jobs—and, as a committee, we are all very pleased with the results. Time to go home, but not time to stop working.

Tomorrow is a community agency day for me. I will start the day, and spend a good part of it, at an agency supervising a graduate student doing her fieldwork. I will spend about a half hour at home preparing for tomorrow's planned activities. I am fortunate in the fact that the student I am supervising is very competent and is a self–starter. Still, I will go over the skill-building activities that will be the focus for our work tomorrow. The student and I will be completing an in-service that focuses on teaching the agency staff the "how tos" of employing successful legislative lobbying strategies. Like today, tomorrow will be a good day.

9:00 p.m. My day is not yet over. I have been asked by a Music Department service club to help judge a fundraising event being held on campus tonight. Music students putting on skits, singing, and just plain having a good time for a great cause—how could I say no! The fundraiser lasts until 11:35 p.m.

I chose social work as a career because it seemed to me to be a great way to live one's life. You cannot integrate the values of the profession without living those values in your life outside of the work you do. Values such as a belief in social justice and respecting human diversity inform one's point of view and life stance 24 hours a day.

I needed to obtain a Master of Social Work (MSW) degree and a Ph.D. to attain the skills I found useful to do the job described. The MSW degree gave me the skills to form helping relationships with individuals, groups, and communities. The Ph.D. gave me the skills to independently research social issues and assisted me in being successful in the educator role.

Think About It

1.   What is it about the values and focus of social work that sets it apart from other helping professions?

2. The writer states that social work is more than a career for him—it is also a way of life. What do you think he means by this statement?

3. Does the job that Stephen Burke "carved out" appeal to you? Is there an aspect of this job that you would like to specialize in?

Chapter 22
Working in an Academic Medical Center

●●●●●●●●●●●●●●●●●●●●●●●●●●●●●●●

by Kristi O'Dell, Ph.D., ACSW, LCSW

Being director of the student affairs department of a medical school is a dream position. I use my social work knowledge, values, and skills to help in the selection and education process of future physicians and in the care of patients. I am an educator, researcher, clinician, and administrator. After a long career as a medical social worker, I was in the right place at the right time to be considered for this position. That is, I was already employed at the medical school as an assistant professor of psychiatry. Much of the work that I describe can be applied to that position as well.

One of the things that I like most about the position is that there is no "typical day." There are seasons and different focuses, depending on whether I am working with premedical (premed) students, medical students, or medical residents (medical doctors in specialty training programs).

Springtime is premed recruitment season. I spend a good deal of my time visiting college campuses, meeting with premed advisors, premed clubs, health professions classes, and individual premed students. We talk about motivation and commitment to medicine, grades, and the Medical College Admissions Test (MCAT). We conduct "mock" medical school admissions interviews. The prime question at interviews is, "Why do you want to be a physician?" This is followed by any number of questions, such as, "What kind of a physician do you want to be? What else is important to you in life? What have you done in your life that has been of service to others? What do you do for fun? Can you improve your grade point average (GPA)? Are you willing to take the MCAT again?" I never cease to be amazed at these young adults.

Springtime is also a transition time for medical students, who are in medical school for four years (MS 1–4), and medical residents, who are in their specialty training programs for a minimum of three years. Students and residents have had the time since the prior summer to adjust to the unique challenges of that year and to look forward to the new challenges that begin each summer. First year medical students (MS-1s) are grateful for surviving biochemistry and anatomy. Second years look forward to getting out of the classrooms and into beginning their "clinical years." Third years look forward to beginning their last year of medical school. Fourth years definitely look forward to graduation, but also feel some trepidation about entering the next level of their education, specialty training. They are leaving the familiar environment of medical school to begin again in a new educational environment, often in a new town and state and with family in tow.

I could not have imagined how much I would use my social work knowledge, values, and skills in nurturing the growth and development of these young professionals at group and individual levels. I get to help them understand their patients from a psychosocial perspective. I get to observe them interacting with their patients, and they observe me with mine. There is an exchange of questions about the impact of illness on life. How do chronic illness, loss and grief, access to health care, and limited resources affect patient, family, and community life? And so on.

On a personal student development level, being "intelligent" is not a shield from life's personal problems and decisions. A typical day as director of medical student affairs includes listening and problem solving with medical students on personal, educational, and professional levels. "Where is the clinic?" "How do I get access to the computer?" "The professor is not fair!" "My classmate/supervising resident is harassing me." "I am failing my class/clinical rotation." "My spouse and I are having problems." "I am sick. What should I do?" "I have been in a car accident." "I need a place to live." "I don't know what kind of medicine (specialty) I want to practice." "How many residency programs should I apply to?"

Summer is a time of heightened activity at the medical school. It is a time of beginnings and special programs. Special programs for premeds generally revolve around the recruitment and support of minority and rural students, both in short supply. Minority and rural students spend time "shadowing" health care professionals and participating in limited ways in the care of patients. The students get additional help with the science curriculum and MCAT preparation, as needed. It is the beginning of the school year for medical students and residents. For all, it is a time of orientation and acculturation into the next level of medical education.

Fall and winter are times of "settling in" for the medical students and the completion of the medical school admissions process for the premeds. It has been my privilege to serve on a medical school admissions committee, a diverse, dedicated group of people who meet one day a week for five to six months per year to decide who will be our future physicians. What a pleasure to meet many of the best and brightest young people from across the U.S. and other countries. These are people from all backgrounds, and not just science majors. That said, it is also occasionally a shock to meet a few students and wonder, "How did they get here?" Admissions committee is an amazing and initially terrifying experience. I help decide who does and who does not get into medical school! Once I became comfortable with the process and saw that it worked, I could relax and have fun. Once the decisions are made, then we all wait to see how it will all "fall out" in June and July. Some students know early on that they have been accepted to one or more schools. Others are on wait lists. Some eventually get in, and some start the admissions process again the next year. The medical schools wait, as well. Will the best and brightest students with multiple acceptances come to our school?

What is personally rewarding about a career in medical student affairs is getting to know the students over time, watching them develop personally and professionally from premeds to medical students to residents, and having a part in that progression. Additionally, as a social worker, it is most gratifying knowing that I had no small part in training these young physicians to care for their patients, not only as biomedical beings, but also as psychosocial beings.

For those with an interest in dealing with thorny issues, the medical school environment is teeming with ethical and policy issues. For example, there are privacy issues as they relate to students and patients, including the Health Insurance Portability and Accountability Act of 1996 (HIPAA). Other ongoing issues include Medicare, Medicaid, managed care policy, right to treatment, right to withdraw treatment, and so on.

What is the "down side" to being a social worker director of medical student affairs? First, I am a social worker in a host setting, and a biopsychosocial and spiritual person in a largely biomedical work world. I need to prove myself as a valuable asset and team member. I need to find and maintain my social work profession connections largely away from my workplace. Fortunately, there are several helpful professional organizations that offer information and meetings. These include the National Association of Advisors of Health Professions, Association of American Medical Colleges, and Society of Teachers of Family Medicine. Second, not everyone who wants to be a physician is accepted into medical school. You listen, console, and advise premed students who are not accepted. Of those students who are accepted, the vast majority graduate. Finally, and most grievously, many of our patients in the medical center clinic and hospital settings have chronic illnesses, disabilities, and some die. There are always loss and grief issues to be faced.

Think About It

1. What abilities and qualities would you look for in a medical school applicant (a future physician)?

2. What ethical and policy issues with students and patients would you face while working in an academic medical environment?

3. What are some differences between the "medical model" that is prevalent in physicians' training and the "person-in-environment" model to which social work students are exposed?

PART 8:
Specialized Roles in the Court System

Chapter 23
Social Service Management Within a Court System

• •

by Jesús Reyes, AM, ACSW

It is 7:30 a.m. and I sit in my car on the Dan Ryan Expressway on the way to my office. As I crawl along at an all-too-familiar pace, the noise of traffic is muted by the sound of Bach played by guitarist Christopher Parkening coming from my car's CD player. The beauty of the music's mathematical precision and recurrent motifs makes me think of how my day as Director of the Social Service Department of the Circuit Court of Cook County will be anything but precise or predictable.

I begin a mental review of the meetings and issues that will fill my day. I organize my thoughts and map strategies for the day. I've often asked myself why I do this every morning even though I know my days seldom work out as planned. I rationalize that having planned ahead for the expected allows me to concentrate better on the unexpected. The real answer is much simpler: it makes me feel better.

I walk in the crowded and noisy lobby of the Criminal Courts Building, where my office is located. The staccato, drill-sergeant voices of sheriff's deputies directing people to remove their watches, belts, and other metal objects can be heard above the incessant chatter of the many people entering. Young men strain to hide their nervousness behind a mask of bravado as they file to have their cases heard in court. Fathers and mothers, spouses, and others look confused as they try to find their way to the correct courtroom. Alongside them are lawyers in expensive suits who seem strangely at home in this chaotic place.

Court employees step into crowded elevators as they make their way to their workplaces. A well-dressed woman holding a book steps into my elevator, struggling to read directions on a piece of paper. I ask her if she needs to go to the jury assembly room on the third floor. She says yes, and asks me how I knew. I respond that people coming to serve on a jury often bring books to keep them occupied as they wait for assignment. My response is only partially true. I also know she is a juror because, even though her hesitancy betrays an unfamiliarity with her surroundings, she lacks the look of nervous defiance that masks the fear and dread often seen in criminal defendants.

I step off the elevator at the ninth floor and walk past our waiting room full of clients who have been court-mandated here because of domestic abuse, drunk driving, petty theft, or other misdemeanors. Caseworkers usher clients into offices for routine status checks and, ideally, to help the person correct whatever brought them under our supervision on a conditional discharge from the court. I know the same scene is playing itself out in my department's other twelve offices with 260 employees across Cook County. We serve 24,000 clients each year, all residing in Chicago and its more than 120 suburbs.

I hear Matt, one of our younger caseworkers, chatting with a client as they walk toward Matt's office. Matt recently completed his undergraduate work in criminal justice and has been with us only a few months. Yet, his sensitivity and ability belie his young age and inexperience. As I make my way to my own office, there is a trace of envy in me for Matt and the work he does. When I entered the profession, I thought I would be a direct provider of services, a clinician, for the duration of my career. Time, opportunities, and too many other factors to recall changed all that. I have not provided direct clinical services to a single client in many years. I still miss that kind of work.

I turn the corner to my office and my nostalgic thoughts are interrupted by the voice of Emma, my secretary, telling me that Vanessa, my deputy director for human resources, has asked to see me right away. As is my practice, I ask Emma to call Vanessa and also call my two other deputy directors (Sharon, who heads operations, and Heather, who oversees clinical services). My three deputy directors and I approach all matters as a team. Each of them heads her own particular area, yet in our meetings there are no boundaries of responsibility and all are free to express opinions and make suggestions across the board. I have found over time that, more often than not, our combined expertise and creativity are more than a match for whatever challenges arise. We work as a team but, in the final analysis, I am the single person responsible to the Chief Judge of the Circuit Court of Cook County for the operations of my department.

Vanessa tells us of an unexpected twist in an employee disciplinary matter that is the subject of a grievance in process. We look carefully at the issues, consult our Collective Bargaining Agreement, and decide what to do. Our caseworkers and our clerical support staff are represented by two different unions. Our operations, working conditions, and almost every aspect of our relationship with employees is affected by our contracts. This means that we must be conscious of operating in an even-handed and consistent way within contractual parameters.

As that matter resolves, we turn our attention to a meeting that Heather, Sharon, and I will attend in the afternoon. The meeting will be with administrators at the office of the Clerk of the Court and will also involve representatives from the Office of the Chief Judge, the Adult Probation Department, and the State's Attorney's Office. The focus of the meeting is on how the Clerk's Office will handle the collection of court fines and some fees for clients of the Social Service Department and the Adult Probation Department. The matter involves tens of millions of dollars yearly, and careful planning and coordination with all parties is crucial.

Our discussion is interrupted as Emma alerts me that the director of the Children's Advocacy Rooms of the court is on the phone for me. I have administrative responsibility for the Children's Advocacy Rooms, and the director of the Rooms reports to me. Before being promoted to direct the Social Service Department, I held that position. When promoted, I asked for, and was granted, the opportunity to maintain responsibility over their operations. A great deal of my early career as a clinician involved work with children and families. Involvement in the Children's Advocacy Rooms allows me to use that background to satisfy the dormant clinician within me. The Rooms provide drop-in day care and specialized services for children of parents who have business with the court at eight of our court locations. The director informs me that a child has suffered a minor hand injury and, as is our practice, she wants to inform me of the incident. We go over what took place and verify that the child is well, parents have been informed, and that our procedures have been observed.

My phone call concluded, Sharon, Heather, and I decide on materials we should take to our meeting in the afternoon and outline how we will make our presentation.

We then turn to the topic of our new caseworker performance appraisal instrument. We have been working for several months with an expert consultant from the Institute of Government of the University of Illinois. He is due to arrive momentarily to begin training our supervisory and management staff on the foundations and application of the instrument. He arrives as scheduled and we join him in our training room. About twenty, or approximately one-half, of our supervisors and regional managers are present. I provide a brief introduction with the important message that the instrument is designed as a tool for supervisors and caseworkers to establish a clear understanding of work expectations and track performance for the purpose of improving our services. The supervisors see past my formal statement and recognize that the heart of the issue is that the instrument is also the basis for determining the distribution of yearly merit pay. This unavoidable requirement has complicated the application of similar instruments in the past.

My presence as director and my statements of support for the supervisors are intended to ease the anxiety involved in implementing the new procedure. I observe the understandable wait-and-see attitude of many supervisors and do what I can to ease their tension. I no longer work as a clinician in the traditional sense, but time and time again I have found that my clinical skills play a positive role in my work. The two-hour meeting goes well, and we break for lunch.

In the early afternoon, Sharon, Heather, and I drive in my car to the Daley Center in downtown Chicago for the meeting at the Clerk's Office. As we discuss technical and procedural details, the complexities of operating within one of the nation's largest unified court systems serving a population of 5.5 million people become very apparent. All in all, we leave the meeting satisfied that the court's interests are not in jeopardy, but in full realization that many twists and turns will appear before this is all in place.

By a little after 4:30 p.m., Emma, Sharon, Vanessa, and Heather have ended their day. I stay behind until almost 6 p.m. to address the more mundane aspects of my job. I review expense vouchers and sign approvals. I respond to e-mails and other correspondence from sources as varied as the Administrative Office of the Illinois Courts, the Illinois Probation and Court Services Association, universities, and social service agencies. Managing a department with a budget in excess of $14 million involves many details. In the after-hours respite from the quick pace and unpredictability of the regular day, I can address such matters quietly and efficiently.

Many signatures and initials later, I pack my briefcase and walk down our still busy corridors to the elevator. Caseworkers see their evening clients while a team of facilitators gathers defendants for a male batterers' group.

I make my way downstairs, and the lobby of the building seems a different place from this morning. The large crowds and the noise are replaced by a few family members anxiously waiting for evening bond court. A cleaning crew quietly mops and waxes the marble floors of this old but still very beautiful building, in anticipation of tomorrow's crowds. A small contingent of Sheriff's deputies oversees security checkpoints.

The drive home is slow, as usual, but uneventful. It is a time to reflect and decompress that I have come to appreciate. I go over the events of the day and briefly ponder what lies ahead tomorrow and beyond. As is often the case at the end of my days, there are at least as many questions as there are answers.

Long after dinner and after time with my wife, I spend the hour from 9 p.m. to 10 p.m. in the solitude of my study, alone with my guitar and simple classical arrangements of Bach, Sor, Tárrega, and others. I spend the hour attempting to bring to life the notes of those masters. My thoughts are far from work as I dwell in the melodic and precise world of music. For now, that is all that exists. For now, tomorrow's unpredictability with its touch of chaos is far away.

Think About It

1. Reyes is the director of a very large bureaucratic agency, yet he still maintains a human touch in his work. How?

2. What skills, knowledge, and experience would you need if you wanted to obtain and be successful in such a position?

3. Reyes says he misses clinical work. How does he maintain his clinical expertise in his current position?

4. How can music help social workers to relieve their own stress? How might it be used with clients?

Chapter 24
International Work on a Domestic Level: Immigration Law

● ●

by Lisa Villareal-Rios, MSW, JD

Hot sun streaming through my window past parrots and palm trees, I look at the clock on this treacherously warm South Texas day and thank the sun for its less than gentle, but less *also* than alarming, reminder to awake for the day's calling.

Coffee in a mason jar, Chihuahuas kissed goodbye, and breakfast eaten on the fly, I am in my old rickety red truck again, making the familiar drive to the home of the South Texas Pro Bono Asylum Representation Project (ProBAR). ProBAR, a joint project of the American Bar Association, the State Bar of Texas, and the American Immigration Lawyers' Association, is the only organization in the Rio Grande Valley (Valley) solely dedicated to the representation of immigrants, refugees, and newcomers detained by the Department of Homeland Security (DHS), formerly known as the Immigration and Naturalization Service. Down in the Valley, an area consisting of a plethora of small towns on the United States-Mexico border, three DHS detention centers—de facto jails—confine adults and children, hopefully separately, as is legally required, in three different detention centers, two for children and one for adults.

As an Equal Justice Works (EJW) fellow hired to represent immigrant children in court, I think of my list of things to do for the day as I bound up the wooden stairs to our second-story office, which consists of three converted bedrooms in an old wooden, peach-painted house. The phones, already ringing, interrupt plans for the day and quickly bring me into the present moment. Immigrants, refugees, and newcomers, tired and hungry, in need of comfort and a kind voice, are calling ProBAR for help. Afraid to go back to their countries, crying for their family members, wanting to know how they can get out of detention, these individuals need legal representation and much, much more.

As a lawyer and a social worker by training, I am cognizant of the multiple levels of help that are so often needed and theoretically justified, yet practically unavailable. The field of immigration is international work on a domestic level. It is a compelling field of rapidly and ever-changing laws whose boundaries are literally, figuratively, and continually challenged by war, poverty, environmental disasters, politics, country conditions, and other limiting and expanding economic and social parameters. Ever committed to using my law degree in the public interest, my joint-degree in law and social work at Washington University, though not specifically required for my attorney role at ProBAR, instilled in me—most importantly—the desire to reach beyond traditional legal boundaries in favor of the global, wholistic perspective of care so needed by my clients.

Just five on staff at ProBAR, we scramble to either find legal representation for our clients, or try to provide it ourselves. And we are stretched further than any phone cords connecting voices across space, as we struggle to meet more than the legal needs of our clients, and of others for whom we can offer little more than a listening ear and a compassionate voice.

As ProBAR's advocate for the children, my calls, as they are every day, are likely from Central American street children, escaping the violence, poverty, child abuse, and inexplicable horrors of their countries. Almost at my desk, I steady myself—physically, spiritually, and emotionally—for the raw sentiment and staggering stories that I will no doubt hear today.

Sipping my coffee, I glance at a magnet placed at eye-level on my ever expanding file cabinet:

PEACE. IT DOES NOT MEAN TO BE IN A PLACE WHERE THERE IS NO NOISE, TROUBLE OR HARD WORK. IT MEANS TO BE IN THE MIDST OF THOSE THINGS AND STILL BE CALM IN YOUR HEART.

(Unknown)

Today is Tuesday, the day my colleagues and I ride the dusty highways through the semi-agricultural Valley towns to a children's detention center in Los Fresnos, Texas. It is there that we will come face to face with mostly Central American children who will meet us eager and moon-eyed, with laughter and with tears.

My colleagues and I ring the buzzer of the locked doors of the detention center and wave into the camera. Once recognized and allowed in, we quickly commence the routine of counting the newly arrived children and discussing the children from last week who have still not had interviews. We are charged with informing the children of their legal rights in the U.S. and providing them with interviews conducted, in part, to ascertain what, if any, legal relief is available to help them stay temporarily or permanently in the U.S. We disperse to fulfill our duties, with intake forms and educational materials in hand.

In a room filled with bunk beds and a makeshift wooden table with aluminum legs that fold in and out as functionally as those on an ironing board, the children and I look across the table at each other, sweaty but smiling. I am admittedly already exhausted as I lapse into the familiar Spanish words I will bestow upon them, in the best efforts I can muster, to explain the situation in which they have found themselves, and its legal, social, and emotional consequences. I explain that I am the child of an immigrant, half-Mexican, but raised in the U.S., able to speak Spanish, albeit not as gracefully as a native speaker. They laugh gently and encourage me on, grateful that I have come, and willing to strain to understand me, so desperate to know what is happening to them.

I begin with a series of questions meant to gauge the knowledge in the room and then start to explain that I will be representing them in court, what the court is (and who will be there), when they might be able to reunite with family members abroad or in the U.S., why they are detained, what confidentiality is, what legal remedies exist that might allow them to legally stay temporarily or permanently in the U.S., and so on. About an hour and a half later, we are ready to start with the confidential interviews to which all the children are entitled.

Through the course of the next couple of hours, I interview as many children as I can, the majority of whom are pre-teen and teenage boys who have trekked across country boundaries as if they were mere streets—with no one to tell them to look both ways before they cross. Many of these children are abandoned, having left their families, sometimes at their encouragement, sometimes at their behest, to come to the U.S. in search of safety, love, protection, and hope. I hear stories of abuse sustained at the hands of their loved ones, of living on the streets, of being raped by smugglers, of having to submit to prostitution, of fleeing rampant gangs (or of being forced to join gangs at the threat of guns and death), of watching their houses and family members disappear in hurricanes and earthquakes, and of using drugs to keep out the coldness of a society that either cannot or will not care for its youth. From Nicaragua, El Salvador, Honduras, Guatemala, Mexico, and other countries, these children are restless and weary. Many of them are without basic education. Still, they are wise beyond their years, often lacking childhoods, often having had to work in the fields or on the streets from young ages, just to survive.

I fill out an intake form for each child, along with the DHS permission form, which is signed by each child and gives me permission to be privy to this confidential communication. I write down how old the child is, why he left his country, and what family she has in her country or here in the U.S. I ask whether or not the child is afraid to return to his country, and if so, why. I nod as tears burn down the children's cheeks, as they tell me that they cannot sleep, that their families will lose their houses because of the debt they have assumed in order to come to the U.S. I feel the almost palpable yearnings of these children—yearning as they are, in part, to work away the unsolvable and solvable problems that they face, yearning as they are to live in a world that provides a decent and humane chance for their existence, yearning as they are to feel loved.

Soon, the smell of cafeteria food and the sounds of plastic trays hitting wooden tables awaken our senses to dinner. The period for interviewing the children is suspended for a week's time, which I know will inevitably seem longer to the children than it will to me. I console children who did receive an interview with promises that we will return and remind them that they can call us by phone. My colleagues and I, thirsty and drained, wait for the beep of the alarm that precedes the unlocking of the door. Outside in the sun, the burdensome heat still threatens movement beyond basic steps, and I wonder how these children—more than 5,000 annually—ever made it here.

Inside the car, with the sun making its appreciated descent, we discuss cases—which children might, as a result of fearing to return to their countries, or having suffered physical, sexual, or emotional abuse, be eligible for legal relief in the form of Asylum or Special Immigrant Juvenile Visas. We identify children who are in need of psychological help and talk about how we can facilitate therapy sessions for them. We converse about children's family members who have filled out the necessary paperwork to liberate their relatives and children from detention, about upcoming cases in court, and, at last—about how the children continue to touch and inspire us.

Back at ProBAR, ready to go home for the day, we say our good-byes, shaking our heads in frustration, and engage in the semi-forced laughter that we need so desperately to get us past this moment into the hope that will convene us—together—in this work tomorrow. We remind ourselves that this is the peace worth fighting for—the peace that comes from a busy day of advocating for those for whom there is no one else, pushing stagnation away for something fairer, better, and saner.

Without saying it, we acknowledge that there are children with similar bleak pasts whom we have helped already—children who were afraid to return to their countries, who have fought their cases in court, testified to atrocities we cannot imagine, and were granted asylum (or some other legal remedy) by an immigration judge.

On the drive home, I ruminate about the voices and faces of the day more than about the route that takes me to my destination. I think of the never ending numbers of immigrants, refugees, and newcomers who flee atrocious conditions, and of how few I can actually help. I contemplate great plans—of enforcing international treaties and conventions, of collaborating with other agencies, of calling non-governmental organizations for help. I dream of legislation that might allow more immigrants to live in the U.S. legally and help them access opportunities for healthcare, school, and work.

At the end of the day, I know that I am making a difference. Exhausted, my dogs and I join the sidewalk in its lonely white expanse below the blue gray dusk of sky. I close my eyes, at once in the present, at once in the past, remembering how I arrived one September day, never suspecting how much I would learn from these children, never imagining how much use I could be to anyone, never realizing how much of me would always stay in this day, and others like it—forever.

Think About It

1. Bilingual skills are important in this job. Why?

2. Lisa has a combination of J.D. and MSW degrees. How does she use her social work skills in this job, where she is employed as a lawyer?

3. Do you think this job is more law or social work? Why?

4. What are the macro level issues and skills that relate to this position?

Chapter 25
Mediation: The Fit for Social Work

• •

by Glenda F. Lester Short, Ph.D., MSW, LCSW

I wake up with a smile on my face. The sun is shining and the birds are singing. I have been smiling since I took a course that prepared me to mediate family issues with clients. What a great fit for a social worker!

Mediation is defined as a "conflict resolution process that is valued as an element of social work practice and as a way to resolve grievances related to violations of ethics or practice standards," according to the *NASW Procedures for Personal Review*. The parties who have a dispute use a neutral third party to facilitate solutions to problems. The mediation process provides equal status for all parties, empowers them to speak to the issues, and encourages them to be creative in their approach to solving the problem.

The mediator role is fairly new to social workers. Currently, the National Association of Social Workers (NASW) uses peers to help mediate grievances pertaining to professional conduct or to any unfair practices of an employer or agency. Some state NASW chapters also use the mediation peer review process for complaints of ethical violations.

To learn about the various types of mediation cases and to improve my mediation skills, I first worked pro bono in the family courts in and around Orlando, Florida. Today, I enjoy working in the court sector, because cases vary from a family dispute about inheritance issues to a business dispute about problems at a construction site. I work for the courts two mornings each week from 9 a.m. until noon. These six hours are often the most exciting part

173

of my week, because I never know what type of case I will be asked to mediate or how many people will be involved.

I once mediated a case about an improperly installed gas line for a housing development. A mistake in the installation plans caused delays, and a manufacturing error caused problems in the transport of gas through the line, putting lives in danger. Twelve people worked on the project, and the mediation process was used to determine who would pay for the cost overruns. The mediation efforts were successful, and all parties agreed to share in the additional construction costs and return to the drawing board to correct the problems. It was fascinating to observe how the laborers and administrators discussed the various problems and accepted responsibility for their mistakes.

Today, I am in private practice with a focus on mediation—specifically, divorce mediation. I also provide mediation services to individuals and groups within social service agencies and teach mediation techniques to judges, attorneys, social workers, and mental health professionals. Clients are referred to me by attorneys, other clients, and agencies.

Divorce Mediation Case

My first private mediation case today is a divorce mediation in which both parties agree to mediate the custody and visitation of their children, the issues regarding marital funds, and the issues regarding the division of marital property. During the pre-mediation phase, both parties talked to me via telephone and agreed to use my services in their divorce mediation. They have agreed to exclude their attorneys during the mediation process and to avoid prolonging the divorce by fighting over the issues. The issues will be settled based on the facts of the case. Both parties initially agree how monies will be divided. The mediation task for the first day is to determine custody of the children and visitation rights. I have allocated four hours in the morning to achieve the custody mediation. If a second time frame is needed, the issues will hopefully be completed within a four-hour time frame tomorrow.

The amount of time needed to mediate divorce issues varies. It can take several hours to one or two days. I prefer to set a time frame of four hours per day, taking breaks as needed. Additionally, I may meet with one party while the other party takes a break. The first four-hour session is to get the process started and to create an atmosphere that will enhance the mediation process.

The parties are charged by the hour and must pay for mediation time whether or not it is used. I also charge hourly rates for any report that is required. I employ a sliding scale rate for mediation services. The lower end of the scale is $10.00 per hour, per party. The higher end is $75.00 per hour, per party. Each party is required to pay in advance. The average time for a divorce mediation ranges from four to 24 hours. If significant issues have not been resolved within that time frame, the parties will generally revert to a court process involving their attorneys.

As I enter my office, I cherish the quiet, knowing that the room soon will be well heated and emotionally charged. To prepare, I tune the radio to relaxing music and make coffee to accompany the donuts and fresh fruit I've brought. Next, I begin to mentally prepare by reviewing my planned approach to the people involved and the issues outlined for mediation.

Sally, my efficient secretary who works three days a week, enters on my heels. She serves as receptionist, billing clerk, and liaison for clients and other colleagues. Sally maintains confidentiality and is trained in the regulations private mediators and social work practitioners are required by law to follow. I can depend on her abilities and ethics in working with clients.

My office is divided into several work areas. In a conversation area there is a large, comfortable couch against one wall, faced by two chairs. A coffee table provides boundaries. Lamps and end tables offer a homelike feeling. Another work space offers a round table with chairs spaced evenly around it. The play therapy area includes individual pillows to sit on during floor work. For the meeting this morning, I decide that the conversation area is the best place to begin. I place my papers on the coffee table and sit on the couch, leaving the chairs for my clients.

Mr. Webb is the first to enter. He is a tall, middle-aged man who has a thin moustache and thinning hair. He is congenial and accepts the offered coffee and a donut. He sits down and begins to read an outdoor magazine. Mrs. Webb enters, a tiny Hispanic woman who appears neat and timid. She selects the hot tea and some fruit. Sally buzzes me and I come out to greet the Webbs. They enter the office while I close the door and instruct Sally to hold all calls. Mr. and Mrs. Webb do not greet or acknowledge each other.

I position myself on the couch and take a deep breath. During the mediation opening, I cover all the necessary comments about confidentiality, proper communication within the mediation, and how I will work with the couple. A quick thought passes through my head and I sigh inwardly, "It's funny to me that poor communication skills are cited as the cause of so many divorces and yet, this couple must communicate well to make final decisions about critical issues. These issues will not only affect them, but their children and extended family members, not to mention future relationships for both parties." I begin to feel the weight of my job as facilitator. I ask about the children. Mr. and Mrs. Webb have two children—Seth is ten and Sam is eight. I ask the parents to put their "parent" hat on and think about what is best for Seth and Sam in regard to custody and visitation.

After my opening, Mr. Webb asks to speak first. He whips out a paper with his position on the issue. He believes that Mrs. Webb is a good mother and capable of caring for the children on a day-to-day basis. However, he wants the children every weekend, while she has them every weekday. He sees this as an opportunity to take the children out fishing, camping, and for other activities he enjoys. He makes a point that he is male and the boys are male and it is his duty to impart certain skills to the boys. Mrs. Webb sits quietly and begins to cry softly. Mr. Webb frowns and gets a bit antsy in his seat. He is irritated and states that she should be happy he thinks she is a good mother. She confesses that she is crying because she thinks he is equally a good parent and that she does not want the divorce. She asks him if he will reconsider and come back home.

One party often wants the divorce and one does not, so I allow him to answer. It is clear that he wants the divorce. He wants the process to be as gentle as possible, but he will not maintain the marriage. He asks his wife if she wants to continue with the mediation and make decisions or engage in a "battle" between their respective attorneys. Mrs. Webb sighs and states that she just had to ask one more time. She says that his position, while seeming generous, is not fair. His suggestion makes her feel that she will bear all the day-to-day parenting responsibilities, and he will get to have all the fun with the children, not experiencing the day-to-day struggle to raise the boys. She suggests that they co-parent, since they have done this successfully from the beginning.

Mrs. Webb is not timid, but quite vocal and clear. She wants joint custody with herself and her husband sharing in decisions about the children's welfare, medical, educational, and other needs. Mrs. Webb wants to have the children each week, with Mr. Webb taking them for Wednesday evening each week and every other weekend. Mr. Webb sits and ponders this suggestion. He wonders out loud if they can split the time evenly—he will take them one week and she will take them the next week throughout the year.

Mrs. Webb asks about holidays. With my help, they discuss the impact of sharing the boys on a weekly basis and the boys' need for stability and consistency. Mr. Webb states that he has some traveling obligations for his work and the weekly idea will not work for him.

The Webbs continue the discussion for an hour and a half and I suggest a 15-minute break. After the break, we return and the decision point has arrived. They decide that the boys' physical custody will go to Mrs. Webb, with Mr. Webb having visitation every other week from Thursday evening through Monday evening. This way, he will have the boys for school nights and experience day-to-day parenting responsibilities. In addition, he will be able to request additional visitation time based on family schedules. The Webbs also decide that if scheduling problems arise when the boys are in their care, they can request that the other parent take the boys. If this is inconvenient, then the parent who is responsible for the boys at that time will get a childcare provider.

It has taken three hours for the Webbs to discuss and resolve the custody and visitation issues. I begin to draft the agreement. Mr. and Mrs. Webb look over the document for accuracy and sign it. Mr. Webb shows signs of sadness. He says quietly, "So, this is what our life with the boys has come down to—three pages." Mrs. Webb begins to cry softly again. I discuss the grieving process and the issues they will encounter in grieving the loss of their relationship. I tell them they can write the next chapter in this book and may want help to do so. I offer them each a booklet of resources for divorcing couples. They will return for tomorrow's mediation session. Both express that the mediation process is a good one and that the experience is better than fighting it out in a court room.

I walk them out to the lobby and return to my office to process my feelings about this family. It is sad, but I count today's mediation effort successful. We achieved a mediated outcome; the Webbs were able to compromise and choose the best custody situation for their boys. I am ready for tomorrow. Money issues can be complicated, but the most difficult issue for divorcing couples to mediate involves custody and visitation.

Estate Mediation Case

It is one o'clock. I drive to the next county to mediate a family dispute over the dispersal of a deceased man's estate. We meet in the attorney's office. I am expected to begin the mediation process at 2:00 p.m. and work with the family until the issues are resolved. I have contracted with the family for a minimum of four hours of mediation time at a rate of $150 per hour and a rate of $75 per hour for travel time. The attorney, Mr. Chitwood, insists that the mediation must be completed today. If the mediation is not successful, he intends to put the matter before the judge for a decision. I know that if the dispute goes to court, the family will have no say in the outcome and may not be able to access estate monies or items such as family pictures or personal jewelry. I do not know any of the parties and have only talked to the estate attorney about the mediation.

When I arrive, the family members are already present. I have a short time to read the paperwork the family has just completed, and I am struck by the wide gap in their positions on closing the estate. There is a son, Roger Dowdy, and a daughter, Sarah Sims, who are eleven and ten years older than the younger daughter, Susan Farmer. The deceased is Susan's father, but she has a different mother from Roger and Sarah. Susan's husband is also in attendance.

The conflict is that the younger daughter wants to keep her parents' home and all the family items and furniture. She is willing to pay her older half siblings a fair price for the home and its contents. Roger and Sarah want the home and family items sold, except for the family pictures, and an antique car that is to be auctioned off. They state they do not want *her* (Susan's) money. They had not spoken to their father for the last 25 years and they have had little contact with their half-sibling, even though Susan had attempted to include them during the last few months of their father's life.

The mediation begins, and I am overwhelmed by the venom emanating from all parties. The attorney expresses frustration, but remains quiet and allows me to do an opening mediation. I decide to be direct about how the communication process will go. I talk about the respect that must be shown to all parties to discuss the issues and congratulate them for agreeing to the mediation process. I inform them that this will be their only chance to determine the outcome of their father's estate, because the attorney is ready to present a motion to the courts giving the judge the power to rule on it.

The setting for this mediation includes a rectangular table with parties seated on either side, the attorney at one end, and me at the other, providing good boundaries. Immediately, a verbal fight occurs among the parties. I ask for a caucus with the elder siblings and the attorney. I request that the younger sibling and her husband leave the room at this time, indicating that I will meet with them next.

After discussing again the need for a respectful attitude from all parties, I ask the siblings to tell me about the situation and discuss their position. They tell me that their father had an affair and fathered Susan. He left their mother and them for his new wife and daughter. They continue to feel abandoned, even though their father made several attempts to visit with them over the years. Their mother's anger caused their father to quit visiting, although he continued to provide monetary support to them. Their hurt and anger are obvious. However, the mediation is about estate issues rather than personal feelings. I begin the tedious and time consuming process of clarifying their position about the estate issues and how they might move to a different opinion. They change slightly, saying they will entertain selling the family home to Susan at a fair market price. They do not want Susan to have any family items that existed when their father lived with them or of his earlier life before he married Susan's mother. A particular sore point is an antique car that their father refurbished when Roger and Sarah were young.

The meeting with Susan finds a sad half-sibling. She realizes that Roger and Sarah feel abandoned and blame her for their father leaving his first family. She has no other siblings and wants to connect with Roger and Sarah. She says that she will pay a fair market value price for the home and will pay for an appraisal. As for her father's personal items, Susan does not want to give them up, but agrees to talk with her husband, particularly about the antique car. She speaks of her love of the car and other items, particularly the pictures of her father in his early years. She agrees that family pictures of Roger, Sarah, her dad, and their mom should go to her half-siblings.

Taking breaks during this mediation is important, as all parties need time to think about what they want to do each time a movement toward conciliation is made by the other party. Sandwiches are brought in at 6:00 p.m. for a supper break. The mediation continues through 8:00 p.m., with a series of caucuses with individual parties. All parties are present for the final mediation and the signing of a mediation agreement.

The agreement includes the following: The real estate appraiser will be selected by the older siblings and the appraisal cost will be paid by the younger sibling. All parties agree that the appraisal value will be the price Susan will pay for the family home and furniture. The proceeds of the sale will be equally divided between Roger and Sarah. Roger and Sarah will share ownership and use of the antique car. Susan will select an appraiser for the antique car, Roger and Sarah will pay the appraisal fee, and the value of the car will be deducted from the purchase price of the home. The family items and pictures will be divided, and all parties will get copies of the pictures they want, regardless of who owns the originals. The person who wants copies of pictures will pay copying expenses. The original pictures and items existing when Roger and Sarah lived with their father will go to them. The items and pictures existing during Susan's time with her father and mother will go to her. The attorney ends the mediation session, explaining the legal implications and the procedures for closing the estate.

As I drive home, I reflect on the impact of my mediation efforts in the custody and visitation case and the estate resolution case. I think about how the decisions that were made will affect the people who were not part of the mediation process, such as Seth and Sam. I feel good about a mediation process that will keep Seth and Sam out of an ugly custody battle and one that perhaps has begun to heal old wounds for disparate family members. As mediator, I have helped to empower these people, allowing them to make decisions that provide social justice for everyone involved. I enjoy the mediation process and the results of my work today. I know that every mediation effort will not be as successful, but I plan to continue my role as a mediator. It is a good fit with my passion for social work and pays me to do what I love most—to help people.

Think About It

1. How difficult do you think it is to be impartial as a mediator?

2. Why does the physical layout of a room have importance in the outcome of a social worker's intervention?

3. If one party is nonassertive, is it the mediator's role to serve as an active advocate for that party's rights during the mediation process?

4. What clinical skills does a mediator need? Advocacy skills?

Chapter 26
A Court-Ordered Program for Divorced and Separating Parents: Is This Social Work?

● ●

by Dana Harmon, MSW, LGSW

Before I introduce you to the part of my life when I was coordinator and group leader of a court-ordered program for divorced and separating couples, there is philosophy I want to share. First, it is and has always been my belief that "all men (and women) are created equal." Therefore, as a social worker, I try to espouse to the primary mission of the NASW *Code of Ethics,* which states:

> *The primary mission of the social work profession is to enhance human well-being and help meet the basic needs of all people, with particular attention to the needs and empowerment of people who are vulnerable, oppressed and living in poverty.*

In addition, I firmly believe that social workers need to be people who are genuinely interested in their clients, and not just doing their jobs to pass the time and get a salary. Okay, that is the thought of the day, but how does it fit with my work as a social worker?

The Tale Begins

We all have a great story to tell about our journey in life. Where do I begin with mine? Well, to tell the story as fully as possible, I think it is most appropriate to begin in Illinois, when I did my field placement as a social work student in an elementary school. Here,

I received a well-rounded experience in all facets of school social work. One of the most rewarding experiences I had at the school was being involved in the Rainbows Program. This program was a group for children of divorce, in which they could express their thoughts and feelings about their parents' divorce. It was not until I was co-leader of one of these groups with kindergarteners and first graders that I understood the effects divorce has on children. As I approached graduation from Loyola University Chicago, I knew that working with divorced families was something I wanted to continue doing.

Two months later, it was a hot summer day in Alabama. It was also my birthday. I was eager to begin working in the profession I had longed for since high school, and I also knew that student loan payments were going to begin in the near future. I was having my second interview at Family Counseling Service for what I thought would be a part-time group leader position. As the interview continued, the director offered me a full-time job, which happened to involve not only counseling individuals and families, but also involved an administrative component. I said to myself, "Administration? That is not what social workers do." Then he said something that I could not believe. "Ms. Harmon, you would be a coordinator of one of our court-ordered programs called Children Cope With Divorce (now called TransParenting)." Wow, I would be working in the area of divorce!

At the Office

My first day at work began at 8:30 a.m. My eagerness got me there about ten minutes early. Boy, that was hard for a person who is not a morning person, but the excitement was high. The first few days and even the first weeks were not that difficult. I became acclimated to the thousands of names in the database of people who had been court-ordered to the program since 1994. I reviewed the policies that were in place and made some modifications where I felt necessary.

One policy change did not occur immediately. The standing policy had been for both parents to attend the seminar together, because it was felt that it would be beneficial for them to hear the same information at the same time. They had to be screened by the coordinator before that occurred, and assessed for the nature of their relationship. In other words, is there "dissention among the ranks"? Well, as coordinator, I had to screen many couples, and Mr. and Mrs. Johnson are ones to remember. When I spoke to

Mrs. Johnson, she said, "I don't care if we attend together or not, I just want to get this over with." Well, then there was Mr. Johnson. He was cordial and said, "My wife and I get along well and I don't think there will be any problem with us attending together." I was on the verge of approving their attendance together, until Mr. Johnson continued talking and adamantly proceeded to tell me, "She will not get the house. because it has been in my family and she is not a Johnson." When I further explored this issue with him, he said, "I will take her to court until the day I die before she gets that house." So I did not approve their attending together and soon changed the policy so no spouses would attend together. Mr. Johnson was one of many who influenced my decision. This is just the tip of the iceberg when it comes to working with divorced and separated couples ordered by the court to attend a program. I will tell you later how some of them are in the group, but I cannot leave out the lawyers and judges, who played a key role in my work as coordinator and even group leader.

The Lawyers and Judges

Let me start with the judges. The family court judges were supportive of the program and of me when I needed to discuss an issue with them. The attorneys were another story. Here are two stories about my interactions with attorneys that made me again say, "This is not what social workers do. We are supposed to help people." One day a lawyer called me, not requesting, but *demanding* information about a client's spouse. I remembered what I was taught in my social work classes and my agency's policy about confidentiality. I said to the lawyer, "I cannot provide you with that information, because it is confidential." On the other end of the phone, he shouted, "What do you mean that it is confidential?! I need to know that information now because my client's divorce is being held up." I again said, "That information is confidential. Would you just give out information to anyone who called your office inquiring about one of your clients?" There was silence on the other end of the phone. The lawyer's response was, "Fine, if you are not going to give it to me, then I will call the judge." My response was, "Feel free to do that." The other situation started by phone, but ended up in the agency. A lawyer called wanting me to break a policy and make an exception for a client. I explained that this was not an option. Again, the phone hung up. A few minutes later, one of the secretaries buzzed me in my office and said, "Dana, an attorney is wanting to see you." An attorney? What about? I did not rush up front, but there he was, the attorney I had just spoken to on the phone, with his client. I guess he thought talking to me face-to-face would change my decision. I used social work skills, but when I was a student, never did I think those skills would be used with attorneys. Thank goodness, I did see clients, and this administrative stuff was not all I did all day every day. Let me move to after five o'clock, to the seminar.

The Seminar

There were and still are strict guidelines for the parents, who were ordered by the court to attend our program. When I worked at the elementary school, I worked primarily with the kids and not much with their parents. Well, now was the time for the parents. Oh my, what a rollercoaster of emotions could fill the room with 15 to 50 people. Anger. Depression. Hate. Oh yeah, there are a few positive ones. There was happiness, but that was usually because "I am finally getting rid of him or her." However, some were happy and content because they could finally get their children out of what was a volatile or unhealthy environment.

Being a co-leader of the seminar was the most rewarding part of this job, because I felt that I was finally "doing social work." This gave me an opportunity to help a group of people going through the same event to see how a decision they had made as adults had and may affect their children. One night I asked a group, and I began to ask every other group after that, "Who is/are the most important person or people in your life?" Most of them said, "My child(ren)." I then asked, "Please raise your hand if you would jump in front of an ongoing train if it meant saving your child's life." Everyone's hand went up. I then said, "How many of you would try to get along with your soon-to-be ex if that meant it was in the best interest of your child or children?" Amazingly, not as many hands stayed raised. One woman said, "Now why would he do that? He has not been there all these years anyway." One man said, "How can you get along with a…" Well, the word is not appropriate to say, but I think you get the idea.

I forgot to mention, we held the evening group at the police department. Is that a message we were sending to the group members? Well, not exactly. However, because many divorcing couples were angry at each other and we (the group leaders) did not know the reason for the divorce, it was for safety reasons. Interestingly, some found this ironic. For example, some women who would come to the office to register for the program would tell the staff that they were getting a divorce because of their police officer husbands having bad tempers. So, they would say, "If you are having the group there because of a safety issue, who is going to provide safety for us?" This is something I had never considered before.

Overall, I think I have touched the lives of many divorcing persons and, indirectly, their children in my county and surrounding counties, and that made the work much more rewarding for me. At the end of the group, I gave the parents their certificate of completion and wished them and their children the best of luck.

Coming Home

Well, it was now 8:30 p.m. and I was finally home. I had worked a 12-hour day and I was tired. There were some days when I was not tired, but just exhausted. Was I ever looking forward to what the next day was going to be like? Yes and no. As with any good story, there is always a moral.

There is a lot of good advice my mother gave me over the years, but I always remember this one as I continue my career in social work. When I started in this profession, I used to tell my mother about my day. Essentially, I would take my work home. One day my mother said, "When you put your feet in the car and point it toward work, that is when you should begin thinking about your work day. At the end of the day, as you put your feet back in the car and point it toward home, leave the events of the work day behind you."

As much as I love my work, I live by these words of wisdom daily and do not worry about work until I put my feet back in the car and start the process over. Although I still work at the same agency, I do not point my car in the same direction every morning as I did for four years, because I am a full-time doctoral student. However, I am involved in another court-referred program and point my car in that direction. I hope your car is pointed in the right direction.

Think About It

1. What factors affect the relationship between ex-spouses after divorce? How do these relationships affect successful co-parenting?

2. How are divorce and death alike? How does the bereavement process related to death differ from adjustment to divorce? Answer these questions from the perspectives of adults and children.

3. Sometimes the administrative role is not one the social worker chooses, but is a necessary part of a larger job description. Do you think that doing administrative tasks is "doing social work"?

4. How important is it for social workers to work with other professionals involved in clients' lives (in this case, lawyers and judges)? What skills does this work entail?

PART 9:
Faith & Spirituality

Chapter 27
Coming Home to Metropolitan United Church

• • • • • • • • • • • • •

by Rob Udell, MSW, RSW

Metropolitan United Church is located in downtown Toronto, Canada. It has a strong ministry of community services and houses or runs many programs for disadvantaged people including two on-site hostels, a nursery school, a drop-in program, a computer centre, an art program, emergency counseling, a housing resource centre, a food bank, a clothing room, and a visiting mental health team. There are also three large community meals each week. A small community services staff of two full-time and three part-time employees is complemented by seasonal staff and up to 100 volunteers each week.

I'm driving down the Don Valley Parkway to my job as Director of Community Services at Metropolitan United Church in Toronto. I live in Don Mills, a suburb of Toronto, in an apartment building on the edge of a park. It's quieter there and a respite from the downtown neighbourhoods where I've been working with street people for the past twelve years. I love the work that I do, but I need to come home to quiet. Also, there's too much addiction in my own family and I want to give my daughter a chance to not get caught by it. In Parkdale, it was heroin, people dying in the alleys. At Met, we're in the centre of a crack epidemic, and Listerine is very popular.

The Parkway is not too busy. The start of a hot, humid, Toronto, summer day. I make good time and get into Regent Park in fifteen minutes. I turn up the blues guitar on the CD player.

At Sherborne and Queen, outside the donut shop, a burly street fighter is yelling at a slim black guy. Intense anger. The big guy

187

whips off his shirt and starts punching and kicking the little guy who doesn't put up much of a fight. It's over really fast. Pure crack.

Moss Park is busy, lots of guys sitting around on the benches waiting out the day. A middle-aged, red haired woman pulls down her pants and pees on the grass. Outside the Fred Victor Centre, there are a few people waiting for the restaurant to open. One very thin woman in tight, tight, white clothing walks off. She's missing teeth, but from a certain quick angle still may have enough allure to bring in a few dollars. At the stoplight, an overweight curly-headed man walks into the middle of the street and taps on my car window looking for money. I shake my head no. It's tough here now. Welfare cuts, higher rents, cost of living soaring, more home-less. The panhandlers are more numerous and sometimes more insistent.

I pull into the church parking lot. There are four or five people sitting against the Church House wall. Hostel residents are kicked out early in the morning and can't go back in until 4:15 p.m. Most of them don't really have anywhere to go; some just hang around.

It's already getting pretty hot. I surprise two crack smokers as I walk by one of the alcoves at the side of the church. On the side-walk on the way into the Church House, there's a man lying with his coat over his head. I ask him if he's okay. He doesn't move much but kind of mumbles at me to leave him alone. Namir, one of the church custodians, comes up to me and says that this guy's been there since 7 a.m. Police on bikes came by and checked on him and left. He seems to be sleeping. I'll leave him for now, see if he's still there after the staff meeting.

Every Tuesday, we have a senior staff meeting attended by the two ministers, the admin staff, the director of music, and the main-tenance coordinator. We have a very small staff and do a lot of business. In the Community Services area alone, we have over a thousand visits a week. The meeting is held in the senior minister's office. It has eighteen-foot high ceilings, mediaeval style windows, and dark wood paneling. It has a great feel to it.

We start the meeting today with a spiritual reading and then discuss it. Not your typical agency staff meeting. I like the spiritual side to my work and have had a deep faith for most of my adult life. Certainly my involvement with God has motivated and guided my work in social work. Previously, Met had employed ministers to run the social service programs—but they were mowed down, couldn't deal with the demands of running a complex agency for street people. My social work training and experience has helped immensely with this. My developed skill set includes program development and management, staff supervision, crisis counseling and intervention, and a wide range of clinical knowledge. I'm really used to and thrive on fast pace and craziness.

My personal and professional values are in tune with the unconditional love and acceptance in practice at this church. All are welcome and valued. Also in keeping with my values, there is no evangelical side to our work. Needs are met with no strings attached, religious or otherwise. No sense of "first pray, then eat." I don't believe that I could deal with that, and certainly it would be in conflict with my social work code of ethics. Interesting though, as well as professional training, all of the community services staff have religious or spiritual foundations. Several of my staff are Christians, one is Buddhist, one is Jewish, one is Christian Rastafarian. Several are in addiction recovery and involved with twelve-step programs that have a spiritual foundation. I guess this makes sense, as people with a spiritual connection would be drawn to work in a spiritual organization.

The meeting continues. We move on to a check in and then new business. I get called away. There is a problem at the Church House. I rush down the stairs and over to the Church House, past the man still lying there. At the entrance, there is a drunk man yelling at a cop who is looking pretty pissed. The director of the refugee hostel is there and quickly explains to me that they found this guy passed out on the second floor and couldn't wake him up. They called the police, and when they arrived the man was immediately awake and immediately angry. Now things are heating up more. The guy seems on a mission. He's yelling and swearing at the cop, who doesn't appear to be too willing to arrest him. I manage to get the guy's attention and get him to take a few steps back from the scene. I talk calmly and keep telling him to calm down, to take it easy, that he's going to get arrested, and that he needs to calm down. I tell him I'm not a cop, that I'm a counselor, that he'll thank me later. Somehow he listens. I tell him to take a walk and get calmer, and then to come back in an hour for lunch. He walks away, still swearing, but going in the right direction. The cop still looks a bit pissed. I talk with him and thank him for coming, telling him that no one should be spoken to in such an abusive way. I shake his hand. I go back to the staff meeting, which is pretty well over now. It gives me a chance to come down a bit.

Back to my office, check messages and e-mails, order water and coffee cups. Our housing worker drops by with bills to sign. She's driving a client out to a treatment centre tomorrow and will be at the Housing Tribunal in the afternoon. The computer centre coordinator tells me that the laser printer isn't working. We search unsuccessfully for the warranty and then decide to call one of the volunteers who's a computer pro to come and look at the printer. A drunk client knocks at the door wanting socks. I send him to one of the counselors.

I glance at the painting on the wall, which I like very much. There appears to be an angelic figure in the centre of a swirl of colours. The man who painted it stayed in our hostel for three years, just drifting. We found him a place to live and began working with him. He started coming to the art group. Very, very talented. The angelic figure seems to have sky for a face.

Another knock on my door. They want the counter for the lunch. It's used to count how many people attend. Each week, we put on two large lunches and one dinner for street people and get up to 400 people at each meal. These events are staffed primarily by volunteers, some of whom have been at it for quite a long time. One of the older volunteers has been involved for over seventy years. She's a wonderful, spiritual, giving woman and I admire her very much. Our volunteers are great, but they can be quirky and a handful. They are happy anarchists and they do so much good. For some reason, they get a little nervous when they don't have the counter. Lately, I've been hearing from a variety of people up to two hours before the lunch that the counter is needed. Today, I give up the counter early but still get multiple inquiries.

I keep the counter in my office so it won't go missing. We buy can openers a few at a time, because they're very popular with street people. Security is always a concern. If you leave a door unlocked, someone will come in. If you leave something unattended, it may well disappear. Most of our clients honour us, but theft would be commonplace if all precautions weren't taken. Recently, some of our needier volunteers have been taking our food supplies home. No doubt the food is being well used, but distribution needs to be equitable. There is great need here.

The kitchen upstairs is busy. However, trouble is brewing. Imran, one of our cooks, has been shouting at the sandwich makers. He's a really accomplished cook, worked on freighters sailing around the world for many years. He is retired now because he lost much of his hearing. He clearly likes to rule the kitchen in a style that is not going to work with our happy anarchists. I am taken aside at least four times to be told that things are not going well. Finally, I get everyone into an office and we sit down and work it out. Imran understands that we love him and truly treasure his wonderful homemade soup *but* that he must stop *yelling* at every-one. Mary is in charge, and he must take her direction about how many sandwiches are to be made and when to put the mayonnaise back into the fridge and when to make more pizzas. Everyone calms down. Everyone agrees to stay calm. Everyone starts to head back to the kitchen, because we have 400 guests arriving for lunch very soon. I hold Mary back to strategize with her about what to do when things start to blow up again. I suspect that this may be very soon.

A number of volunteers tell me about the man on the sidewalk. Eleanor, one of the counselors, comes to tell me about the man on the sidewalk. We go to see him again. It's getting really hot outside, and he's been lying there on the pavement in the sun with his coat over his head for five hours now. He refuses to move into the shade. We still can't get him up, so we call for an ambulance.

Lunch begins. Things are going well. There's a wonderful spirit of community. Our volunteers are a mix of ex-street people, church members, and people from the wider community. All are enthusi-astic about helping. The patio, where we serve lunch, is sunny and breezy, and everyone feels good. A man comes up and gives me a $100 donation. I've never seen him before. Much of the food that we serve is donated.

I spend time talking with Harold. He is from Virginia, from the Blue Ridge Mountains. He is Canadian now. He's a big man, 245 pounds, a gentle ex-trucker. When Harold first came to us, he was drinking, depressed, and suicidal. One of my counselors, Phil, in Recovery, a Buddhist, gentle and patient, got Harold into a treat-ment centre. Harold is much better now. He volunteers with us, usually daily, at the lunches or at our drop-in. He also helps with the heavy lifting. I talk with other street folk. There is a good feel-ing here. The sandwiches are good, the pizza is good, the weather is gentle, and the feeling of God is tangible.

It's interesting—over the years, many people have asked me how I deal with the burnout that apparently is so prevalent in the helping professions. But for me, the act of helping itself keeps me going because it makes me feel really good. This is what drew me to social work and what keeps me in it: being given the opportu-nity to pass on what has been freely given to me. God's grace. God's love.

As we're speaking, a small drunk Russian man swaggers up to us. He says that one of the ministers has sent him over to see me. His name is Ijor, not Igor, that's Ijor with a J. Very drunk. I sense the con. He wants money to get to Regina because his sister is dying. One of the kitchen volunteers draws me aside and tells me that Ijor was just in the kitchen creating problems hassling and grabbing at one of the women. They had a hard time getting him out. Now Ijor starts shouting, calling Harold out, wants to fight. Taunts him: *C'mon, c'mon you fat F. C'mon to the sidewalk, LET'S GO.* Instead, Phil and I go with Ijor to the sidewalk and send him away. Not a good start, but perhaps we will have a chance for something better tomorrow.

People come and go. The regulars. Robert is not too drunk today. Seems quiet and depressed. Al, who's been banned, comes to the edge of the patio and asks for food. He broke another client's nose for little reason. We were very sad; we'd been making good progress with him. Shauna stands lost. In a thick parka and holes in his/her shoes. Doesn't want to be engaged. Today he/she is hallucinating. Muttering angrily to someone we don't see. I spend time talking with Sam. He's got a place to live now and had the operation on his leg. He's doing volunteer work in a seniors' home, runs the tuck shop. He's so much less angry now. I tell him that. Sam feels that it would be a good idea to bar the drunk Russian for life. He savours the idea. We laugh. I feel really good.

Lunch ends—345 people today, and still some food left that we can use in the drop- in tomorrow. I help bring in tables and chairs. I speak with the counselors about closing off different sections of the building. I check with the maintenance staff about how the clean up is going and let them know that I'll be around if needed, and I'll be back later.

I go over to the main church to the sanctuary for a brief time out. The church is huge, originally built in the 1870s as a Cathedral of Methodism. Most of it burnt down in the 1920s, but it was quickly rebuilt. Some of Toronto's well known families were members here: the Masseys, Eggerton Ryerson. Old dark wood and carvings and richly coloured, beautiful stained glass—I sense that this is a place of power. People have been praying and meditating here for a hundred and thirty years. It's haunted. Ghosts have been seen here a number of times. The senior minister thinks that one of the earlier ministers is still here or visits. However, the feeling is warm and loving, not spooky. These are good spirits.

Mid-afternoon—it's quiet. I take my time, and when I open my eyes, the light has shifted so I am surrounded by it.

On the way back to the Church House, the sleeper is still there. The ambulance has still not arrived. It's been seven hours, and he's still in the sun. Now, though, I am able to get him up. Eventually, he comes inside with me and he drinks and drinks water. He's edgy and erratic. Keeps bursting into tears. He tells me that he's going to go to Lake Ontario and swim across. He says he just lost his job and has been using Tylenol Threes for days, not eating or sleeping. I think that other drugs are on board, as well, but I don't say that. I cancel the ambulance and phone a psychiatric crisis team. They come. They know him. After a while, they go off with him.

The van arrives with a load of food. Phil goes and gets some of the street guys and we unload the van. I carry one box at a time. Several of the street guys pick up two or more. They want to prove that they're strong and healthy, which they're definitely not. Too much testosterone here. I worry about someone hurting himself. Phil developed a hernia from one of these sessions. One older man gets really winded but, at my suggestion, allows himself to take a break. I thank everyone for helping. They are so pleased to be part of our mission to help.

Inside, Irena, one of my other counselors, is speaking to a man on the stairs. He looks at me and comments on my spiritual development and seems impressed. He tells us that he is psychic. He says that he has a social phobia. He can't stand to be inside. He lives in the Don Valley ravine. We speak quietly, and I can feel the energy flow back and forth between us. A quiet connection. We give him some food from the food bank. When he leaves, he tells us that he needs to restore his "rainbow eyes."

Everything shuts down and I go for a run down by the lake. I find that this helps to break up the really long days. I have to attend an Outreach Committee meeting tonight, which will be fun. Most of the Outreach Committee members are quite elderly. We will talk and talk and sidetrack all over the place. A great visit. I have much respect and love for these people. Our Elders. They are very committed. The chair of the committee is younger and very bright. An architect, he's been a Christian all of his life. He grew up on a farm.

I sense that his early life and mine must have been quite different. I grew up in the city and was addicted to drugs and alcohol at a young age. I spent thousands of hours in self-help meetings and reconnected to my spirituality. I was very fortunate to heal. At some point, I decided to become a social worker and went back to school.

As a child, I attended the United Church regularly. My grandfather and his brother were both Methodist ministers and involved in the formation of the United Church of Canada in the 1920s. As a teenager, I left the church and hadn't been back until I took the job at Met. I just needed work really.

While undergoing my professional training and throughout my career, it never occurred to me that I would end up working for a church. But Met has a way of growing on you. Very enriching. During my first week here, we had a special service for the 9/11 tragedy. I felt a sense of belonging then, like returning home after a long journey. Even a sense of answering an intergenerational calling. I suspect that Met is one of the few churches where I would feel comfortable working. It is open to everyone, active with the surrounding community, with the gay and lesbian community, with street people.

I believe that I can stay here. Perhaps I am meant to.

Think About It

1. Some social work positions carry a greater threat to personal safety than others. How important is safety and security in your choice of job setting?

2. Is the "calling" of social work consistent with having strong spiritual values? What are some common values between social work and those who engage in helping others because of their religious convictions?

3. What are some ways in which this particular faith-based setting might be similar to or different from other faith-based settings? Do you think it is typical of faith-based settings in general?

4. How does Rob avoid or counteract burnout?

Chapter 28
Spiritual Social Work

●●●●●●●●●●●●●●●●●●●

by Carole A. Winston, Ph.D., LCSW, ACSW

It was 1992, and my career as a clinical social worker and supervisor had already spanned over twenty years when I accepted the position of Associate Director of Social Work Services in a large municipal hospital's community primary health care consortium. The consortium was comprised of a main primary care clinic and four smaller satellite clinics located in several medically underserved communities. The majority of the patients who sought care were members of families described as poor and working poor. Along with primary medical care services, the clinics offered social work screenings, short-term counseling, HIV/AIDS services, and referral services for more intensive psychosocial treatment options.

The main clinic was housed in a large office building that was home to other municipal services, including a mayoral ombudsman's office, a tenant/landlord mediation center, and a city personnel division. On the ground floor, tucked away in a corner, was an unpretentious suite of rooms housing the Harlem Interfaith Counseling Service, Inc. I noticed that on Wednesday afternoons, several elderly women entered that office, often in pairs, but more often alone. It seemed to be the same women each week, and I wondered if they were taking part in a group.

I didn't spend too much time thinking about what was going on there, but I was intrigued. There were more pressing matters to be considered: "customer satisfaction" surveys to be evaluated, interdisciplinary team meetings to be convened, end-of-year evaluations to write. Besides, I was looking forward to treating myself to a conference on innovative social work intervention methods. Even though I was hired as an administrator, I continued to work with clients, an aspect of the job that I truly enjoyed. I did not want to lose touch with clients. As a trained clinician, treatment was at the heart of my professional life.

After registering for the conference, I decided to attend a workshop on a "nontraditional psychospiritual" approach to mental health care services. The workshop was led by Doris Dennard, a social worker who was described as the Program Development Administrator for...the Harlem Interfaith Counseling Service, Inc.! When I entered the large meeting room, I beheld Mrs. Dennard, a richly brown-skinned woman with a crown of snow white natural hair and a sonorous voice that insisted you listen to what she had to say. Her presence filled the room. She began by telling her audience that it was possible to become fully responsible and consciously participate in our own personal and collective unfolding. The process would happen naturally. "You just need to get outta the way and let it happen!" She challenged us to challenge our clients to assume responsibility for their part of the co-creative process and look within to seek their own truth. To do otherwise was to do the "same old inauthentic thing," live their lives by the borrowed truths of others' ideas about how things ought to be. In this life, we have free will, and anything that comes into our lives from a higher source comes only at our invitation.

I was hooked. I wanted to know how I could help our clients to understand and accept that they had the power to change their lives, the power to heal and feel whole. I didn't know what it was called, but I knew it was a model that could be adapted for use in working with individuals and families who presented with a range of concerns including anxiety, depression, grief and bereavement issues, substance abuse, and family violence, to name just a few.

At the end of the workshop, I introduced myself to Mrs. Dennard and had the opportunity to sit and talk with her for a few hours. She described her program as a community-based outpatient treatment facility offering culturally competent services to its constituents using a non-traditional psychospiritual approach to help clients "respond creatively to the challenges of learning, behavioral, emotional, social, and mental disorders." A strengths-based perspective was the core of the development and implementation of the comprehensive services offered to its clients. The Harlem Interfaith Counseling Service clients were primarily Black and Hispanic individuals and families who had been through several programs and had received services offered in the traditional mental health system, but at "HICS," they found social workers, peer counselors, physicians, and psychiatrists who looked like them, under-stood their plight, and invited them to begin to affect change and renewal through a process of psychospiritual integration. When I explained that I worked in the building where her agency had its offices, we realized that we were serving the same population of community residents. I mentioned the elderly women I saw each Wednesday, and she shared that they were members of a support group for grandmothers parenting their grandchildren as a result of the incarceration or death of the parents. When the group met, they addressed issues of grief and loss as they took on the respon-sibility of surrogate parenting for children ranging in age from in-fancy to young adulthood. In her role as facilitator, Mrs. Dennard encouraged the women to call on their collective spirit to address the conflicting feelings of anger, resentment, guilt, and redemption as they attempted to sort out their feelings toward their absent children, the burden of caring for their grandchildren, and the place of God in their lives.

I had been aware that several women whose children were fol-lowed in our Pediatric Clinic acknowledged they had struggled with substance abuse for many years. After my meeting with Mrs. Dennard, I decided to invite a number of the mothers with a his-tory of substance abuse to form a support group. The women had to have been clean and sober for a minimum of six months. The group was formed, with an initial membership of seven mothers. Under Mrs. Dennard's tutelage, and with my understanding of the centrality of religion and spirituality in the lives of many of our clients, I would encourage the participants to share with one an-other those things that helped them to abstain from drug and alco-hol use. Each woman spoke at length about her close relationship with God and her prayerful relationship with that Higher Power. As the meetings continued, it occurred to me that the women's prayers were active and self-assertive, rather than passive and acquiescent. With the support of one another, they began to talk about their expectations of God and how they expected support and encouragement. In the past, they had begged for forgiveness and plead for help. As their confidence grew, they began to ac-knowledge their feelings of anger toward themselves and their God, speaking openly and honestly about their disappointments in God, "because God can handle it!" Validating their both/and relation-ship with God rather than the dualism of either/or freed them to accept the conflicts within themselves as they struggled to main-tain sobriety.

In my years as a clinical social worker, I have found that prayer is a significant coping device for people of African descent (I use the terms people of African descent, Blacks, and African Americans interchangeably to describe Black people living in America), particularly women, as they cope with mental health issues. To assess the role of spirituality in the lives of Black clients, Knox (1985) uses spirituality as a tool, specifically for the assessment of African American alcoholics and their families. Her findings provide insights into the ways spiritual beliefs have sustained American Blacks and become an integral part of their system of survival. Boyd-Franklin (2003) argues persuasively that spiritual reframing is a very useful technique with Black families given the significance of spirituality and religiosity in Black communities.

Social work, defined broadly, has always drawn inspiration from religion. In the United States, the profession has its roots in the church-based charities of the late 19th century. But as social work practice became professionalized and sought parity with the "hard" sciences, its relationship to religion and spirituality became marginalized. More recently, the argument for teaching spirituality in schools of social work has become more compelling, and the audience more receptive. For social workers to provide culturally competent services, it is essential that they understand the material and spiritual needs of their clients, many of whom are people of color. Always remembering to "Begin where the client is," the social worker might do well to inquire about a client's spiritual life, how she operationalizes her beliefs either through prayer, attendance at religious services, reading the Bible or other religious tracts, watching or listening to religious programming, or other manifestations of spiritual connectedness. Recognition of this manner of coping must be acknowledged and incorporated in the therapeutic process.

Think About It

1. How would you begin to assess a prospective client's spiritual coping strategies?

2. What are the distinctions between spirituality and religiosity?

3. Should administrators continue to work with clients? Explain.

PART 10:
Domestic Violence

Chapter 29
Hospital-Based Domestic Violence Advocacy

●●●●●●●●●●●●●●●●●●●●●●●●●●●●●●●

by Jill Rodriguez, BSW, and Monica Sierra-Mayberry, BSW

As domestic violence advocates in a hospital setting, our experiences are unique yet similar to one another. We both work in a hospital and provide services to women and children who are dealing with issues related to domestic violence.

Jill: My interests are in healthcare and in domestic violence. So, when I heard about a position working with victims of domestic violence in a hospital setting, it was perfect for my career goals and aspirations. Luckily, I got the job and am happily working 40 hours a week making a salary that I can easily live on.

Monica: I have worked with families and children in crisis for six years and have recently found an agency where I can grow and achieve many of my goals. I have found a profession that allows me to provide service to others. I want to empower individuals to find their own strengths that bring them integrity, dignity, and worth. I also strive to find social justice for the underserved and work through challenges and barriers society places upon individuals.

Monica/Typical Day

We both work for the Bridge Program, which is a part of the full continuum of care offered by Rose Brooks Center. Rose Brooks Center offers crisis intervention and other supportive services to thousands of victims of domestic violence each year. The Bridge Program employs four advocates who serve six hospitals and several clinics. Some weeks, we alternate being on call after hours and on weekends. However, on an average day, I will receive referrals from other social workers and healthcare professionals requesting that I meet with a patient who has screened positive for Intimate Partner Violence (IPV). After making contact with the patient, I arrange a time to meet in a confidential location, usually the hospital room, to discuss the situation. Because I work with victims of domestic violence in a hospital setting, I offer an array of services. I provide access to community resources, education, and support. I take pictures of injuries and help the victim develop a safety plan. I provide free and confidential services to patients, employees, and students who have experienced IPV. If clients want to go into a shelter, I can assist them in finding which shelter is the best fit for their needs.

Sometimes, clients want to go home; in those cases, I can help them fill out and file an order of protection. In addition, many days consist of providing educational resources and training to nurses, physicians, medical students, and social workers on how to routinely screen for domestic violence using the PVS (Physicians for a Violence Free Society) course.

As a young BSW social worker fresh out of college, walking into a room of physicians can be very intimidating. We are not only teaching them about an issue they may not think is very important, but we are also trying to change the way they screen their patients. One time, while I was speaking to a group of ER doctors and nurses, someone asked the question, "So, are you are saying that if a woman comes in with an ear infection, she should be screened for domestic violence?" My response was, "Yes, every female patient over the age of 14 should be screened, as well as males 14 and older with indicators of abuse. Just because they may not present themselves with an injury doesn't mean that they are not experiencing abuse at home." The room went up in a roar of laughter. You would have thought I had just told a joke, but I was completely serious. I was quite embarrassed at first, but then I realized: *That is why I'm here—to educate them so they won't miss any potential victim of domestic violence.* After the training was over, one of the doctors came up to me privately and said how much he appreciated what I was doing. It made all the laughing and embarrassment worthwhile. Fortunately, most of the healthcare professionals I train are very respectful, listen, and ask informed questions. Actually, the trainings and inservices have become one of my favorite parts of this job.

My public speaking has greatly improved, and it's never a bad idea to make friends with people who may have your life in their hands one day.

Jill/Bridge Call

Every patient we see is very different. There is no "typical situation" in a domestic violence referral. We may see a woman who has been verbally abused by her husband of 30 years or an 18-year-old girl who was beaten with a baseball bat by her new boyfriend. One hot summer day in July, I got a call from the hospital telling me I needed to come in and talk to a patient who had just arrived and was in crisis.

Upon arrival to the emergency room, I saw a very young looking 26-year-old woman who had obvious physical wounds. The nurse gave us some privacy as I talked to "Carrie" about what had just occurred. Before getting started, I introduced myself and had her sign our consent form. Now that HIPAA has been implemented, we must get permission from the patient before performing a service. As I do with all my clients, I let her tell me what she was comfortable disclosing while actively listening, making a mental note of what services might be best for her. Carrie shared with me that she had been held hostage in her own home and repeatedly beaten by her boyfriend. She was scared to go home and needed a safe place to stay for herself and her children.

After discussing with me what resources were available, Carrie decided that going to a shelter would be best for her and her children. I helped facilitate placing them into the shelter that met their needs. I also took photographs (to be used as evidence in court) of the burn marks, bruises, and gashes covering Carrie's body.

Although most clients we serve are women, we do see approximately 15 men a year, most of whom are in same-sex relationships and are being abused by their partners. One patient, Tom, had been admitted into the hospital and was never asked if he was experiencing domestic violence. He saw a brochure for the Bridge Program and called me. It was very difficult for him to disclose the abuse, but he had an even harder time telling me he was gay. He wanted to leave his partner but had nowhere to go. Unfortunately, there are no domestic violence shelters for men in our area, and he didn't want to go into a homeless shelter. We talked about his support systems, and he figured out that he could probably go stay with a cousin who lived out of town. I also gave him numbers of local and national organizations that specialize in helping victims of same-sex abuse. I called Tom a few days later to follow up and see how he was doing. He told me that his partner had visited him in the hospital and convinced him not to leave. They were living together again, and Tom said things were okay at the moment.

In the short time spent with patients in crisis situations, we become attached and want to see them thrive away from the violence. Because of the right to self-determination, we must sometimes accept their decisions to return to an abusive relationship, even though we may feel differently. I was disappointed when I found out Tom was still with his partner, and that is a very natural feeling to have. Not all clients leave their dangerous situations, but I know that at least they have been given information that can help them in the future. However, each time a victim returns, we listen, support, and educate them on how they can live free from abuse.

Jill/Macro Social Work

As a social worker, I feel it is important to give back to the education of future professionals in the field. One of my responsibilities outside of work is sitting on a committee that is helping a university develop its BSW program. I use my experiences as a former BSW student to help formulate the best possible curriculum for future social workers. I am also on the Domestic Violence Task Force at the hospitals I serve. This group meets once a month and works on developing policies and protocols to address domestic violence issues relating to employees and patients. Finally, as all social workers know, our jobs can be very stressful. That is why I became part of the Wellness and Fun Committee at Rose Brooks Center. The goal of this committee is to make the workplace an enjoyable environment through activities, retreats, and team builders.

Monica/Macro Social Work

I come from a very diverse background professionally and culturally. Since I'm bilingual in Spanish, I use my language skills when working with Spanish-speaking victims of Intimate Partner Violence. There are many barriers immigrant women face when they want to break free from abuse. They are often more isolated because of cultural differences and language barriers. I have been able to provide training to community social service providers and agencies on cultural differences when working with the immigrant population.

I have joined various committees, such as the Women's Mosaic Network, which works on the prevention of harm to foreign-born women; the Justice Committee in Kansas City, Kansas, which works at addressing gaps in service to victims of crime in the judicial setting; and the Urban High Crime Committee, which is working on establishing a community advocate in Kansas City and developing a community resource book for the community. I'm also co-chair for the Immigrant and Refugee Committee for Wyandotte County, Kansas. This committee addresses gaps in services to immigrants who have experienced domestic violence and addresses their concerns regarding service delivery. We identify both agency and community needs, including training, education, and community outreach. Our goal is to work on breaking barriers down, so the community can better serve this population. Finally, I serve on the University of Kansas Hospital task force for suspected abuse, which looks at ways to screen and identify victims of domestic violence. As I stated earlier, I believe in empowering not only victims, but also the community, even when it looks as though there is no hope for change.

Conclusion

There are several qualities that are essential for social workers who are healthcare domestic violence advocates. First, one needs to be aware of one's own limitations to not get burned out. Because of the severity and sensitivity of the cases we see, there are times when we need to find support from our co-workers or supervisors. Another important quality is that of being comfortable speaking in front of 15-70 people at one time, which is something we do quite often when training other professionals about domestic violence. One way we promote screening for domestic violence is through articles we write for hospital and community newsletters and newspapers. A social worker in this position must be knowledgeable about writing styles and how to cite resources. One must be comfortable networking and collaborating with others in the same field, including healthcare providers who can at times be intimidating, in order to provide effective services.

As we look back on being BSW students, we realize how valuable it was having three great mentors in our field. Jan Hockensmith,

Michael Lareau, and Gary Bachman were very instrumental in providing a foundation for what we needed to become as social workers and strive for within our profession. Much of what we do today stems from their inspirational stories, life experiences, and their strong belief in the NASW *Code of Ethics,* which each social worker should know by heart.

Think About It

1. How does patient privacy affect how a social worker works with clients?

2. How do one's own biases get in the way of working with victims of domestic violence?

3. In the examples of interactions with the patients, Carrie and Tom, what types of therapeutic messages would you give to them?

4. What steps does a domestic violence advocate need to take to prevent the occurrence of secondary/vicarious trauma?

5. What effect do you think Monica and Jill's in-service trainings (and ones like them) will have on the healthcare delivery system?

Chapter 30
It's All in the Family: Working in a Shelter for Victims of Domestic Violence
● ●

by Wanda Whittlesey-Jerome, Ph.D., LMSW

I was a BSW student when I first came to volunteer, and then to work as an employee, in a small shelter for battered women and children who were escaping life-threatening situations in a small, north Texas college town. The shelter was located inside an old home that was, in its past life, a well-known local brothel. The house was built in the 1880s, so it was full of history and "that antique smell" that old Victorian houses are known for. The wooden floors creaked and the doors and walls were a little crooked, but we were glad to have this safe place—the only one of its kind for nearly 50 miles in every direction.

The shelter was almost always full. We had room for 16 people, including women and their children. We had a kitchen, an office, a playroom/artroom/childcare room, and a bathroom downstairs (mostly for staff). Upstairs were the family rooms, with a bathroom located in the hallway. It was small but comfortable, and we felt safe when we were there.

One day that I will never forget started out like any other day. Around 2:00 a.m., the phone rang and a woman on the other end of the line spoke in whispers: "I need help—he's passed out in the living room on the couch. I'm calling from the phone in the bathroom. Can you help me? He beat me with a phone cord and tied me up. I've got myself loose, and I think I can sneak out. Can you meet me somewhere, please? I'm afraid if he wakes up, he'll really kill me this time."

I told her of our safe place meeting spot, and that I would meet her there in 10 minutes. I hopped in the shelter van and off I drove.

I found her in her car outside the convenience store where we always met our new clients, had her gather her things, and told her to join me in the van. Later, I'd go pick up her car and drive it to the shelter.

She was very scared, yet relieved. I noticed her nicely manicured fingernails. But the rest of her—especially her clothing—was very messed up. Her ash blonde hair was sticking out in all directions, and even though she tried to hide it, I could tell her face was bruised. I got her to the shelter and found a room for her. She was lucky—usually two families had to share a room. But this morning, one room was empty. She lay down on the bed and went fast asleep. I would wait until she awoke to do my intake later that morning.

Around 6:00 a.m., the shelter came alive. Children were up and wanting breakfast; mothers were cooking and the halls resounded with women's, children's, and babies' voices. The director arrived, and the office opened for a regular business day. But, there was no such thing as a regular business day in a crisis environment like this shelter—and this day was no exception.

My client awoke around noon, and I popped my head in her door and decided to meet after lunch for my intake appointment. I got my intake paperwork in order and waited to greet her. She didn't come. I got worried and went looking for her. I found her in the downstairs bathroom huddled in a corner. She was wearing a gray sweatsuit that had been donated. Her beautifully manicured red fingernails seemed all that was left from her previous life up until that point. That was, until she saw me and spoke.

In that bathroom, I learned of the horrors that face our clients. As a social worker, you never know what you are going to hear when a client begins to speak—and you have to be prepared to hear anything and everything. But what I heard that morning has stayed with me until this day.

She and the abuser were a part of a Satanic cult. Members of the cult had held her and made her watch as the abuser killed her two children by driving over them—right in front of her. This had happened within the past week. Prior to this, she had been mutilated with knives, and her breasts had been partially cut off. I couldn't believe what I was hearing. With tears in her swollen eyes, she lifted her sweatshirt and showed me the scars. I began to cry, too.

What did I, a BSW student, know about this? I felt so helpless. I just held her as she cried. Within a few minutes, she stopped crying and said that she was ready for the intake appointment. We walked together into the office, and we began. We decided that she would need to be sent on the "underground railroad" to a state somewhere in the East where she could have a new identity and be safe. I will never forget what I heard and saw that day, and I often wonder how she is doing, and if she is still alive, because from what I learned about them later (getting to know this woman sparked my interest in the subject), Satanic cults often have ways of finding members who have escaped from their influence.

Around 3:00 p.m., it was time for after-school music and art with the children. This was one of my favorite times, because I could play my guitar and sing along with them. I taught them songs like "Magic Penny" and "I'm Glad to be Me." Today, I had about eight children to work with. One little seven-year-old boy, who had just come to the shelter the day before, was acting withdrawn and angry. He wasn't going to participate—he sat in the corner with a frown on his face. But when I pulled out the guitar, his face lit up like a Christmas tree. He immediately came over and grabbed for the guitar. Now, this guitar was special to me (it was the nicest one I'd ever had), so I told him how to hold it and play it. He obliged. He started strumming some nondescript chord and singing, "Daddy, please don't hit mommy…daddy, please don't drink that beer." The other children sang with their own words and we had a moment of intense sharing that only the guitar could have brought to us—out of their sadness and pain. Music does that, you know.

Art does, too. After our sing-along, I got out the magazines. The shelter often received donations of magazines from local businesses. We did a project called "My World," in which the children cut out pictures of things they liked. Then they glued the pictures on a styrofoam ball that would hang by a string from the ceiling in their room so everyone could see what "mattered" to them. These little "worlds" were, for me, glimpses into what really mattered to these children, and were often avenues for discussion about hopes, fears, joys, and sadnesses. I will never forget them.

After the children's group, it was time for dinner. The women cooked together (the ones who were there at the time and not working) and then we all ate together. The shelter was lucky in that it received commodities from the local food banks and donations from restaurants and bakeries. I remember a red velvet chocolate cake that was probably too old to eat, but eat it we did anyway! It was so yummy. I still laugh when I think of the children's faces with chocolate cake all over. Much of the donated food had to be eaten right away. Much of it was also full of fat and cholesterol, but since we were hungry and poor, it didn't matter. It was food. And, it was free.

After dinner, while the women had their therapeutic group, I worked with the volunteers to take care of the small babies, and another student worked with the children doing playdough baking and other fun things. This evening, one of the older boys started acting out in group, and I was called to intervene. In the shelter, when a child needed help with inappropriate behaviors or words, we would do "time-out." We didn't hold or restrain. I asked him if he'd like to go outside and sit with me under the backyard tree. He said "Yes—that playdough was for kids." So we did. The sun was setting and the sky was a shade of pink. We just sat there for a long time, listening to the crickets. Finally, he said that he didn't want to be here. He wanted to go home. He missed his dad. I asked him what he missed about his dad and he said, "He buys me things." I knew from my intake with his mother that the boy would hit her in the breasts just like her husband would do—that he was mimicking the behaviors he saw his dad exhibit, and she felt that he was getting dangerous.

I asked him about his angry feelings and shared with him the analogy of the shaken-up Coke can. I said, "Pretend you have a Coke, all right? Suppose you shake it up real good, and then you put it in the freezer. What do you think will happen?" He looked at me sort of puzzled, and then said, "It'll explode." "Yes," I said, "and that is what anger does—we explode if we get shook up and don't have a safe place or someone safe to share our feelings with. Without hitting, of course, because hitting is not a good thing to do. People can't hear your words when they're being hit. They don't know what you are thinking, because they are just afraid of being hurt." He listened intently, and even today, I wonder if my little story made any difference to that young boy. Unfortunately, he and his mother returned home to the batterer the next day, so I would never know.

Later that evening, I received a call from a woman who had found the shelter's number in the phone book. She had run away from her abuser and was homeless now, but had a job working at the local truckstop. She was sleeping under a bridge in a nearby park. (Our town didn't have a homeless shelter.) I told her I would come pick her up and take her to the shelter, which I did.

This woman was in her mid-forties. Her red hair was dull and lifeless. Her face was weathered and wrinkled. Her nails were clean, and she was wearing brown polyester pants, a white shirt, an apron, and dirty white tennis shoes. On the way to the shelter, she told me that her boss was going to fire her if she didn't get a pair of brown shoes to wear. And, here was the bad part, they had to be the kind nurses wear for support—SAS shoes. I asked her what size she wore, and she said her feet were so swollen that she was thinking it would be size 9 extra wide. I had my mission! I took her to the shelter and found her a room. She went to sleep, but was supposed to work in two days back at the truckstop.

The next morning, I started calling shoe stores around town. To my deep disappointment, none of them would donate what she needed—brown SAS shoes size 9 extra wide. I even thought of driving to the SAS shoe store and buying a pair, but they were expensive (around $45.00 a pair), and I was just a poor undergraduate social work student. That wasn't an option.

Then, I remembered that we had received a fairly large donation (about 20 some-odd black garbage bags) of clothing and other items the day before. The bags were piled in the garage—they actually filled it up so we couldn't park in it. So, I went to the garage and started picking through the donations. Hours passed, and the sun had set. I checked on the woman and she was going to bed, worried about how she would be able to work the next day. She told me "Goodnight" with tears in her eyes, and shut the door to her room.

I went back to the garage, crying. I wiped the tears from my eyes, and began again to rummage through the black garbage bags. I found nothing. What was I looking for? A miracle—that was what this woman desperately needed.

I finally ended up at the last garbage bag. I dug through clothes and a purse or two. I was about to quit when my fingers touched what felt like a pair of shoes. I dumped the clothes out of the bag, pulling out a pair of brown SAS shoes, size 9 extra wide! I couldn't believe my eyes. They were in really good shape, too. My heart almost jumped out of my chest, I was so happy.

I searched through the bags and found a little red plastic flower and some ribbon. I cleaned the shoes the best I could, and put the flower in one and tied them together with the ribbon. Then, I went upstairs to her door and placed the shoes outside. I went back downstairs to the office, wishing I could be there when she opened her door in the morning, but I would need to be in class.

My next day at the shelter was not until one week later. I heard from the other social worker that the woman believed that the shoes had come from an angel. I still smile to this day just thinking about that. And, I share this story with my social work students in their first practice class as an example of faith—and that we must never give up in our quest to find the resources our clients need.

I often think about the shelter, and how the women and children who lived there during my time, those that followed, and those who continue to find safe haven there, albeit briefly, are doing. Are they alive? Are they doing better, worse, the same? Are they among the 90-95% that return to their abusers time and time again, or did something, or someone there, help them realize that they deserved to be treated with respect and love—often for the first time in their lives? I have to believe that it is so.

Think About It

1. Do you feel that Wanda was obligated to report the woman's story about the murder of her two children to the police? Under what circumstances can a social worker ethically break confidentiality?

2. If Wanda could have afforded to purchase the shoes, would it have been appropriate to do so? To what extent should a social worker be expected to, or be willing to, provide resources to clients when the agency cannot or will not do so?

PART 11:
Therapeutic & Case Management Roles

Chapter 31
To Touch With Your Knowledge and Your Heart

●●●●●●●●●●●●●●●●●●●●●●●●●●●●●●

by Heidi Ann Karns, BSW

I was in my last six months of college, broke, ready to quit school, and only a few months away from graduation. I wanted to enter the field of social work and stop working these "mall jobs" where respect is rare. I went to my professor at Hawaii Pacific University and informed her of my frustrations. After we talked for a few minutes, she pulled up an e-mail she had received that day. A family was looking for a companion to work with their 18-year-old son who had Down Syndrome. "Could you possibly be interested in this?" I jumped at the opportunity, even though I didn't know much about Down Syndrome except for a mention in class.

Something about the job appealed to me, and I interviewed with the family. Over the next six months, I worked with "Steve," teaching him to live independently by riding the city bus, budgeting, and preparing and cooking meals (even though we burned the spaghetti!). Steve and his parents introduced me to a new population, a group that goes unrecognized by the rest of society all too often—those with developmental disabilities/mental retardation, and their families. I was "hooked."

Now I work for the Hawaii Department of Health's Developmental Disabilities and Mental Retardation Division. Although many people think it is exotic to live in Hawaii, and we love it here, we work hard and encounter many of the same challenges as social workers on the mainland.

I hear the music, roll over, and hit the snooze button one more time. The music plays again, and I am out of bed by 5 a.m. Who do I visit today? Will I finish my case notes from a home visit three days ago? Maybe I can use some of my comp time to run some personal errands. These are a few of the many thoughts that run through my mind this morning.

7:15 a.m.: My boss stops me before I enter my cubby to inform me that budgets for each of our clients receiving Medicaid Waiver Services (day programs, personal assistance) need to be reviewed, corrected, and submitted by the end of the day. I enter my cubby with my morning cup of coffee that I will probably never get to drink, and pick up my mail and messages from yesterday. Sarah's guardian wants her to move into a new home. Sam's mom is canceling tomorrow's visit. I have an assessment meeting at 9:30.

"Heidi, call on line one." It's Jack's day program. He has had a seizure that lasted six minutes, longer than usual. He has been rushed to the hospital; his caregiver will pick him up when he is stable. I schedule a meeting with our unit nurse, since his seizures have been more frequent the past few months. Jack will be asked to move out of his care home if the seizures cannot be brought under control. He has moved so many times, and there are so few homes that will take clients needing this much supervision for seizures. Before I get distracted with other things, I contact Jack's caseworker at the Office of the Public Guardian, a state agency for those with no one else to take responsibility for them, to inform him of the seizure this morning. Then paperwork—case notes for the file regarding Jack's seizure and what I did.

8:48 a.m.: My list of parents willing to attend the "transition meeting" (from school to adult life) must be submitted by today at 11:30.

8:49 a.m.: Begin calling parents regarding the transition meeting.

9:02 a.m.: Telephone caregiver regarding Jack's seizures. She is on her way to the hospital to pick him up. She sounds discouraged. Assured her that we are working on his medical situation.

9:12 a.m.: Return telephone call to Sarah's guardian. She would like Sarah moved from her current independent living home right away, since she is unable to care for herself. I call the foster care certification unit for a current listing of available homes.

9:20 a.m.: Speak to supervisor regarding a case that was just assigned to me. Case notes from the previous worker are not up to date, and I am unsure when the last contact was made, or what is going on with the client. Supervisor advises me to start from today.

9:30 a.m.: Attend annual assessment meeting on Diane, a client with autism. She is doing well, although her mom expresses difficulty in finding and paying for a sitter who understands Diane's needs. I tell Mom about some programs through the Department of Health that assist families in paying for respite, and she is very interested. Diane has to be wait-listed, because of limited funding. We will explore other resources as well.

11:00 a.m.: Call Jody's mom to let her know the process to have her daughter's finances handled by the Public Guardian. Like many adults with developmental disabilities, Jody has parents who are now elderly and having difficulty meeting their own needs. At one time, so many of the developmentally disabled did not live through childhood. Now, I am seeing more and more who have no one to look out for them. If our clients didn't have us, and a range of community services, I don't know what would happen to them. They're an easy target for abuse and exploitation.

11:05 a.m.: Call from an irate parent. Where is Andy's wheelchair? It was *promised* by the end of last month. She is calling the Ombudsman's office to put in a complaint about us. I check the file—the previous case manager filled out a requisition, but there is no indication that it was ever submitted. I call the wheelchair vendor to see if the chair was ever ordered, and then call the Department of Health, the Office of the Public Guardian, and the Ombudsman's office. The wheelchair will be delivered on an emergency basis within two days. Notify mother. Update client's records. Make a note to myself to call in two days to see if the wheelchair was received.

11:40 a.m.: Complete and mail letters introducing myself as new Case Manager to the five new individuals who have been assigned to me. Briefly review the five new case records.

12:25 p.m.: Update my home visit schedule, so my unit will know where I will be in case of an emergency. If there is a situation where I do not feel comfortable going into the home, I can request my supervisor or someone from the unit to call the home, or on my personal cell phone, to check on me throughout the meeting.

12:40 p.m.: Finally, a break. Grab a quick cup of coffee, since mine is cold from this morning. I then remember to fax in the list of parents that was due at 11:30.

12:55 p.m.: Contact five homes for Sarah, one possibly interested; however, Sarah would have to share a room.

1:15 p.m.: Contact guardian—she does not want Sarah to share a room.

1:22 p.m.: Contact other available homes on the list. There is one possible placement with a private room. Others in my unit congratulate me—it is unusual to find something this fast.

1:30 p.m.: Sarah's guardian agrees to look at the potential placement once she returns from vacation. In the meantime, I can visit the home and provide them with information about Sarah—if the guardian consents. Without her consent, it is illegal for me to tell them anything (HIPAA regulations). Guardian agrees to my sharing information.

1:35 p.m.: Contact potential placement and schedule a date to visit the home. Provide potential caregiver with basic information on Sarah.

1:40 p.m.: Meet with unit nurse to discuss Jack's seizure this morning. Since he has had several seizures in the past few months, we schedule an appointment to consult with a doctor on this case. Jack is on several medications that may be lowering his seizure "threshold." The nurse is not sure whether anything can be done, since he needs those medications. I worry about what will happen to Jack if he loses his present placement.

2:00 p.m.: Leave the office. I have a brief walk to my car. This helps to clear my mind. Stop at the drive-thru for another "healthful" lunch while driving to home visit.

2:30 p.m.: Home visit to meet with a new client. I sent a certified letter one week ago to schedule the visit. No one home, and the apartment looks empty. I track down the resident manager. He says that the family, and my client, moved to Las Vegas. I will close the case when I return to the office.

3:00 p.m.: No chance of taking comp time today. I head back to the office to complete the budgets as requested this morning.

3:20 p.m.: I have completed eight of the ten budgets when I hear, "Heidi, call on line three." Jack's caregiver has decided she would like Jack placed in another home. I inform her that I will contact his guardian, and obtain a listing of available homes. Budgets are completed.

4:30-5:00 p.m.: Leave message for Jack's guardian, and fax consent for release of information to be signed. Research available care homes online. Shut down computer, make list of things to do tomorrow. Another 45 minutes of overtime.

Today, I planned to have two home visits and catch up on paperwork. As my former professor says, "If you want to make God laugh, make plans." It's pretty typical that I don't complete what I've planned, because other things come up. Everything I did or said is documented. This helps to protect me when a case is reviewed or questioned. It also helps me remember where I am in the midst of all my cases.

This job is not for everyone. You have to love working with individuals of various ages who have developmental disabilities and/or mental retardation. You have to be able to change gears at a minute's notice, be organized, flexible, and have excellent time management skills. I currently have 40-45 clients. That's a lot, when I am responsible, to a large degree, for their welfare. It can be frustrating at times, but I take one day at a time. The good days do outweigh the bad ones. We are underpaid, and there is a lot of paperwork (I mean A LOT of paperwork!) that coincides with each home/field/school visit, telephone call received or made, consultation with another professional, letter received, incident report, and any budget action for services. There are days when I feel as though I am more like an accountant or secretary than a social worker, but then I realize that social work is about seeing that vulnerable people are taken care of, whatever it takes. We make sure the individual's wants and needs are met, and that they have assistance if needed to accomplish their dreams and goals. And yes, people with developmental disabilities have wants, needs, dreams, and goals that are just as important to them as mine are to me.

I do not do this job for the recognition, and definitely not for the money. As I told my husband when I married him, "If you are looking for a woman who is going to make a lot of money, you are looking in the wrong place." He laughed and said, "Heidi, you love getting up each morning to help make a difference in others' lives. You are always concerned that others get what they want and need. I admire you." For that point of view, I admire *him*.

That mail I was opening this morning, when I got the call about Jack's seizure? I finally get to it. It is a note from a mother. She says that I am an angel, and have no idea how much I have not only affected her son's life, but her family's as well. "You have touched us all with your knowledge and heart for my son."

You can't have a better day than that.

Think About It

1. What feelings do you think you would have in working with this population?

2. How important do you feel documentation is? How and when might case documentation help you?

3. How important do you think it is that social workers love the population they serve? And if they don't, what type of results may occur?

Chapter 32
Sex Therapy and the Private Practice Social Worker

● ●

by Mark O. Bigler, LCSW, Ph.D.

My mother wasn't exactly impressed when I told her toward the end of graduate school in social work that I had decided I wanted to become a sex therapist. We were a fairly traditional Mormon family from Utah, and sex wasn't something we had talked about much growing up. In fact, I remembered only two things about my sex education as a child—there was something about tampons I wasn't supposed to hear (Mom would race to turn off the television whenever a tampon commercial came on), and a book about puberty and reproduction for teens had mysteriously appeared on the coffee table shortly after my 12th birthday. I tried to ease her concerns by explaining that my interest in sexuality, while similar to that of other young men in their early 20s, was a bit unique and that I was interested in the intellectual stimulation of the topic as much as anything else. I also reminded her that people in Utah had sex, too (yes, even Mormon people) and one thing I had learned while in graduate school was that concerns about sexuality were pretty common among social work clients.

Yet, despite the prevalence of sexuality concerns, it seemed to me that there were few qualified professionals in our area who were prepared to deal with these types of issues. I felt our community needed someone with proper training and experience to handle such specific and sensitive concerns, who also had an insider's view and understood the cultural nuances of our "people" when it came to intimacy and sexual relationships. I told my mother I thought I could be that person, and besides, I didn't want to have a career that might eventually get old and mundane after a few years. I figured a career in sexuality would never become boring (which I have found to be true after 17 years of practice).

I think my mother thought this was another phase I had to go through and didn't take my career plans seriously at first. But the more I thought about it, the more I felt this was something I needed and wanted to do. However, like many who come to me today for advice on how to become a sex therapist, I didn't have much of a clue. To make matters worse, I wasn't acquainted with any sex therapists myself to whom I could turn for guidance and direction. For several weeks, I spent a lot of time in the reference section of the university library (this was a few years before the Internet became widely available) looking for graduate study programs that might prepare me to be a sex therapist.

I found out early on that there wasn't a degree in sex therapy, nor was there such a thing as a sex therapy license. Instead, I was told by a representative of the American Association of Sex Educators, Counselors, and Therapists (AASECT) that sex therapists came from a variety of professional counseling backgrounds. With the right training, work experience, and supervision, physicians, psychiatrists, psychologists, marriage and family therapists, professional counselors, and even social workers could be certified by AASECT as sex therapists and practice this specialty within their own discipline.

Because my training as a social worker did not include any sort of concentration in sexuality, it was clear to me that I needed additional training. My search for programs that granted graduate degrees in sexuality led me to New York University where, much to my mother's surprise, I began doctoral studies the semester after I completed my MSW. Although the NYU program was in health education rather than social work, the emphasis in sexuality was what I needed and it quickly became apparent to me that social work practice and health education were similar in process and objective.

While I was working on my Ph.D. in human sexuality, an opportunity for additional preparation in sex therapy fell into my lap. Through my work in a large, residential drug treatment center in New York City, I was invited to participate in a two-year, post-graduate training program in sex therapy with Dr. Helen Singer-Kaplan, a renowned psychiatrist who had been a pioneer in the development of modern approaches to the treatment of sexual dysfunction. (Dr. Kaplan has the distinction of having trained another well-known sex therapist by the name of Dr. Ruth Westheimer.) Over a period of two years, as I finished my doctoral courses and worked on my dissertation, I spent one day a week under the watchful eye of Dr. Kaplan and her colleagues, seeing sex therapy clients, participating in case presentations, and learning about sex therapy techniques from the best.

When I left New York City after five years to return to Utah, I had my Ph.D. in sexuality in hand, sufficient hours and supervision to qualify for my professional license in social work back home (LCSW), two years of intensive training in sex therapy, and the time and training I needed for AASECT certification as a sex therapist. I quickly went to work establishing a practice, placing an ad in the Yellow Pages, contacting old friends and key health and mental health practitioners in the community, and making personal appearances at staff meetings in counseling centers and organizations of helping professionals where I would describe my personal history and my unique professional background. Although I made a conscious choice not to do sex therapy full time (I also do a great deal of HIV prevention and recently joined an undergraduate social work faculty in Northern Utah), my practice has been very successful, always challenging, and never boring. Best of all, my mother is now very proud to introduce me to friends and strangers as her son, the sex therapist.

In many ways, a typical day in my professional life is not much different from that of other social workers in private practice. The principles, values, ideals, and skills I talk about as a social work educator are the foundation of my practice as a sex therapist. I spend a portion of the day speaking with other professionals about possible referrals and returning phone calls to prospective clients. Except for the fact that our conversations center around a very intimate and often sensitive part of people's lives, these discussions tend to address the same questions that other social workers have to answer: How do you work? How long does it take? How much does it cost? A quick assessment of the situation is essential for me to understand the nature of the concerns and help me determine if I am the most appropriate source of professional help. Sometimes a visit to a medical professional is a better beginning point. In other cases, the sexual problems a couple is experiencing are really secondary to interpersonal problems and relationship conflicts, and general relationship or marriage counseling is more appropriate than sex therapy. Most often, however, referring professionals and would-be clients have come to the right place when they finally get around to contacting me. Many have already been to doctors and marriage counselors with little improvement in their sex lives. I pride myself on being able to create a comfortable, non-threatening environment where my conversations with clients feel more like arranging for yard care or dry cleaning than discussing the intimate details of one's sexuality.

On an average day, I meet with anywhere from three to six clients. For the most part, my clients are couples. This reflects my personal bias (and my social work training) for looking at relationship problems from a systems perspective. A systems approach helps diffuse blame, allows me to observe relationship dynamics firsthand and work with them as they occur, enhances communication between partners about the therapeutic process, and gives the couple the chance to explore the impact of family of origin systems. My experience as a sex therapist working from a systems perspective also supports my belief that social workers are ideally suited for this type of clinical work.

One of the most important tasks with any social work client is to perform a comprehensive, multidimensional assessment. This is especially important in sex therapy, where client concerns are particularly sensitive, often complicated, and may involve issues that are well outside the client's conscious awareness. Within the first few minutes of meeting clients face to face, I begin to gather a thorough sexual history, including what Dr. Kaplan referred to as a sexual status exam (a detailed description of the clients' most recent sexual interaction from first thoughts to final reflections). This process is purposeful, not a random, voyeuristic peep show, and requires tact, empathy, and a well-developed interviewing technique. In early meetings, we also complete a genogram, outlining family dynamics and generational patterns from both sides. The outcome of this information gathering process determines, to a large extent, the nature and course of treatment.

In sex therapy, treatment varies according to the specific phase of the sexual response cycle that is affected—desire, arousal, or orgasm. While I address a wide range of sexual dysfunctions in my practice (for example, erectile dysfunction, involuntary or rapid ejaculation, difficulty achieving orgasm), inhibition or discrepancy in sexual desire is by far the most common complaint. In any case, a typical course of treatment involves ongoing examination of systems dynamics, exploration and personal insight, and the application of a variety of behavioral techniques. Behavioral assignments have several advantages that facilitate progress in sex therapy. First, the client couple is engaged actively in their treatment, completing specific tasks and discussing the outcome in regular sessions. Second, such techniques are both diagnostic and therapeutic. Third, assigning behavioral exercises carries treatment beyond the bounds of the office and the therapeutic hour.

The most common assignment I give my clients is something Masters and Johnson referred to as sensate focus exercises. Briefly, this is a sensual touching assignment, the focus of which is more on sensual awareness than sexual arousal. The couple is instructed to begin the task by creating a relaxing environment (with music, candles, dim lights, and so forth). Both partners disrobe. Next, one person lies face down and the other person begins to caress her/ his partner gently from head to toe. The person being touched then turns over and the process continues in a similar manner. The partners switch roles and repeat the process. In the early weeks of therapy, touching is restricted to non-sexual body parts (anything except genitals and female breasts) to encourage a focus on sensuality. In either role, each partner is instructed to concentrate on physical sensations, emotional responses, and cognitive processes. Conversations in weekly sessions typically revolve around the outcome of these exercises and the thoughts and feelings that were evoked by these activities. With experience, I have become pretty good at anticipating couples' responses to therapy and the specific behavioral tasks I assign, but one of the exciting aspects of my work is that there are always surprises, which keeps things interesting and challenging.

In my role as a social work and sexuality educator, I often have students who indicate an interest in pursuing a career in sex therapy and want to know how to go about it. My first advice is not to follow my career path. Instead, I suggest they will need a professional degree, preferably in social work, that will help them develop clinical skills and establish professional credibility. I also recommend that, as they look into graduate studies, they identify experts in sex therapy who teach in their chosen field and consider applying to these programs where they will be more likely to have mentors who will support their professional interest in sexuality. Finally, I encourage them to go to the AASECT Web site, where they will find information on sex therapy certification and related requirements.

All in all, there are many more ups than downs in a day in the life of a sex therapist. The pathways to this place are varied, and where to begin the journey is often unclear. Being one of few can feel lonely on occasion, and in conservative times and places, friendly faces can seem rare.

The job is demanding, but my mother will tell you that I love my work and I'm good at what I do. Sex therapy easily satisfies my need to help others. I thrive on the challenge of working effectively with an issue from which many other professionals shy away. Most importantly, I believe 100% in the value of the outcome. Sexuality is an inherent and pervasive part of being human and should, in my opinion, be a balanced, positive force in every person's life. Sex therapy gives me the opportunity to help make that happen.

Think About It

1. Why was additional training beyond the social work degree necessary for practice in this specialty area?

2. How is this practice the same as or different from other kinds of private practice?

3. How does the systems perspective come to play in this work?

4. The writer does HIV prevention. What are some other macro level roles for social workers with training in sexuality, sex education, or sex therapy?

Chapter 33
Client Centered Play Therapy, Student Centered Instruction
• •

by Ann Biddlestone, MSW, LISW

A day in my life as a social worker now is a result of my experiences at a small family service agency in northwest Ohio many years ago. I began my work at Regional Family Counseling as a bookkeeper. By the time I left several years later, I had completed both my undergraduate degree in psychology and my MSW. I believe reaching this goal was possible because of the encouragement and mentoring of the agency's social workers. I was truly fortunate to have found this place, because it is how I found my social work career.

Since high school, I had hopes of working with children and families in the mental health field. Happily sidetracked from this goal by marriage and babies of my own, and now in my thirties, I still wanted to pursue a mental health career. At Regional Family Counseling, I was surrounded by people who valued social work. These friends helped me understand how pursuing social work in graduate school was the preferred way to reach my professional goal and prepare me to work with their clinical team. And so I was allowed to get my bookkeeping work done at odd hours and still take college coursework. I could ask the most basic social work questions of people who had been working in the field for years and benefit from the open sharing of their clinical experiences. I felt I was in social work heaven.

As a graduate student, I was able to learn the art of play therapy from these same social workers. Regional Family Counseling had a play therapy program that was fascinating to me. The therapists were knowledgeable, enthusiastic, and effective. These social workers *were* the play therapy program. I was amazed at their skill and honored that they would share their knowledge of play therapy with me. It was a remarkable learning environment. Without it, I believe I would still be a bookkeeper.

I share this history because it has such an impact on my current work day. One of those play therapists from years ago is a dear friend who has provided ongoing supervision and feedback, something that I believe is essential to be successful. The other is currently a professor of social work at the University of Toledo and recommended me to the department to serve as a Field Associate for the BSW program.

So much for history—and now my day begins. This morning at the university, I check my voice and e-mails. There are requests for recommendation letters from two students who are applying to the program. Another student needs some clarification about an essay assignment. I respond to the students and grade some papers before going to an Admissions Committee meeting scheduled for mid-morning. Our committee is working hard on fine-tuning our BSW policy and procedure and is also in the beginning stages of developing policy for our proposed MSW program. Sometimes I think it is tedious work. This morning, however, there is an interesting exchange of ideas about the use of the GRE as a measure of success in graduate school. Although no decision is made today, I enjoy listening to the different perspectives and ideas.

It's time for the Senior Field Lab class. The students are working on presentations related to their fieldwork. Today, a student begins to discuss a very pertinent issue about the availability and portability of health care. She begins well, giving several examples about how the high cost of health care and lack of insurance coverage can be financially devastating to families. She has identified the problem and holds her classmates' attention. This is great, I think to myself. But then the presentation seems to end prematurely, with little follow through on possible solutions. As I walk back to the office, I worry. This is one of the first presentations of the semester. Maybe I have not expressed my expectations clearly enough to the students. I know that, for the benefit of the students presenting over the next few weeks, I need to think of ways to make them more clear next week.

By now it is late afternoon—time to drive downtown to Family Service. Time to play. These are long work days, balancing the academic and direct service, but I like it. At Family Service, I work with young children who are having difficulty with their behavior, mood, or both. Some of the children have been placed in foster care. Many have experienced abuse or loss.

It is rewarding to help children feel better through the use of play. A strong positive relationship develops between the therapist and the child, the foundation for the healing that takes place. I use a client centered approach, which can be a powerful experience for both the child and the social worker. Having complete control over this hour every week is truly empowering for kids who have experienced the powerlessness of victimization. Play is the language they use to express their thoughts and feelings when words fail them, and this is healing.

I have been working for several weeks with a young girl who has returned to her mother's home after a foster care placement of about 18 months. She was previously removed from her home because her mother had serious substance abuse problems that were interfering with her care of the children. The degree of neglect and trauma that the child experienced during this time in her life is currently unknown. Her symptoms include anxiety, nightmares, and refusal to follow her mother's directives. She also appears to "zone out" on occasion.

Today in the playroom, she seems to have moved on from the early stages of rapport building and limit testing to the next stage of the process. For several weeks, she had been engaged in "safer" play; not so much symbolic of her past experience and feelings, but cautious play, testing the safety of the environment and of our relationship. Jane begins this play session by instructing me to sit in a small chair in the corner. She directs the play in short clear statements for the next several minutes. First, my character is confined to a very small area. Then Jane uses items that restrict the movement of my hands and feet. She speaks forcefully and with some anger. She is clearly in control. She collects all of the blankets from the playroom and, one by one, places them over my head. I cannot see. For a second, I think to myself how glad I am that no one except Jane can see me either, because I feel a little goofy. Fortunately, I am able to return very quickly to Jane's purpose and I begin reflecting back in words the feelings she is trying to share through her play. Unable to move or see, I feel fairly certain of how Jane must have felt at one time in her young life. As I reflect back fear and anxiety, the play intensifies, indicating that these are indeed the emotions she wishes to share within her story.

Jane chooses a monster character and a plastic ax, acting out very threatening play within inches of my feet. I briefly consider stopping the process and reminding Jane that the playroom is a safe place for everyone. I have a feeling that she is trying to share her story with me in more depth, and I decide to allow the play to continue. She hands me a toy symbolic of communication, instructs me to ask for help, then denies that help. She directs that I repeat this part of the play several times over, all the while maintaining my character in a very vulnerable position. My character feels helpless and hopeless. I believe that Jane has finally decided that the playroom is a safe enough place to share her traumatic story. I reflect back the feelings of powerlessness that my character is experiencing. Although I believe this is Jane's way of sharing her own personal story, I decide that it is too early in the play therapy process to connect her play to her history. The timer rings, and the symbolic play ends. Jane's voice tone and manner soften and she seems grateful for the sharing of these strong feelings and experiences. She appears to leave these struggles in the playroom, and happily returns to her family, who wait for her in the lobby.

I am exhausted! Thankfully, there is a cancellation following Jane's therapy, and I am allowed the luxury of processing this powerful session with my supervisor. He stands in the playroom door, trying to follow my recollection of the session as I return each toy to its place. It is as intense in the retelling as during the session, and I can only imagine the fear that the younger Jane actually experienced. I know because she was able to share her story with me in this way that some relief is hers in return.

It is the top of the hour again, and I go out to the waiting area to meet Paul and his family. He is smiling. His mother is not. She shares her frustration about some unfavorable reports from his teacher. Paul is often in trouble at school. We decide that we will meet after his play session to go over some parent strategies. Paul is bored with this "school talk" and is eager to get started. He runs to the playroom. His play is more direct than symbolic. He also discusses school issues, but through his play. He takes the role of the teacher and relates to a playroom character who tries very hard to follow the rules, but the effort is not recognized. It is fun to interact with Paul and help him learn, within the play, ways to cope with his learning disabilities and increase his ability to appropriately share his frustration with his teacher and her aide. He has many strengths in other areas, and he makes it easy to reinforce them throughout our time together this evening. I also enjoy working with his mother, who is open to input intended to increase her ability to both advocate for Paul within the school system and at the same time work collaboratively with the academic team. Mother seems hopeful and even enthusiastic. I am hopeful for this family, too. This is fun social work.

Next, I greet a long time client who has "graduated" from the play therapy process. She is a teenager now, but continues to need ongoing care for serious depression and other environmental problems. She is currently struggling as the psychiatrist works with her to adjust medication. Although she has been very involved in previous therapy sessions, today it is all she can do to shrug her shoulders in disinterest. I attempt to use some structured play to engage her, but am unsuccessful. I decide to review some coping skills she has mastered in the past. Nothing. As the session progresses, Sue picks up some art materials and begins to draw. I am pleased, maybe even a little smug, that I have successfully engaged her in a process that I have known to be therapeutic for her in the past. Our time together draws to a close and she hands me her art. I look at the paper, and then at her face, and I am somewhat embarrassed, certainly humbled. Sue has written "blah blah blah, blah blah blah," in several colors and styles of writing on the paper. She nods her head and leaves until next week. I get the message. I have said too much. I took too much control over her session. I need to learn to respect the therapeutic value of silence. I know that for as many years as I am able to practice, I will continue to learn from my clients. I certainly did today.

There is one more session scheduled this evening. As I approach the waiting area to get Mary, I think about her previous play therapy. She is only three years old and has been placed with her step-grandmother following reports of abuse and neglect. Her biological parents both have substance abuse problems, and she has had little contact with them for about five months. Mary has been involved in play therapy for several weeks and focuses on the use of paint. I try to think of the potential symbolism in what she has shared so far. I am baffled and wonder how therapeutic these sessions actually are for Mary. I think about talking to the grandmother regarding a more structured approach to Mary's care, yet I really don't find that option especially appealing, particularly since Mary is so young.

Sometimes social work is messy work, and I look down to ensure I am wearing washable clothing. I laugh to myself. I have on a skirt worn during a previous contact with Mary. I see faint stains of green and red paint. I anticipate what is ahead of me. Mary smiles broadly and races to her playroom. There is no surprise to me that she immediately opens the red and green paints. But this evening, instead of rather aggressive use of the paints at the easel, Mary takes one of the baby dolls from the cradle and gently places her on the table. She pours out red paint and methodically covers the baby with the paint. I wonder where she is going with this new behavior and if I should consider setting a limit with this. (Clinically, I am certain that I need to let her continue, but pragmatically, I am thinking about the mess I will need to clean up later.) I regain my focus as Mary turns to me and states that the baby is hurt. I am astonished to hear Mary talk to the baby in a very nurturing way about how hurt she is, and I realize only at this moment that Mary's previous use of art materials was purposeful, used as rapport building and to develop a sense of safety and security in this playroom environment. Mary then takes the green paint, and assumes the role of a doctor. She calls the green paint "medicine" and she takes care of the very hurt baby. I use reflective statements to connect the hurt of the playroom baby to Mary's past hurts. She looks at me and begins to cry. She looks to the ceiling and wails "Why didn't you take care of me?" It is heartbreaking to experience Mary's level of pain. I know from this session that she will be able to work through some of her hurt in this playroom. I am grateful that I did not stop the messy paint play.

After cleaning up the paint, it is time to get these sessions documented. I tend to think through the symbolic messages of the children's play as I complete my documentation. This takes time. I scramble to complete the notes, knowing that the security guard would like to lock up and go home. I complete some notes and process further on my car ride home. This work day is over, and I feel good about it. I will be back for more tomorrow.

Think About It

1. Play therapy is a non-directive process. The client controls the pace and, therefore, length of treatment. In these times of limited resources and managed care, how can the provider explain to funding sources the desirability of play therapy as a preferred intervention?

2. A community member voices her concern about the close relationship that develops between the child and play therapist. Her impression is that this therapeutic relationship might sabotage the parent/child relationship. How could you respond to this as the child's play therapist?

PART 12:
Employment & Hunger

Chapter 34
Employment Outreach With America's Heroes

• •

by Doris Nelson, LMSW

It is a busy Tuesday morning. I press the control key on the computer keyboard to find that there is another client on the log. "I just finished with one person and now there is another one. It has been steady since we opened at 8:00 a.m.," I think. It seems that each client I have seen for the past two hours is "desperately" looking for work, realizing, after six months of hit and miss job hunting, that they are at their last week of receiving unemployment benefits. I think, "Don't these veterans remember those days of being in the military, of getting things done and done on time, never to procrastinate? What are they thinking about?" Anyway, I hit the F1 key to see if the veteran has looked up three jobs on the job site intranet, so I can give him more details about where the position is located, the salary, and job description of the position of interest. There are no jobs selected. No other notes have been keyed in to reference what the veteran needs. "Well, what does this person need?" I wonder.

The Department of Labor is not just a place to file for unemployment benefits and look for a job from the job site intranet the agency lists every day. The agency is now known as the one-stop career center, where people can file for unemployment, look for jobs, and get assistance in going to school if they qualify. Partner agencies are at the labor department on assigned days to receive referrals for clients needing public assistance, such as food stamps, housing, vocational rehabilitation, training for those over 55 years old, and more. There is a resource center that offers computer classes, résumé and cover letter classes, interviewing classes, and classes for those who are transitioning from incarceration. We see hundreds of people every day seeking assistance in job placement, academic/technical training, or social service assistance. Because our time is limited with each client, an average of 15-20 minutes, we work fast and, in turn, a few clients become revolving clients, fall through the cracks, or leave with a bad taste in their mouths that they did not get the help they needed. I am the only licensed master's level social worker in the agency. Many of my colleagues do not possess any degree, but newcomers to the agency are expected to have at least a bachelor's degree or four years of experience in a human service agency and familiarity with unemployment insurance. Being fresh out of graduate school and passionate about working with America's heroes are the factors that drove me to accept the position, even though the pay is lower than that of a secretary.

Many of my clients have recently gotten out of the military through retirement, finished their enlistment term, or have been out for many years. Many have stated to me that they still think back on their military days and the "can do" attitude they had in getting tasks accomplished when told to, but now it seems since they have hung up the BDUs (Battle Dress Uniforms), the drive they once had has dwindled away. Many of my clients are used to a structured environment—when their supervisor or NCO (Non-Commissioned Officer) told them to do something, it was done without question. I remember my own experience in the military. I liked the structure, the traveling all over the world, the "yes, sergeant" or "no, sergeant" or "can do, sir" remarks. There wasn't a dull moment in the military! I had many dreams and goals to accomplish, but they ended very quickly because of a disability that I incurred. I couldn't see a light at the end of the tunnel. I asked, "What am I going to do? Where am I going to live? What can I do to obtain suitable employment that I would enjoy and be capable of doing with a lifelong challenge that I have to accept?" Many of my veteran clients have similar challenges that have them wondering, "What, when, where, how, and why?"

My next client is a retired Army Vietnam/Persian Gulf veteran. As I call his name, he gets up and follows me to my cubicle office. I greet him and he speaks softly. At my cubicle, I introduce myself, saying, "My name is Doris and I will be working with you today." He says, "Thanks," and holds his head down slightly. I ask about his military career and what job he is seeking. He talks briefly, but his sad facial expression speaks louder than his words. I listen and watch. He states, "I got to be honest with you, ma'am. I lost my job, my marriage is over, and my spouse took all my money. My bills are overdue and I am getting ready to be put in the street."

"What a mouthful to swallow," I think. I look at him—silence. He covers his face. My brain is rolling with questions. I know my counseling will be limited to finding a career and landing a job. All the other issues this veteran has going on are things I am not to address very much. It isn't part of my job. I know I can only work with him no longer than twenty minutes, but he has many concerns and issues that cannot be brushed away. How can he effectively get back in the job market and obtain a stable job and deal with his other worries at the same time? What does he have as far as other family support, community, and other personal resources? What is his mental capacity? Any suicidal thoughts or harmful intentions to others or himself? I begin to talk softly, showing concern and asking questions. Thankfully, he does not have any intentions to hurt himself or anyone else. His eyes fill with tears.

He reports that half of his military retirement check is allotted to his minor child. He has a few friends he did some landscaping and carpentry work for, and they have offered him extra money to help him stay above water. "I do with what I got, but it is getting harder and harder. I feel like I am sinking and I can't get up," he tells me. We begin to work on what strengths he has right now and how to utilize them in the areas that are causing concerns or hindrances.

The client opens his briefcase and pulls out his credentials—a résumé that needs to be updated, a DD 214, a Social Security card, certificates, awards. I look at his résumé and the other articles. "This is good," I tell him. The résumé is well written and states all his skills from his military career. I see many skills that could help him in two positions we currently have listed on the job intranet. He has supervision and leadership skills. I tell him about the positions and we begin to review them.

After three meetings and six telephone counselings, the veteran revises his résumé to target the positions that we have reviewed—one for a local charter school as a superintendent of housekeeping and a federal position on the military base. I feel that he would want something paying a lot more than $30,000 a year that is being offered for the position—Custodial Superintendent. He doesn't. He states, "I had to wax floors, clean rooms and toilets in my military career, so I don't mind the work."

The tasks seem hard and tedious. In the military, everything was done when it was supposed to be done, he says. He is used to everything being structured and done on time. I tell him it has to get harder before it can get better, but hold on and continue to do what is necessary to meet your goal. After the veteran has faxed and re-faxed the needed paperwork for the positions, I advocate and negotiate with the employers, playing phone tag to set up interviews. The light at the end of the tunnel begins to appear. My client is able to work out housing accommodations with his friends. He has been offered both positions, and has to make a choice. Success! He calls me from time to time to say hello and to thank me for helping him. I tell him, "It was the determination in you to get the task accomplished."

It's not all in the money you want to make, prestige you want to hold up in lights, or the recognition in everything you do. It is the gratification in helping human beings who felt that their whole world would crumble, and we as social workers let them know that the power is within them. We are just the vessel used to give guidance and allow them self-determination in setting their own goals that are suitable for them and not us. Everything that may be right for us is not always right for them.

Working with veterans is a challenge within itself, because many have so many skills from their military experience and want to utilize them in the workforce. Many employers do not realize that the skills veterans have learned while serving in the military in just a few years is as much experience as someone working a whole lifetime. The challenges they face, especially those who served in wartime, make them able to see beyond the surface of what we see. They feel that they are not appreciated. The benefit that they have given us is the freedom to come, go, and sleep at night while they, the veterans, have stayed up all night in the cold, the heat, or sleeping on the ground, giving their lives to ensure that those not serving will be safe.

These are the heroes that I give honor to and ensure that they are able to give back to us the experience that keeps us free.

Think About It

1. What are your feelings about working with veterans? Do you feel employers should treat them differently from those who did not serve in the military? Explain.

2. In what way would you work with this veteran, knowing you had only 20 minutes to come up with a plan? Would you have done any more or less than the worker did? Why or why not?

Chapter 35
Food for Thought

● ● ● ● ● ● ● ● ● ● ● ● ● ● ● ● ●

by Regina D. Cassidy, MSW

I walk into the dining room, where lunch is being served. It's grown warm already, though the air conditioning has been on all morning. People are lined up at a long battered table for the tuna salad and soup, and I greet them as they take their trays. Most have smiles for me, though not all.

I make my usual rounds to the tables, commenting on the weather and last night's Yankees game. Some people respond in kind, while others simply stare down at their food. I see children with their mothers, and I am pleased to tell them that I've received new donations of books. One parent asks, "Do you think that I could get a voucher for clothing? They're growing so fast—I can't keep up with it!" I'm happy to be able to comply with her wish as I hurry to get the pink form—this is an easy request, after all.

People begin to gather their belongings so the others standing outside can have a chance to come in. We have to keep the flow of traffic moving, as our soup kitchen's neighbors do not want clients loitering outside our building. We receive complaints on a regular basis, and we don't want to further antagonize anyone, having been generally accepted into this community.

A new woman gives me a silent summons to follow her as she prepares to leave. I walk with her to the office that I share with several other workers, so we can have a small measure of privacy.

"How are you doing today?" I ask. I am surprised to notice her youthfulness, hidden beneath disheveled hair and oversized clothing.

Her eyes rise to meet mine and I guess there's only one way to describe them— bewildered.

Twenty-four hours ago, Hannah was released from prison. She wandered the streets last night, and today, at lunchtime, found her way to our soup kitchen for her first hot meal on the outside.

She has difficulty focusing on one topic, as her eyes move restlessly around the room and her hands pick at stray objects on my desk. Standard questions lie before me on the regular intake form, but they seem a bit daunting, given her apparent state of mind. Instead, I encourage, "Tell me a little bit about yourself."

"I have kids...I want to see my kids," she answers haltingly. "I'm pregnant, too."

"Go on," I say. "Do you have a place to stay tonight?"

"I can stay in the basement of a friend's house," she whispers. "But only until Friday."

"And then...?" I continue.

She shakes her head and stands. "I have to get a job. My mother, she's got my kids. I have until next week to go pick them up."

"Have you applied for public assistance? Food stamps? Medicaid?"

"No. They told me that I got to get into a program first. Do you know anything around here?" She paces around the room.

"What kind of program do you need?" I probe.

"I don't have any meds." She shrugs as I look at her uncertainly. "And I drink."

"How are you feeling? Have you had anything to drink today?"

"I cry real easy...I only had a beer or two." She shakes her head impatiently and I know it is time for me to stop asking questions. "I don't remember...but look, I need a job."

All of a sudden, her face brightens. "I can clean houses."

"That's good." I smile, too. This is something I can work with. "There's an agency nearby that hires women to cook and clean on a day-to-day basis. How about I give you that address?"

She looks at me. "But can't I clean for you? I'll do a good job." Her voice becomes vaguely tinged with hysteria. "Please, I gotta get an apartment by next week. I gotta get my kids. You must need help at your house. Let me clean for you. Please. I won't even charge you."

Now it is my turn to stand. "Can you excuse me for a moment? I'll be right back."

I need to walk around for a moment. I need to clear my head. I need to believe that this woman must have had someone to work with her before her release from prison. She must have been given a discharge plan, with an appointment to show up at a local treatment program, bright and early. No one would just be released into the streets homeless, still addicted to alcohol, and pregnant, without a way to get her children and her psychiatric medications. Right?

Entering the dining room, I see that now there's a line of people waiting to see me. I am torn—I want to listen to them, but I know I'll have to return to Hannah in a moment. I'm glad that I took my clipboard with me. I ask everyone to wait as I list a variety of requests—from the concrete needs of furniture, toiletries, and housing to a regular who insists, "I need to talk to you *today*, in private. Nobody listening to us." It's starting to grow noisier and hotter, and I feel increasing pressure to move quickly.

I take a breath and return to my office. Hannah jumps up and says, "You found an apartment for me? A job?"

"Let's both sit down, " I say. "Let's start again."

And, in this way, I begin the work that comprises the greatest portion of my day—making connections between people and the resources in our community.

I am a social worker in a New York City soup kitchen, one that is run by a nonprofit agency, with some government support. Volunteers from local churches staff the kitchen, where meal preparation is begun early each morning. Anyone who comes to the door is welcomed for lunch; many will also leave with a bag of food, as well.

Our population is widely mixed. Many are homeless, and these are the people upon whom we focus our attention, as we also run a shelter at another location. A good portion is marginally housed, living temporarily with friends, in SROs, or in transitional placements. Most have one or more issues of substance abuse and mental illness. Others are recent immigrants, who lack access to basic benefits, given their tenuous status in this country. Some are people we help just for a short time, in response to sudden unemployment or health problems. The remainder are clients who have been regulars for years, a fact not necessarily discouraging in itself. There's a good sense of family at some of the tables. For example, a gentleman known only as "Popi" always has a kind word and a smile for the younger men and women. They in turn watch out for his safety, when they leave the center together.

Upon my graduation from social work school several years ago, as an older student, I chose this field as my first position. Why? Since I was a teen, I had been troubled whenever I saw people lying about in our city streets, huddled in doorways, or asking for food at our ferry terminal. A part of me was afraid of them, but I was also confused. These were people, too—they had been babies once. What had happened, to bring them to this point?

When I became a mother, living in a more suburban environment, my young children and I would regularly pass a bus stop at our corner. Often, we saw a man sleeping on its bench, wrapped in soiled blankets and coats. Whether the temperature was freezing or scorching, he was there. We would return home, remembering to include "the man on the bench" in our evening prayers—the extent of my involvement at that point in my life.

When offered the position at this agency, I jumped at it eagerly, idealistic in spite of my 43 years. Finally, I was presented with a chance to do something. I was now a social worker, with abilities and skills. Problems in our community were overwhelming—poverty, illness, prejudice, and crime were rampant—but at least I could give out food and clothing.

Well, as it turns out, the least of what I do is give out food. It seems that perhaps the best, or only thing I can really do, is listen. There are no easy answers to the situations that I am confronted with each day. I would like to say that low-income housing is available down the street. I would like to suggest that jobs are easy to get, benefits and training included. I would like to promise that the salary they will earn will be sufficient to support themselves and their families. But this is often not the case.

And so, my door is open for an hour or two after lunch each day and people file in, just to talk. I can predict Will's mood—basically, he is always angry. He debates the state of the world and his ideas to improve it. Then, on most days, he rants bitterly about his upbringing and the unfairness of his situation, his temper barely controlled. After a short time, I remind him gently that I must move on to the next person. He leaves a bit calmer and I am grateful for this small sign of progress.

Joe, disabled with degenerative diabetes, gives me daily reports about his attempts to get SSI benefits. We share our frustration with the system—his need is obvious. Thankfully, we can usually find a moment of humor in the tangle of paperwork and phone calls, a process confusing to both of us.

It's a good sign when Matthew finds his way to my door. I don't know how he'll be from one day to the next. He's a chronic alcoholic, and at times, he'll be sober and remorseful; other days, his clothes will reek of the beer he drank earlier that morning. Recently, he came in to tell me about his best friend, someone I also knew. His eyes filled with tears as he explained that his friend had fallen while inebriated, and died from a head injury. Matthew resolved then and there to stop drinking, and I offered to help him get into a detox program. Though he's been in programs before, we both know that this could be the time it will work.

Why do I want to work in this soup kitchen, if the problems are beyond the scope of what I can do? Why would you want to work here? Challenge is one answer, change is another, compassion is a third. Some people want to climb Mount Everest—I'd rather tackle food and housing shortages. Also, I have the potential to be an instrument of reform. Just because I don't have the answers at this present moment doesn't mean that I won't have them one day. At this point in my career, I need to heighten my awareness, I need to learn about the problems. Already, I can say that in three short years, my sheltered eyes have been opened and a great deal of my "naiveté" has been replaced by realism. Finally, the faith that I profess encourages me to care for the hungry and homeless. So why not be there in the soup kitchen, among people who at this point in their life need my help?

There is one remaining reason why I choose to work here. I love it. Making connections, offering comfort, listening to stories—I can do that and I can do it well. Yes, there's much more to be done, and many a day, I walk out the dining room doors, laden with frustration and sadness. But tomorrow, I know that Hannah, or someone like her, will be waiting to see me. She must be there, and so must I.

Think About It

1. What services does a social worker in this type of setting provide, in addition to handing out food and clothes?

2. Many social workers in a soup kitchen will need to deal with issues of stark contrasts between their own lives and those of

their clients. How may clinical supervision best be utilized to deal with such issues?

3. How may changes in public policy be brought about so that the need for soup kitchens and food pantries may be eliminated? Could or should this type of advocacy work also be a part of the responsibility of a social worker in this setting?

Appendix A—Organizations and Web Sites of Interest to Social Workers

This is a partial listing of professional associations, organizations, and Web sites that may be useful in exploring social work in general or specific areas of practice presented in this book. Please use these resources to find further information about the areas of social work that are of interest to you.

Administration on Developmental Disabilities
http://www.acf.dhhs.gov/programs/add/index.htm

Alliance for Children & Families
11700 W. Lake Park Drive
Milwaukee, WI 53224
414-359-1040
http://www.alliance1.org

American Association of Grant Professionals
http://www.grantprofessionals.org

American Association for Marriage and Family Therapy
112 South Alfred Street
Alexandria, VA 22314-3061
703-838-9808
http://www.aamft.org

American Board of Examiners in Clinical Social Work
Shetland Park
27 Congress Street, #211
Salem, MA 01970
800-694-5285
http://www.abecsw.org

American College Personnel Association
One Dupont Circle, NW, Suite 300
Washington, DC 20036-1188
202-835-2272
http://www.acpa.nche.edu

American Public Human Services Association
810 First Street, NE, Suite 500
Washington, DC 20002
202-682-0100
http://www.aphsa.org

American Society of Association Executives (ASAE)
1575 I Street, NW
Washington, DC 20005-1103
202-371-0940
888-950-2723
http://www.asaenet.org

America's Second Harvest
35 E. Wacker Drive, #2000
Chicago, IL 60601
800-771-2303
312-263-2303
http://secondharvest.org

Association for the Advancement of Social Work with Groups (AASWG)—An International Professional Organization
Raymie Wayne, General Secretary
30 N. Canton Road
West Simsbury, CT 06092
866-90-AASWG
860-651-7089
http://www.aaswg.org

Association of Baccalaureate Social Work Program Directors
c/o Stacy Barrentine, Membership Coordinator
P.O. Box 151463
Alexandria, VA 22315-9998
703-971-6715
http://www.bpdonline.org

Association for Community Organization and Social Administration
20560 Bensley Avenue
Lynwood, IL 60411
708-757-4187
http://www.acosa.org

Association for Conflict Resolution
1015 18th Street, NW, Suite 1150
Washington, DC 20036
202-464-9700
http://www.acrnet.org

Association of Fundraising Professionals
1101 King Street, Suite 700
Alexandria, VA 22314
703-684-0410
http://www.afpnet.org

Association of Jewish Center Professionals (JCC Association)
15 E. 26th Street, 10th Floor
New York, NY 10010
212-532-4949
http://www.jcca.org

Association of Jewish Family and Children's Agencies
577 Cranbury Road, Suite 2
E. Brunswick, NJ 08816
800-634-7346
http://www.ajfca.org

Association of Social Work Boards
400 S. Ridge Parkway, Suite B
Culpeper, VA 22701
540-829-6880

800-225-6880
http://www.aswb.org

Canadian Association of Social Workers
383 Parkdale Avenue, Suite 402
Ottawa, ON, Canada K1Y 4R4
613-729-6668
http://www.casw-acts.ca

Center for Law and Social Policy
1015 15th Street, NW
Washington, DC 20005
202-906-8000
http://www.clasp.org

Child Welfare League of America
440 First Street, NW, 3rd Floor
Washington, DC 20001-2085
202-638-2952
http://www.cwla.org

Children's Defense Fund
25 E Street, NW
Washington, DC 20001
202-628-8787
http://www.childrensdefense.org

Clinical Social Work Federation
P.O. Box 3740
Arlington, VA 22203
703-522-3866
http://www.cswf.org

Coming Up Taller: Arts and Humanities Programs for Children and Youth at Risk
http://www.cominguptaller.org

Council on Social Work Education
1725 Duke Street, Suite 500
Alexandria, VA 22314-3457
703-683-8080
http://www.cswe.org

Difficult.net
http://www.difficult.net

Family and Corrections Network
32 Oak Grove Road
Palmyra, VA 22963
434-589-3036
http://www.fcnetwork.org

Family Preservation and Child Welfare Network
http://www.familypreservation.com

Family Violence Prevention Fund
383 Rhode Island Street, Suite 304
San Francisco, CA 94103-5133
415-252-8900
http://www.endabuse.org

Federal Register
http://fr.cos.com/

Federation for Children with Special Needs
1135 Tremont St., Suite 420
Boston, MA 02120
617-236-7210
http://www.fcsn.org

The Foundation Center
79 Fifth Avenue/16th Street
New York, NY 10003-3076
212-620-4230
800-424-9836
http://www.fdncenter.org

The Innovation Center for Community and Youth Development
6930 Carroll Avenue, Suite 502
Takoma Park, MD 20912
301-270-1700
http://www.theinnovationcenter.org

Institute for the Advancement of Social Work Research
750 First Street, NE, Suite 700
Washington, DC 20002
202-336-8385
http://www.iaswresearch.org

Institute for International Connections (IIC)
137 West County Line Road

Suite 240
Littleton, CO 80129
http://www.iiconnect.org.

Interfaith Alliance
1331 H Street, NW, 11th Floor
Washington, DC 20005
202-639-6370
http://www.interfaithalliance.org

International Federation of Social Workers
Postfach 6875
Schwarztorstrasse 20
CH-3000 Berne, Switzerland
41-31-382-6015
http://www.ifsw.org

Joint Commission on Accreditation of Healthcare Organizations
1 Renaissance Blvd.
Oakbrook, IL 60181
630-792-5000
http://www.jcaho.org

The Library of Congress: Thomas, Legislative Information on the Internet
http://thomas.loc.gov

National Academy for State Health Policy
50 Monument Square, Suite 502
Portland, ME 04101
207-874-6524
http://www.nashp.org

National Association of Advisors for the Health Professions
P.O. Box 1518
Champaign, IL 61824-1518
217-355-0063
http://www.naahp.org

National Association of Black Social Workers
1220 11th Street, NW
Washington, DC 20001
202-589-1850
http://www.nabsw.org

National Association of Human Rights Workers
Joe Cooper, President
5719 Cooper's Ridge Lane
Charlotte, NC 28269
704-875-8812
http://www.nahrw.org

National Association of Social Workers
750 First Street, NE, Suite 700
Washington, DC 20002-4241
800-638-8799
http://www.socialworkers.org

NASW PACE (Political Action for Candidate Election)
http://www.socialworkers.org/pace/default.asp

National Coalition Against Domestic Violence
P.O. Box 18749
Denver, CO 80218
303-839-1852
http://www.ncadv.org

National Coalition for the Homeless
1012 14th Street, NW
Suite 600
Washington, DC 20005-3471
202-737-6444
http://www.nationalhomeless.org

National Dissemination Center for Children and Youth with Disabilities
P.O. Box 1492
Washington, DC 20013-1492
800-695-0285
http://www.nichcy.org

National Human Services Assembly
1319 F Street, NW, Suite 402
Washington, DC 20004
202-347-2080
http://www.nassembly.org/

National Network for Social Work Managers
1040 W. Harrison Street, 4th Floor
M/C 309
Chicago, IL 60607
312-413-2302
http://www.socialworkmanager.org

National Youth Leadership Council
1667 Snelling Avenue N., Suite D300
St. Paul, MN 55108
651-631-3672
http://www.nylc.org

The New Social Worker Online
P.O. Box 5390
Harrisburg, PA 17110-0390
717-238-3787
http://www.socialworker.com

North American Association of Christians in Social Work
P.O. Box 121
Botsford, CT 06404-0121
888-426-4712
http://www.nacsw.org

On The Issues: Every Political Leader on Every Issue
http://www.ontheissues.org

Physicians For A Violence Free Society
1001 Potrero Boulevard
Bldg. 1, Room 300
San Francisco, CA 94110
415-621-3582
http://www.pvs.org/index.shtml

Play Therapy International
Fern Hill Centre, Fern Hill
Fairwarp, Uckfield,
East Sussex TN22 3BU
United Kingdom
Phone: 44-1825-712360
http://www.playtherapy.org

Rose Brooks Center
http://www.rosebrooks.org

School Social Work Association of America
P.O. Box 2072
Northlake, IL 60164
http://www.sswaa.org

Sexuality Information and Education Council of the U.S. (SIECUS)
130 West 42nd Street, Suite 350
New York, NY 10036-7802
(212) 819-9770
http://www.siecus.org/

Society for the Scientific Study of Sexuality (SSSS)
P.O. Box 416
Allentown, PA 18105-0416
(610) 530-2463
http://www.sexscience.org/

Society for Sex Therapy and Research (SSTAR)
P.O. Box 96920
Washington, DC 20090-6920
(202) 863-1644
http://www.sstarnet.org/

Society for Social Work Leadership in Health Care
1211 Locust Street
Philadelphia, PA 19107
866-237-9542
http://www.sswlhc.org

Society for Social Work Research
http://www.sswr.org

Substance Abuse and Mental Health Services Administration (SAMHSA)
www.samhsa.gov

U.S. Administration for Children and Families
http://www.acf.dhhs.gov/

U.S. Department of Health and Human Services
http://www.os.dhhs.gov/

U.S. Department of Homeland Security
http://www.dhs.gov

U.S. Department of Justice
http://www.usdoj.gov

U.S. House of Representatives
http://www.house.gov

U.S. National Institute of Mental Health
http://www.nimh.nih.gov

U.S. Senate
http://www.senate.gov

Victim Offender Mediation Association
c/o Center for Policy, Planning and Performance
2233 University Avenue W.
Suite 300
St. Paul, MN 55114
612-874-0570
http://www.voma.org

Washington Center for Internships and Academic Seminars
2301 M Street, NW, 5th Floor
Washington, DC 20037
202-336-7600
www.twc.edu

World Wide Web Resources for Social Workers
http://www.nyu.edu/socialwork/wwwrsw

Youth Service America
1101 15th Street, Suite 200
Washington, DC 20005
202-296-2992
http://www.ysa.org

Appendix B—Additional Reading

General

Doelling, C. N. (2004). *Social work career development: A handbook for job hunting and career planning.* (2nd ed.). Washington, DC: NASW Press.

Fox-Piven, F., & Cloward, R. (1982). *The new class war.* New York: Pantheon Books.

Ginsberg, L. H. (2000). *Careers in social work.* (2nd ed.). Needham Heights, MA: Allyn & Bacon.

Grant, G. B., & Grobman, L. M. (1998). *The social worker's internet handbook.* Harrisburg, PA: White Hat Communications.

Grobman, L. M. (2005). *Days in the lives of social workers.* (3rd ed.). Harrisburg, PA: White Hat Communications.

National Association of Social Workers. (1999). *Choices: Careers in social work, where commitment and opportunity meet.* Washington, DC: Author.

Perlman, H. H. (1979). *Relationship: The heart of helping people.* Chicago: University of Chicago Press.

Perlman, H. H. (1989). *Looking back to see ahead.* Chicago: University of Chicago Press.

Reyes, J. (2002). *The social work graduate school applicant's handbook.* Harrisburg, PA: White Hat Communications.

Shulman, L. (1999). *The skills of helping individuals, families, groups, and communities.* (4th ed.). Itasca, IL: F.E. Peacock.

Wells, C. C. (1998). *Social work day-to-day: The experience of generalist social work practice.* (3rd ed.). New York: Longman.

Chapter 3—Transferring Micro Experience to Macro Practice: Working at the Child Welfare League of America

Allen, M., & Nixon, R. (2000). The foster care independence act and John H. Chafee foster care independence program: New catalysts for reform for young people aging out of foster care. *Clearinghouse Review: Journal of Poverty Law and Policy, 34,* 197–216.

National Low Income Housing Coalition (NLIHC). (2003). *Out of reach 2003: America's housing wage climbs.* Available online: http://www. nlihc.org/oor2003.

Courtney, M. E., Terao, S., & Bost, N. (2004). *Midwest evaluation of the adult functioning of former foster youth: Conditions of youth preparing to leave state care.* Available online: http://www.chapinhall.org/article_abstract_new.asp?ar=1360&L2=61&L3=130.

Robertson, M., & Toro, P. (1999). Homeless youth: Research, intervention, and policy. In Fosberg, L. B., & Dennis, D. L. (Eds.), *Practical lessons: The 1998 symposium on homelessness research.* Washington, DC: U.S. Department of Health and Human Services. Available online: http://aspe.hhs.gov/progsys/homeless/symposium/3-Youth.htm.

Roman, N. (1995). *Web of failure: The relationship between foster care and homelessness.* Available online: http://www.endhomelessness.org/pub/fostercare/web.htm.

Chapter 7—Managing a Hospital Social Work Department

Berkman, B. (1996). The emerging health care world: Implications for social work practice and education, *Social Work, 41* (5), 541-551.

Ell, K., & Northen, H. (1990). *Families and health care: A psychosocial practice.* New York: Aldine de Gruyter.

Kayser, K., Hansen, P., & Groves, A. (1995). Evaluating social work practice in a medical setting: How do we meet the challenges of a rapidly changing system? *Research on Social Work Practice, 5* (4), 485-500.

Osman, H., & Perlin, T. M. (1994). Patient self-determination and the artificial prolongation of life. *Health and Social Work,* 19 (4), 237-244.

Toby-Brown, J. S., & Furstenberg, A. L. (1992). Restoring control: Empowering older patients and their families during health crisis. *Social Work in Health Care, 17* (4), 81-101.

Chapter 10—Representing the Faith Community in the Policy Arena

Karger, H. J., & Stoesz, D. (2002). *American social welfare policy: A pluralist approach* (4th ed.). Boston: Allyn and Bacon.

Schneider, R. L., & Lester, L. (2001). *Social work advocacy: A new framework in action.* Belmont, CA: Wadsworth.

Chapter 11—It Takes a Village: Reclaiming Our Youth Through Community Partnerships

Brueggemann, W. G. (1996). *The practice of macro social work.* Chicago: Nelson-Hall.

Kahn, S. (1982). *Organizing.* New York: McGraw Hill.

Specht, H., & Courtney, M. (1994). Social work in the 21st century: Replacing psychotherapy with community education. In H. Specht & M. Courtney, *Unfaithful angels: How social work has abandoned its mission* (pp. 130-152). New York: The Free Press.

Chapter 12—Policy Supervisor in a State Government Setting

Ginsberg, L. (1999). *Understanding social problems, policies, and programs* (3rd ed.). Columbia, SC: University of South Carolina Press.

Kane, R. A., Kane, R. L., & Ladd, R. (1998). *The heart of long-term care.* New York: Oxford University Press.

Milne, D., Chang, D., & Mollica, R. (2004). *State perspectives on Medicaid long-term care: Report from a July 2003 state forum.* Portland, ME: National Academy for State Health Policy.

Netting, F., Kettner, P., & McMurtry, S. (1993). *Social work macro practice.* New York: Longman Publishing Group.

Chapter 13—Interning on Capitol Hill

Haynes, K. S., & Mickelson, J. S. (1997). *Affecting change: Social workers in the political arena* (5th ed.). New York: Longman.

Oleszek, W. J. (2003). *Congressional procedures and the policy process* (6th ed.). Washington, DC: CQ Press.

Chapter 14—Training in Eastern Europe

Austin, M. J., Brannon, D., & Pecora, P. J. (1984). *Managing staff development programs in human service agencies.* Chicago: Nelson Hall.

Bard, R., Bell, C. R., Stephen, L., & Webster, L. (1987). *The trainer's professional development handbook.* San Francisco: Jossey Bass.

De Shazer, S. (1988). *Clues: Investigating solutions in brief therapy.* New York: Norton.

De Shazer, S. (1992). Solution-focused therapy. In C. W. LeCroy, *Case studies in social work practice.* Belmont, CA: Wadsworth Publishing.

Dodson, L. S. (1991). The dying process of a conscious woman—Virginia Satir. *The Journal of Couples Therapy, Vol. 2(1/2).*

Satir, V. (1967). *Conjoint family therapy.* Palo Alto, CA: Science and Behavior Books, Inc.

Satir, V. (1988). *The new peoplemaking.* Palo Alto, CA: Science and Behavior Books, Inc.

Satir, V., & Baldwin, M. (1983). *Satir step by step: A guide to creating change in families.* Palo Alto, CA: Science and Behavior Books, Inc.

Scannell, E. E., & Newstrom, J. W. (1991). *Still more games trainers play.* New York: McGraw-Hill.

Schon, D. A. (1987). *Educating the reflective practitioner.* San Francisco: Jossey Bass.

Quick, T. L. (1991). *Training managers so they can really manage: Confessions of a frustrated trainer.* San Francisco: Jossey Bass.

Chapter 16—Doing Social Work Research

Cherry, A. (2000). *A research primer for the helping professions.* Belmont, CA: Brooks-Cole.

Klein, W., & Bloom, M. (1995). Practice wisdom. *Social Work, 40* (6), 799-807.

Nasuti, J., York, R. O., & Henley, H. C. (2003). Teaching social work research: Does andragogy work best? *Journal of Baccalaureate Social Work, 9* (1), 149-175.

Padgett, D. (1998). Does the glove really fit? Qualitative research and clinical social work practice. *Social Work, 43* (4), 373-381.

Chapter 17—A Day's Work at the Institute for the Advancement of Social Work Research

Solt, B. E. (2002). Blending service and financial security: An analysis of a fraternal benefit society. *Social Thought: The Journal of Religion in the Social Services, 21* (1). 21-37.

Zlotnik, J. L., Biegel, D. E., & Solt, B. E. (2002). The Institute for the Advancement of Social Work Research: Strengthening social work research in practice and policy. *Research in Social Work Practice, 12,* (2), 318-337.

Chapter 18—A Life-Altering Experience as a Social Work Researcher

Bloom, M., Fischer, J., & Orme, J. G. (2003). *Evaluating practice: Guidelines for the accountable professional* (4th ed.). Boston: Allyn and Bacon.

Mason, J. (2002). *Qualitative researching* (2nd ed.). Thousand Oaks, CA: Sage.

Royse, D. (1998). *Research methods in social work* (2nd ed.). Chicago: Nelson-Hall.

Rubin, A., & Babbie, E. (2001). *Research methods for social work* (4th ed.). Belmont, CA: Wadsworth.

Chapter 19—FUNd Writing: Working as a Grant Writer

Geever, J. (1993). *The Foundation Center's guide to proposal writing.* New York: Foundation Center.

Quick, J. A. (2001). *Grant seeker's budget toolkit.* New York: John Wiley and Sons.

Chapter 20—The Field Office: Teaching and Supervising Student Internships

Caspi, J. (2002). *Educational supervision in social work: A task-centered model for field instructors and staff development.* New York: Columbia University Press.

Gardner, D. (1989). *The anatomy of supervision: Developing learning and professional competence for social work students.* Milton Keynes, UK: Society for Research into Higher Education and Open University Press.

Kadushin, A. (2002). *Supervision in social work* (4th ed.). New York: Columbia University Press.

Chapter 21—Carving Out a Career: Academic and Community Collaboration

Burke, S. C., & Draina, L. K. (2004, February). Interdisciplinary problem-solving: Enriching social work doctoral education. *Social Work Today, 4* (2), 18.

Burke, S. C., & Bromwell, J. (2003, November). Faith-based TANF services: A leap of faith? *Social Work Today, 3,* 26.

Burke, S. C. (2003, Fall). Student-faculty collaborations: Making a difference in foundations courses. *BPD Update, 25* (3).

Chapter 22—Working in an Academic Medical Center

Schamess, G., & Lightburn, A. (Eds.) (1998). *Humane managed care?* Washington, DC: NASW Press.

Maguire, L. (1991). *Social support systems in practice: A generalist approach.* Washington, DC: NASW Press.

Chapter 24—International Work on a Domestic Level: Immigration Law

Nugent, C., & Schulman, S. (2003, February 19). A new era in the legal treatment of alien children: The homeland security and child status protection acts. *Interpreter Releases, 80,* 233.

Nugent, C., & Schulman, S. (2001, October 8). Giving voice to the vulnerable: On representing detained immigrant and refugee children. *Interpreter Releases, 78,* 1569.

Chapter 25—Mediation: The Fit for Social Work

Chandler, D. B., & Chandler, S. M. (1987). Mediating the end of love. *Journal of Social Work and Human Sexuality, 5,* 123-136.

National Association of Social Workers. (2001). *NASW procedures for professional review* (4th ed.). Washington, DC: Author.

Saposnek, D. (1991). *Mediating child custody disputes.* San Francisco: Jossey-Bass.

Severson, M., & Bankston, T. (1995). Social work and the pursuit of justice through mediation. *Social Work, 40* (5), 683-692.

Stuart, R. B., & Jacobson, B. (1986-87). Principles of divorce mediation: A social learning theory approach. *Mediation Quarterly, 14-15,* 71-85.

Wallerstein, J., & Kelly, J. (1980). *Surviving the breakup: How children and parents cope with divorce.* New York: Basic Books.

Chapter 26—A Court-Ordered Program for Divorced and Separating Parents: Is This Social Work?

Amato, P. R., & Booth, A. (1994). Parental marital quality, parental divorce, and relations with parents. *Journal of Marriage and the Family, 56,* 21-34.

Amato, P. R., & Keith, B. (1991). Parental divorce and the well-being of children: A meta-analysis. *Psychological Bulletin, 10,* 26-46.

Cancio, J., Orbuch, T. L., & Thornton, A. (2000). The impact of marital quality, divorce, and remarriage on the relationships between parents and their children. *Marriage and Family Review, 29,* 221-246.

Emery, R. E. (1999). *Marriage, divorce, and children's adjustment.* California: Sage Publications.

Chapter 28—Spiritual Social Work

Boyd-Franklin, N. (2003). *Black families in therapy: understanding the African American experience* (2nd ed.). New York: Guilford Press.

Knox, D. H. (1985). Spirituality: A tool in the assessment and treatment of Black alcoholics and their families. *Alcoholism Treatment Quarterly, 2* (3-4), 31-44.

Martin, E. P., & Martin, J. M. (1995). *Social work and the black experience.* Washington, DC: NASW Press.

Small, J. (1994). *Embodying spirit: Coming alive with meaning and purpose.* San Francisco: HarperCollins.

Chapter 29—Hospital-Based Domestic Violence Advocacy

Flitcraft, A. H., Hadley, S. M., Hendricks-Matthews, M. K., McLeer, S. V., & Warshaw, C. (1992). *Diagnostic and treatment guidelines on domestic violence.* Chicago: American Medical Association.

Alpert, E. J. (Ed.). (1999). *How to recognize and treat victims of abuse. A guide for physicians and other healthcare professionals* (3rd ed.). Waltham, MA: Massachusetts Medical Society.

Warshaw, C., & Ganley, A. L. (1998). *Improving the health care response to domestic violence: A resource manual for health care providers* (2nd ed.). San Francisco: Family Violence Prevention Fund.

Chapter 32—Sex Therapy and the Private Practice Social Worker

Leiblum, S. R., & Rosen, R. C. (Eds.). (2000). *Principles and practice of sex therapy* (3rd ed.). New York: Guilford.

Kaplan, H. S. (1983). *The evaluation of sexual disorders: Psychological and medical aspects.* New York: Brunner/Mazel.

Kaplan, H. S. (1995). *Sexual desire disorders: Dysfunctional regulation of sexual motivation.* New York: Brunner-Routledge.

Kaplan, H. S. (1999). *How to overcome premature ejaculation.* New York: Brunner-Routledge.

Kaplan, H. S. (1999). *The illustrated manual of sex* (2nd ed.). New York: Brunner-Routledge.

Kaplan, H. S. (1999). *The new sex therapy: Active treatment of sexual dysfunctions.* New York: Brunner-Routledge.

Kaplan, H. S. (1999). *Sexual aversion, sexual phobias, and panic disorder.* New York: Brunner-Routledge.

Masters, W. H., Johnson, V. E., & Kolodny, R. C. (1980). *Ethical issues in sex therapy and research: Volume 2.* Boston, MA: Little, Brown.

Rosen, R. C., & Beck, J. G. (1988). *Patterns of sexual arousal: Psychophysiological processes and clinical applications*. New York: Guilford.

Schnarch, D. M. (1991). *Constructing the sexual crucible: An integration of sexual and marital therapy*. New York: W. W. Norton.

Chapter 33—Client Centered Play Theapy, Student Centered Instruction

Axline, V. M. (1969). *Play therapy*. New York: Ballantine Books.

Carroll, J. (2002). Play therapy: The children's views. *Child and Family Social Work, 7,* 177-187.

Gil, E. (1991). *The healing power of play: Working with abused children*. New York: Guilford.

Kaplan, C., & Telford, R. (1998). *The butterfly children: An account of nondirective play therapy*.

O'Connor, K. (2002). The value and use of interpretation in play therapy. *Professional Psychology: Research and Practice, 33* (6). 523-528.

Chapter 34—Employment Outreach With America's Heroes

Clark, E. J. (2004, March/April). Mapping the profession's future. *Social Work Today, 4* (3), 10.

Covey, S. (1989). *The 7 habits of highly effective people*. New York: Simon & Schuster.

Robb, M. (2004, March/April). 7 habits of highly effective social workers. *Social Work Today, 4* (3), 24.

Chapter 35—Food for Thought

Berzoff, J., Flanagan, L. M., & Hertz, P. (1996). *Inside out and outside in: Psychodynamic clinical theory and practice in contemporary multicultural contexts*. Northvale, NJ: Jason Aronson.

Jucovy, L. (2003). *Amachi: Mentoring children of prisoners in Philadelphia*. Philadelphia, PA: Public/Private Ventures.

Kozol, J. (1995). *Amazing grace*. New York: Crown.

Parent, M. (1998). *Turning stones*. New York: Fawcett Columbine.

Waterston, A. (1999). *Love, sorrow, and rage*. Philadelphia: Temple University Press.

More Social Work Books from White Hat Communications

DAYS IN THE LIVES OF SOCIAL WORKERS:
54 Professionals Tell Real-Life Stories from Social Work Practice
3rd Edition
edited by Linda May Grobman

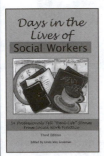

Did you ever wish you could tag along with a professional in your chosen field, just for a day, observing his or her every move? In this third edition of our "best seller," you can read about social workers in 54 different settings, including mental health, schools, prisons, adventure-based therapy, private practice, HIV/AIDS, public health, hospice, nursing homes, international social work, public policy, and more.

410 pages • 5 1/2 x 8 1/2 • ISBN 1-929109-15-6 • 2005
$19.95 plus shipping

THE FIELD PLACEMENT SURVIVAL GUIDE:
What You Need to Know to Get the Most
From Your Social Work Practicum
edited by Linda May Grobman

Field placement is one of the most exciting and exhilarating parts of a formal social work education. It is also one of the most challenging. This book brings together in one volume over 30 field placement-related writings from THE NEW SOCIAL WORKER magazine. A goldmine of practical information that will help social work students take advantage of all the field placement experience has to offer.

253 pages • 5 1/2 x 8 1/2 • ISBN 1-929109-10-5 • 2002
$21.95 plus shipping

Order from White Hat Communications, P.O. Box 5390, Dept. MD, Harrisburg, PA 17110-0390 with order form in the back of this book.

ORDER FORM

I would like to order the following:

Qty.	Item	Price
_____	Days in the Lives of Social Workers @ $19.95	_____
_____	More Days in the Lives of Social Workers $16.95	_____
_____	Field Placement Survival Guide @ $21.95	_____
_____	Social Work Grad. School App. Hdbk. @ $19.95	_____
_____	1-yr New Social Worker sub. ($15/U.S. delivery)	_____

Please send my order to:

Name _____

Organization _____

Address _____

City_____ State____ Zip _____

Telephone _____

Please send me more information about ❑social work publications and ❑nonprofit management publications available from White Hat Communications.

Sales tax: Please add 6% sales tax for books shipped to Pennsylvania addresses.

Shipping/handling:
❑Books sent to U.S. addresses: $6.00 first book/$1 each add'l book.
❑Books sent to Canada: $7.00 per book.
❑Books sent to addresses outside the U.S. and Canada: $12.00 per book.

Payment:
Check or money order enclosed for $_____
U.S. funds only.

Please charge my: ❑MC ❑Visa ❑AMEX ❑Discover

Card #: _____

Expiration Date _____

Name on card: _____

Billing address (if different from above): _____
_____

Signature: _____

Mail this form with payment to:
WHITE HAT COMMUNICATIONS, P.O. Box 5390, Dept. MD
Harrisburg, PA 17110-0390
Questions? Call 717-238-3787.
Credit card orders: call 717-238-3787 or fax 717-238-2090
or order online at http://www.socialworker.com

ALSO PUBLISHED BY WHITE HAT COMMUNICATIONS:

BOOKS

Days in the Lives of Social Workers
edited by Linda May Grobman

The Field Placement Survival Guide
edited by Linda May Grobman

*Improving Quality and Performance
in Your Non-Profit Organization*
by Gary M. Grobman

*An Introduction to the Nonprofit Sector:
A Practical Approach for the Twenty-First Century*
by Gary M. Grobman

The Nonprofit Handbook
by Gary M. Grobman

The Nonprofit Organization's Guide to E-Commerce
by Gary M. Grobman

The Social Work Graduate School Applicant's Handbook
by Jesús Reyes

*Welcome to Methadonia: A Social Worker's Candid
Account of Life in a Methadone Clinic*
by Rachel Greene Baldino

MAGAZINE

*The New Social Worker—The Magazine for Social Work
Students and Recent Graduates*

VISIT OUR WEB SITES

www.socialworker.com
www.socialworkjobbank.com
www.whitehatcommunications.com